PARTICIPATORY RESEARCH

WHY AND HOW TO INVOLVE PEOPLE IN RESEARCH

DIRK SCHUBOTZ

Los Angeles | London | New Delhi
Singapore | Washington DC | Melbourne

Los Angeles | London | New Delhi
Singapore | Washington DC | Melbourne

SAGE Publications Ltd
1 Oliver's Yard
55 City Road
London EC1Y 1SP

SAGE Publications Inc.
2455 Teller Road
Thousand Oaks, California 91320

SAGE Publications India Pvt Ltd
B 1/I 1 Mohan Cooperative Industrial Area
Mathura Road
New Delhi 110 044

SAGE Publications Asia-Pacific Pte Ltd
3 Church Street
#10-04 Samsung Hub
Singapore 049483

Editor: Alysha Owen
Assistant editor: Charlotte Bush
Production editor: Martin Fox
Copyeditor: Gemma Marren
Proofreader: Neil Dowden
Indexer: Martin Hargreaves
Marketing manager: Susheel Gokarakonda
Cover design: Bhairvi Gudka
Typeset by: C&M Digitals (P) Ltd, Chennai, India
Printed in the UK

Library of Congress Control Number: 2019937403

British Library Cataloguing in Publication data

A catalogue record for this book is available from the British
Library

ISBN 978-1-4462-7336-4
ISBN 978-1-4462-7337-1 (pbk)

At SAGE we take sustainability seriously. Most of our products are printed in the UK using responsibly sourced
papers and boards. When we print overseas we ensure sustainable papers are used as measured by the PREPS
grading system. We undertake an annual audit to monitor our sustainability.

CONTENTS

About the Author   vii

Abbreviations   ix

Introduction   1

Part I: History, Theory and Ethics of Participatory Methods   **7**

1   The History and Nature of Participatory Research Methods   9

2   Theoretical Perspectives on Participatory Research   23

3   Approaches and Populations in Participatory Research   42

4   Research Ethics in Participatory Research Practice   69

Part II: Applications of Participatory Methods   **95**

5   Participatory Action Research   97

6   Participatory Approaches to Participant Observation   119

7   Group Discussion Methods in Participatory Research   148

8   Participatory Survey Methods   183

In Conclusion   211

Glossary   215
References   217
Index   241

ABOUT THE AUTHOR

Dr Dirk Schubotz is a Senior Lecturer in Social Policy at Queen's University Belfast and studied Social Sciences and Education in his home city Berlin, in Belfast and in Kassel. Dirk initially held a three-year research post at Ulster University and then joined Queen's University Belfast in 2003. Dirk has since then been a member of ARK (www.ark.ac.uk) – Northern Ireland's Social Policy Research Hub.

Dirk's research focuses on children and young people in relation to a broad range of issues, including attitudes to community relations and education, sexual and gender identity, sexual and mental health and wellbeing, and children's and young people's rights. Dirk's interest in and passion for participation and participatory research methods goes back to his time as a full-time youth worker. In his academic career, Dirk has conducted a range of collaborative studies that involved children and young people as advisors and/or as co-researchers. Dirk is a member of the Centre for Children's Rights at Queen's University Belfast and the Centre for Evidence and Social Innovation (CESI) at Queen's University Belfast. Outside of university he chairs Common Youth, a sexual health charity for young people in Northern Ireland.

ABBREVIATIONS

AI	appreciative inquiry
AO	assertive outreach
AR	action research
CAPI	computer-assisted personal interviewing
CAQDAS	computer-assisted qualitative data analysis
CATI	computer-assisted telephone interviewing
CBPR	community-based participatory research
CJS	criminal justice system
CRAG	children's research advisory group
CRYM	Child and Youth Resilience Measure
CSE	child sexual exploitation
CSO	Civil Society Organisation
IE	institutional ethnography
IRB	Institutional Review Board
NABU	Naturschutzbund
NCB	National Children's Bureau
NGO	non-governmental organisation
NICCY	Northern Ireland Commissioner for Children and Young People
NSPCC	National Society for the Prevention of Cruelty to Children
OD	organisational development
PAR	participatory action research
PLA	participatory learning and action
POR	participatory organisational research
PPA	participatory poverty assessment
PRA	participatory rural appraisal
REC	Research Ethics Committee
RSPB	Royal Society for the Protection of Birds
UNCRC	United Nations Convention for the Rights of the Child
VIPER	Voice, Inclusion, Participation, Empowerment, Research
YLT	Young Life and Times

INTRODUCTION

I was approached to write this book by a representative of SAGE shortly after I had given a presentation at a conference of the European Sociological Association (ESA) on a participatory research project that I was involved in. The project was a mixed methods study led by the National Children's Bureau (NCB) with the aim to explore to what extent children and young people in Northern Ireland were involved in school policy making on bullying in their own schools (Schubotz et al., 2006). In the presentation I had talked about working on this study with children and young people of different abilities as co-researchers, including children from special schools, and how they all had different rationales for their active participation in this project. Some wanted to use their experience to support their applications to study social sciences at university, whilst others had experienced school bullying themselves and wanted to improve the way schools dealt with this issue. I talked about the need and the challenges to accommodate different perspectives of children in that study and how we tried to find different roles for all co-researchers which suited their diverse interests and abilities. I also reported back on some of the personal outcomes for the co-researchers and the participating schools, as well as the guidance to all schools that was published by the office of the Northern Ireland Commissioner for Children and Young People (NICCY) as a result of this study, encouraging schools to involve children and young people more proactively in the running of schools, including on bullying policies.

So, when I was approached about writing this book I was both delighted and hesitant. With many years of experience in community youth work in Berlin, my home city, and now many years of experience in participatory youth research and children's rights-based research approached in Belfast, my adopted second home, I certainly felt confident that I could make a contribution to the field of collaborative and participatory research methods. Teaching qualitative research at undergraduate and post-graduate level at university has also helped me acquire a more comprehensive understanding of various collaborative research approaches. In the role as Chair of my School's Research Ethics Committee I have gained a good understanding of ethical challenges faced by collaborative research practice and have tried to implement and facilitate sensitive and flexible approaches required to accommodate participatory research in university settings. Nonetheless, writing a textbook like this as a single author ultimately means that I am covering areas of research in which other people have a far greater expertise than I have.

At the end of a quite long process of completing this book, I feel assured by different peer reviews from practitioners in various areas of participatory research practice that I have done a reasonable job of covering the main issues that arise in participatory research. I read several hundreds of publications in the ever increasing body of literature on collaborative research practice. This growing body of literature must be comforting for most researchers involved in participatory research, as there is clear evidence for what I think is a participatory turn in social health and educational research. Ultimately I had to be selective in what publications I cover in this book and what case studies I present. In that I was guided by my desire to showcase the diversity of participatory approaches. I think it is this diversity that is the strength of this field and shows the flexibility that researchers involved in participatory approaches have to have in order to accommodate the varied needs of the individuals, groups and communities that they work with.

Rationale

The main aim of this book is therefore to provide a compendium of the history of participatory research methods as well as a practical guide to researchers who are considering the involvement of people as active participants and co-researchers in their research projects. I will address both the 'why' and the 'how' of participatory research methods, taking into account the aforementioned growing diversity of participatory and collaborative research practice.

Because it would be hard to imagine that social science research could be conducted without people participating, from the onset, the term 'participatory research' requires some attention. As Silver (2008: 104) puts it, even in document analysis, there are elements of indirect participation by those who produced these documents. Although the levels of participation and visibility of participants in social research may vary, without a minimum level of direct or indirect participation of people, research could not take place. So, should the term 'participatory research' not be considered as something of a truism? The answer to this question is in my opinion two-fold.

Firstly, there is a definitional dimension to this question, which concerns the nature of 'participation' that we are referring to when the term 'participatory research methods' is used. First used in the 1970s, the term participatory research is by no means new, but since then, and in particular in the three decades or so prior to the publication of this book, there has been an upsurge in the number of research projects which use the word *participatory* when describing their methodology. Hence, I argue that we are experiencing a *participatory turn* in social research. I will discuss the manifold reasons for this in Part I of this book, which is dedicated to the history and nature of participatory research approaches and to the rationale and ethics of involving people actively in research. One of the main reasons why we have seen such an expansion and diversification in the use of participatory approaches is the failure of what I will call 'conventional research methods' to address the needs of people and local communities who give their time to research – especially the needs of under-privileged communities and groups of people who participate in research in the hope that this may bring about positive change and action to address their very disadvantage. In response to this failure, some research is moving towards new participatory bottom-up approaches and a more equal paradigm which aspires to 'give voice' – a controversial term in itself, as I will show – to excluded and under-represented groups and communities. Participatory research is not just about researchers understanding the lives of people and communities who are the subject of a research study, but about mutual understanding and collective action to make positive changes. Some of the questions this book seeks to answer in Part I are therefore:

- Why should we actively involve someone as co-researcher who has had no research training or qualification? What is the purpose of these participatory or collaborative approaches and what is their promise?
- What is the added value of participatory approaches? Do they not overcomplicate matters and result in less rigorous research?
- What are the ethical issues related to inclusive participatory and collaborative research approaches?

Secondly, due to this participatory turn in the previous three decades or so, we have witnessed a remarkable diversification of participatory and innovative collaborative research methods. Increasingly, research participants are regarded as potential collaborators in the co-production of knowledge and become co-researchers with responsibilities to different degrees that can range from quite small tasks to essentially directing the research process. This has fundamentally changed the dynamic of research projects, which, in my view, not only justifies a systematic contextualisation of these methods and approaches, but also merits the provision of some guidance for both novice and experienced researchers who may contemplate the utilisation of participatory methods and may seek reassurance on how to do this. Part II of this book therefore discusses in more detail specific participatory approaches and methods.

Part II starts with a discussion of action research (AR) and participatory action research (PAR). AR and PAR are still regarded by many as the original and most complete approaches to participatory and collaborative research practice. Here I discuss not only their theoretical origins, but also many of the practical design principles that have influenced a variety of participatory approaches. This is followed by a discussion on participatory approaches to participant observation and ethnography. As PAR approaches, collaborative ethnographic research projects, such as feminist ethnography or action ethnography, utilise a range of research methods. However, what we can learn from participant observation is good practice in terms of long-term studies, especially their initiation phase, but also the need to leave the field at the right time with an ethically appropriate exit plan which is sensitive to the field and its actors. I finally focus on two specific research methods – group discussions and surveys. Group discussions are very commonly, if not most commonly, used in participatory projects. Surveys are also frequently used, but the perception is very much that surveys follow a positivist, objectivistic and deductive rationale which is primarily informed by theory testing and the ideas of the professional survey researchers and is therefore much more in line with **conventional research**. I want to show that this is not necessarily the case and that surveys can meaningfully be incorporated in participatory co-production designs.

In addition to the more ontological and epistemological reasons why participatory approaches have grown so much in popularity, there are also technological advances that have fostered this development. The last 30 years or so have seen a digital revolution which has resulted in the computerisation/digitisation of most spheres of life. Despite the fundamental changes we have already witnessed, this development still appears to gain momentum. We are now seeing the introduction of computer technology which is increasingly responsive to, and interacts with, human behaviour. In general, IT and computer technology has fundamentally changed the way we communicate with each other, and this has had profound effects on how we collect human and other data. The affordability and proliferation of digital technology, in particular digital media technology (e.g. visual and audio recording) and data processing technology, has created opportunities for the development and advancement of data collection and analysis techniques that were difficult to anticipate a generation ago. Most people today carry a smartphone in their pocket which has a significantly larger capacity and speed than desktop PCs only 20 years ago. Hand-held and mobile computer devices, such as smartphones or tablet computers allow for the collection and movement of large quantities of different kinds of data, such as text, audio and visual data, as well as background data about the movement of people, their likes and dislikes as consumers, activity levels and so forth. Humans leave a digital data trail, and social research has to adapt to this new reality. Using the right software and applications, handheld mobile computer devices can also be used to conduct face-to-face remote video interviews, to record and transcribe, and upload and share, interviews, to take fieldnotes, record geographic co-ordinates, to set up and complete surveys, and to harvest online data.

Whilst the core methodologies and methods we use to collect data have changed only a little, the digital revolution has extended the scope and range of what we are able to do. Fundamentally, advances in IT technology also allow us to involve people in the data collection, transfer and analysis in way that were unthinkable or impractical just a few years ago. The IT revolution has not just enhanced our ability to collect, store and process data, but it has also changed the attitudes towards the recording and sharing of data and information. Even outside the formalised research process, people have increasingly become active data collectors and distributors, even though this may not be in a systematic manner. Examples for this are social networking sites, but also consumer and business interactions. Some of this data is already harvested for commercial purposes. However, these new opportunities are also creating new challenges and pose questions for ethical research practice, which will also be discussed in Part I of this book.

Both the participatory turn and the digital revolution have consequences for the way we conduct research and they do not lead automatically to better research and more effective ways of conducting research. One of the main challenges is the need to re-assess the way we involve people in research practice and what implications increasing participation in a data-rich world has for the way we generate data and draw conclusions from our research.

Content and structure

In Part I, I focus on why people are increasingly involved as active participants and co-researchers in research projects. In Chapter 1 I will discuss the history and nature of participatory research methods, their fundamental principles and character, and their fit with social science theories. I will also address ethical issues that arise when using participatory methods which involve people actively in the research process, for example the issue of power relations in projects which involve co-researchers. This is followed by a discussion of theoretical perspectives and principles of participatory research methods (Chapter 2) where I also address epistemological and ontological issues surrounding the work with co-researchers and the consequences for the way we generate data. I will discuss the different levels of participation in research from being a participant to being an initiator of a research project. This is followed by a synopsis of applications and approaches that have been used under the umbrella term of participatory research methods (Chapter 3).

More practical guidance about the 'How' of participatory methods will be provided in Part II of this book. The first three chapters in this second part focus on more traditional participatory methods. Chapter 5 introduces participatory action research. Whilst not a distinct research method as such, PAR is closely associated with the origins of participatory methods and is most directly driven by the desire to bring about change. I will discuss PAR's origins and practice, but also the risks involved in undertaking research with the ambition to initiate change and impact. This is followed by a chapter on participatory observation (Chapter 6) with a particular focus on ethnographic approaches. In Chapter 7 I will focus on group discussion methods, a method very commonly associated with participant involvement. I will discuss the dynamics of group discussions, which can both be an advantage and a significant challenge.

The final chapter in this volume focuses on survey methods, which are less commonly associated with participatory approaches (Chapter 8). Whilst participatory researchers predominantly employ qualitative data collection methods, one of the key characteristics of participatory approaches is that they are often informed by, and orientated towards, praxis needs. Surveys may for that reason also play an important role in participatory projects, but as survey design and analysis require a unique technical skills set, there are very particular challenges that arise from this. There remains a perceived need of standardisation and generalisability in policy making, so in order to convince policy makers to make changes, surveys remain an important research tool.

It is appropriate to note here that – maybe with the exception of PAR – the research methods discussed in the second part of this book are not necessarily per se and automatically action-orientated or participatory in nature. Rather, they are discussed here because they are suitable to be used in projects which share a philosophy of action and participation. Thus, it is this underlying principle of social action and participation which connects these chapters on more 'traditional' social research methods, such as survey methods (Chapter 8) and group discussions (Chapter 7), with the chapters more directly associated with participatory approaches like participatory action research (Chapter 5).

Who should read this book?

This book is written with a broad audience in mind – researchers at various career stages, including students, novice researchers and more experienced researchers. Participatory research methods per se cross disciplinary boundaries. Rather than focusing on one particular subject area, the aim throughout this book is therefore to provide an inter-disciplinary focus on participatory research methods, and the range of examples of applications discussed in each chapter serve this purpose.

Like with all textbooks, readers may find that some material is more relevant to their own work than others. The more conceptual first two chapters may appeal more to those who wonder how their own epistemological standpoints connect with current collabora-tive research approaches. The more practical second part of this book may be of greater appeal to those embarking on participatory projects for the first time. Case studies, text boxes, tables and figures, and ideas for learning activities and exercises are used through-out the book. Further readings and resources are recommended at the end of each chapter.

In one of the most often quoted articles on participatory research practice, Cornwall and Jewkes (1995: 1667) criticise the 'unproductive debate surrounding the qualitative–quantitative divide' and argue that it is the contexts in which the research takes place rather than their methods that are important. Key is not whether quantitative or quali-tative methods are being used, but how issues of agency, power and representation are being handled during the research process. In the authors' view it is the attitudes of researchers towards their respective projects and towards the participants, which 'deter-mine how, by and for whom research is conceptualized and conducted' (1995: 1667). I wholeheartedly agree with this position, which also reflects my own multi-method research practice and experience. With the inclusion of a chapter on participatory sur-vey research I want to make the specific point that in my view participatory research practice is not reserved for explorative, qualitative enquiry.

PART I

HISTORY, THEORY AND ETHICS OF PARTICIPATORY METHODS

1

THE HISTORY AND NATURE OF PARTICIPATORY RESEARCH METHODS

What you will learn

In this chapter you will be introduced to the origins and principles of participatory research methods. The chapter defines what we mean when we refer to 'participatory' or 'collaborative' research. The conceptual and epistemological arguments for the use of participatory and collaborative research approaches are discussed. There are several theoretical approaches and frameworks which explain and/or support the use of participatory approaches, and this chapter refers to these and their usefulness for conceptualising collaborative research practice. The chapter alludes to reasons why participatory approaches may or may not be appropriate to be adopted for a research study. The chapter concludes with a critical review of participatory methods and the promise of change attached to these methods.

The origins of participatory methods or: the participatory turn

Whilst it is true that research in the social sciences to a large extent involves, and relies on, people and their participation, the term 'participatory research methods' is not normally used to simply refer to the presence of people in the research process. Rather, the term emerged in response to the way in which research participants were often treated and viewed in what have been called 'conventional' research projects. Admittedly, the term 'conventional research' is a bit of a container word which covers a range of diverse research methods and does not account for differences in approaches in a hugely diversified research landscape. However, for some time, and in the quest for objectivity and an 'objective truth', it was seen as desirable and good practice for a researcher to minimise the impact of the relationships that research participants had with researchers or with other people on the research process, and to treat these relationships as redundant or superfluous. Essentially, whilst the relationships with participants are *very* central for collaborative research practice, historically they were simply of secondary importance in conventional research. The active involvement of research participants or volunteers in the research process was also simply unthinkable as they could 'spoil the scientific study' as Krueger and King (1998: 3) put it. If anything, researchers were striving for clear boundaries between themselves, research participants and the public. This in part can be explained with ontological and epistemological convictions and conventions that have dominated the social sciences, such as positivism and **objectivism** and the related search for an objective truth *in* human interaction but paradoxically independent *from* it. I will revisit this point in Chapter 2.

In particular, positivist approaches, which dominated social research practice for many years, were found to be inadequate in their capacity to generate *practical and applicable* knowledge, as Hall (1975) and Susman and Evered (1978) pointed out as early as the 1970s. This failure to produce practically useful and applicable knowledge was perhaps the main trigger for the development of what we are now referring to as 'participatory research approaches'. It is thought that the term 'participatory research' itself was first used, and perhaps coined by, Marja Liisa Swantz in the 1970s in her 'experimental pilot survey of skills' in rural Tanzania (Swantz, 1975). Alongside Hall and Susman and Evered, Swantz was a pioneer of the participatory turn in social research, and it is this period of the mid-1970s that can perhaps be regarded as the launch pad of participatory research methods as we understand them today. The shared perception of these pioneers of participatory practice was that conventional research methods were inadequate in addressing the research questions they had. Having said that, although Hall (1975: 24) thought that 'the case for alternative methods [...] seemed compelling', when he published his iconic article on participatory methods as an approach for change, he saw his publication simply as 'a call for assistance' and did not claim that he had a 'completed product nor step-by-step instructions for researchers to follow'. However, as we know now, Hall pushed on an open door with his quest for support, demonstrated by the development and diversification of participatory methods in the subsequent four decades since the publication of his article.

Beresford and Carr (2012) point to the emergence of social movements in the 1970s and 1980s, such as the disabled people's movement or equal rights movements, including LGBT groups, and the re-emergence of the notion of 'human need' prompting a participatory turn in research practice. Issues around shortcomings of the welfare state, which led to or failed to address inequality, focused research interests on those most disadvantaged, and at that time conventional research often failed to represent their experiences.

In fact, the emergence and diversification of participatory and collaborative research methods has also helped to redefine conventional methods of data collection, analysis and interpretation itself. The broad range of participatory and collaborative approaches that is in use today helps us realise that these methods have not only changed the way we look at the relationships that research participants have – these relationships themselves have also fundamentally changed. In my view it is therefore appropriate to use the term 'participatory turn' when referring to the changes that have occurred in research practice over the last four or five decades. Whilst the term 'participatory turn' itself is actually not new and has been used in relation to increased civic engagement in decision making processes (Saurugger, 2010), I am adopting this term here to refer to the increasing number of studies where non-experts are actively involved in research processes (see, for example, Lengwiler, 2008). Increasingly the term **co-production** is also being used to describe these approaches. According to Carr (Beresford and Carr, 2012), the term 'co-production' first emerged in the *Putting People First* document published by the British Department of Health in December 2007. The publication was praised as a 'landmark protocol' in relation to government ambitions to involve all stakeholders in social care reform for independent living for adults, using a joined-up and collaborative partnership approach. This chapter is concerned with the rationale for and the practicalities of such partnership approaches.

Discussing participatory approaches in science and technology and reflecting on their advantages and limitations, Lengwiler (2008) identifies four main periods which characterise the relationship between expert and non-expert knowledge since the late nineteenth century, and he names these as (1) hybrid, (2) politicised, (3) autonomous and (4) participatory relationship. Lengwiler argues that the initial impetus for a closer relationship between the public and the research community arose with an increasing emergence of popular science, fostered, for example, by scientific exhibitions and popular science societies, but also with social reformist attitudes of academic researchers themselves. Early attempts in social planning around the times of the emergence of welfare states contributed to an increasing politicisation of science, and according to Lengwiler (2008: 192), some science associations embraced and promoted the notion of fundamentally democratising science. The *autonomous* period occurred approximately between the end of the Second World War and the early 1970s, when the lessons from the abuse of science during Fascism in Germany and concerns about the political instrumentalisation of science during the Cold War period led to calls about autonomous and independent science. It was not until the late 1960s and the early 1970s that systematic concerns about the social relevance of science reintroduced the participatory question systematically, and this changed the nature of research practice.

The nature of participatory research practice

As we have seen above, participatory and collaborative approaches to research developed with the aim of providing a critical perspective to existing research practice and in response to concerns about its lack of social impact, relevance and usefulness for those who were the subjects and the centre of this research. Conventional methods had persistently failed to capture the voices and experiences of under-represented, marginalised or hard-to-reach groups in society. Krueger and King (1998) state that concerns about the lack of utility of research for the communities and individuals commissioning it, led to stakeholder involvement in the 1970s and a first step towards more participatory approaches. For Aldridge (2015), this shift towards greater collaboration in research and practice has contributed to the facilitation of the participant voice, particularly for vulnerable people who in the past were too often under-represented, overlooked, denied full participation in research or completely left out. This also reflects Cornwall and Jewkes' (1995) view that the fundamental difference between participatory approaches and other types of research involving people is the shift in power relations towards co-researchers. In participatory practice, the voices and the stories of participants are placed in the centre of the research project rather than at the margins as would often be the case in conventional approaches. Central to the participatory turn in research is the growing acceptance that academic researchers should not and do not have a monopoly on asking important questions. Linked to this conviction is the belief that more active involvement of the subjects or target audience of research may help ask more appropriate questions and ultimately provide better answers to the questions posed.

Aldridge (2015) argues that as a result of this participatory turn, disciplinary boundaries have become more fluent. I would add that the boundaries between the researcher and the researched continually intersect and are redefined. Participatory and collaborative approaches to research encompass a range of methods which share an underlying philosophy but may have different foci (Silver, 2008). Central to this shared philosophy are the principles of 'action' and 'participation' (Stoecker, 1999); in other words, the main aim of participatory research is to address particular social problems by using the expertise of the people who are affected by these problems within the research process (Chambers, 1998). As Stoecker (1999) puts it, unlike in conventional research, undertaking the research is not the actual goal in participatory research practice, but only one of several means to achieve the ultimate goal, namely to bring about change.

Involvement, participation and inclusion in participatory practice

McTaggart (1997) makes a useful distinction between participant *involvement* and actual *participation*. According to the author, authentic participation is ultimately linked to a degree of ownership of a research project. Participatory research practice not only acknowledges the active contribution – or *involvement* – of research participants in the generation of knowledge, but it often actively encourages the co-production of knowledge, through the collective analysis, interpretation and dissemination of findings. Using Heron's (1996) terminology of 'co-operative inquiry', Reason and Torbert (2001: 20) explain how those involved in a research project as co-researchers contribute 'to generating ideas, designing and managing the project, and drawing conclusions from the experience' whilst at the same time being 'co-subjects, participating in the activity which is being researched'. Research participants in these collaborative and participatory projects contribute to the sense-making process, whether this is via participation in the project planning, the data collection and analysis, or their involvement in the interpretation and dissemination of findings. Figure 1.1 shows different levels of co-production and participation. The figure is loosely based on Arnstein's famous 'ladder of citizen participation' (1969), although the bottom two rungs of the ladder – 'manipulation' and 'therapy' – are here not included

Level 1 Being informed	• Participants may be consulted about the research and will receive information about it. They may take part in participatory data collection without having any influence on the way the project is run.
Level 2 Giving advice	• At this level, participants may be involved as research steering group members or have an advisory role. They are consulted about the research process and its results and they provide feedback to the researchers.
Level 3 Co-design	• Participants are involved in all aspects of the research planning process as equal partners. They may have identified the research topic, or have been approached and asked by a professional researcher to help conduct the research. They may also contribute to data collection analysis and dissemination.
Level 4 Co-production or Peer research	• Participants may not have had the original idea for the study, but they are involved and may even be paid to help run the study. They will help with the collection and the processing of the data and will contribute to the report writing and dissemination. Co- or peer researchers will normally receive some training before they embark on their involvement in a research study.
Level 5 Leading the research	• Participants initiate and lead the research process and are involved in all stages of the project. They decide what direction the project is going to take. They may ask a professional researcher to join the project or they may seek other advice or support, but they are the decision makers throughout this process.

Figure 1.1 Forms of participation and levels of participant involvement

on purpose. Arnstein's original ladder was focused on the different levels of power that citizens have in relation to urban redevelopment. This has been criticised as being too simplistic and hierarchical (e.g. Tritter and McCallum, 2006), but in my adaptation of this model I want to demonstrate the different levels of control participants have in collaborative research practice. Whilst Figure 1.1 emphasises that there are different levels and degrees of participation, which can be interpreted as being hierarchical, in my view, in each research project we should aim to achieve the most sensible and appropriate level of participation, and it may well be that this falls short of true partnership approaches or taking control of the research project, as would be the case in level 5 projects.

I would argue that not all projects lend themselves to full co-production, for example due to lack of resources or time. The degree of active participation can therefore vary significantly between projects but, as I already stated above, just because we cannot achieve the highest level of participation all the time does not mean that we should not try. I would agree with Stoecker (1999) that we always need to ask the question: how much research and participation does a group or community actually need or want?

Advocates of participatory and collaborative research approaches argue that participatory methods have an underlying democratising rationale and challenge conventional 'dichotomous, elitist and exploitative' methods (Silver, 2008: 116). Using the example of the specific developments in disability research, Zarb (1992) further distinguishes between *participatory* and *emancipatory* research, alluding to the aspiration that participatory research practice should have an emancipatory effect on the communities involved. Involving local people actively as participants in research and planning has been shown to potentially both enhance the effectiveness of the research and to save time and money in the long term. For Krueger and King (1998: 5), there are four main reasons to involve co-researchers in a research project:

1   The inability of professional researchers to collect the same level of in-depth inside data that a community member or volunteer could.
2   The ability to collect information in settings where a more traditional research design would be too expensive or unfeasible to undertake. Geographic areas that are hard to access are an example for this, but also culturally sensitive subject areas.
3   Participatory approaches mean that people care more about the research.
4   Benefits to the individuals and communities who are involved in the research.

What is common to all participatory and collaborative approaches is that they challenge and redefine the hierarchical power relations that exist between the researcher and the researched. Academic/professional researchers are encouraged to be more reflective about their research praxis, but again, this is by no means an automatic process. In fact, Aldridge (2015: 4) argues that practitioners in participatory research need to demonstrate clearly and rigorously how this closer collaboration between the researchers and participants can be achieved:

In order for researchers to address these challenges effectively, greater clarity, rigour and consistency are called for in P[articipatory] R[esearch] that demonstrate the validity and rigour of participatory methods and that can, for example, also give clear directions for policy and practice.

Aldridge (2015) refers to Walmsley and Johnson (2003: 31) who argue that it was the responsibility of the participatory researcher, in particular when involving vulnerable people, to make sure that the research is being used to positive effect in society. Aldridge (2015) states that many researchers use participatory methods because they want to 'give participants a voice' or provide them with better opportunities. However, as the author warns, this not a straightforward process. In fact, the very notions of 'giving people a voice' and **empowerment** have come under critical scrutiny, because they assume top-down approaches where power is handed down from the powerful *to* the powerless (Eylon, 1998). In that sense I can agree with Aldridge (2015: 4) that the challenge for adopting more inclusive ways of undertaking research is 'to adopt approaches that recognise [participants'] competency and agency [...] while at the same time work within research governance and ethical frameworks and classifications that define them as vulnerable'.

Unlike in conventional research, emancipation is then not just a *coincidental by-product*, but a *planned outcome* of the research process. The key principles of participatory research practice promote understanding, mutuality and collaboration and thereby facilitate a more empathetic, inclusive and democratic approach to undertaking research. If we accept this as an underpinning principle of participatory and collaborative approaches, then we may indeed conclude that the early 1970s mark the beginning of a participatory turn, even though the actual roots of participatory research practice go back to the development of action research several decades earlier (see Chapter 5). In his often-quoted article on inter-group relations Kurt Lewin (1946: 35), who is regarded as the forefather of action research, identified this emancipatory outcome-focused approach as what he felt should be the ambition of social research:

> The research needed for social practice can best be characterized as research for social management or social engineering. It is a type of action-research, a comparative research on the conditions and effects of various forms of social action, and research leading to social action. Research that produces nothing but books will not suffice.

In Lewin's view social research should be guided by two aims: (1) finding out things, and (2) making positive changes – two aims that are central not just to action research but to various participatory and collaborative approaches today. Silver (2008) agrees with Hart and Bond's view (1995) that Lewin's original notion of action research has developed over time into a broader, fundamentally anti-positivist approach to social research.

Discussing critically attitudes to the active involvement of children and young people as co-researchers in participatory research projects, Brownlie (2007) poses that the issue of who is carrying out the research is linked to questions about *for what* and *for whom* the knowledge is produced. Brownlie argues that participation has become both a 'strategic' aim connected to the notion of citizenship as well as a 'knowledge' resource. The two aspects linked to participation are therefore *efficiency*, meaning that participation leads to better research and policy outcomes, and *empowerment*, in the sense that participation has the capacity to improve or change people's lives for the better. This debate leads us directly to the issue of how epistemological and ontological considerations influence participatory approaches. Whilst I discuss these theoretical underpinnings for participatory research approaches in detail in Chapter 2, I will now look at some of the reasons *why* people participate.

Why do people participate?

Brady et al. (2012) remind us that participation itself can be a contested and ambiguous term. Using the example of children's participation in research and the way this is presented and promoted in inclusion manuals and guidebooks, Brady and her colleagues argue that substantial differences can be found between participation as a means of meaningfully taking part, being present and being consulted. This is advocated by Boyden and Ennew (1997) for example. Promoting participation as a process enables children and young people to actually influence decisions and can bring about change for themselves, their peers and communities, and the services they use and need, as described by Treseder (2004) and Burke (2010). Brady et al. (2012) also state that participation practice shows that there are disparities in the kind of activities different children and young people participate in and in the decision-making power they have. A good example to illustrate this is that disadvantaged children have fewer opportunities to participate.

Whether related to children and young people or to adults, participation is very closely linked to the issue of active citizenship, and as Jupp Kina (2012: 205) puts it, 'the belief in participation as a "good thing" is clearly a starting point for many'. Some researchers involved in participatory research practice may hope that the experience will contribute to the participants becoming politically more involved, for example in advocacy work. Often this has been shown to be the case, but it is important to acknowledge that people do not always have this agenda.

─ BOX 1.1 ─

Brodie et al. (2011) undertook a three-year research project to explore in more detail the factors that trigger participation and contribute to sustained participation. The authors found that 'people participate in a myriad of ways, depending on what has meaning and value to them' and they concluded that participation generally 'is primarily about individual choice and personal preferences, and a person's capacity to take action' (Brodie et al., 2011: 7). The authors found a variety of personal reasons that motivated people to participate, such as the desire to help others, attempts to gain more influence or the desire to form new social relationships, as well as personal values and beliefs. All these motifs are no different from those people commonly refer to when asked about their volunteering activities. However, Brodie et al. found that participation and volunteering were dependent on external context factors as well, which were often beyond the control of participants. Other important factors were people's upbringing, their family and social connections and the presence or absence of a culture that encouraged and supported participation in their immediate environment, for example in voluntary and community groups or schools. Brodie and colleagues also concluded that people's attitudes to and perceptions of participation influenced how and why they participate. Interestingly, there was a somewhat negative bias towards politically motivated participation, and a reluctance to be considered a 'do-gooder'.

The willingness to participate in research is equally founded on a diverse set of reasons. According to Corbin and Morse (2003: 342), participants who agree to participate in a research study 'usually do so because they want something in return even though they themselves might not be consciously aware what this is'. The authors observe that there is always a level of reciprocity in the researcher–participant relationship. Corbin and Morse specifically refer to qualitative interviewing when they make these observations, however, many of the issues they raise transcend this particular research method. The desire to share one's views, to have these validated or simply to be listened to non-judgementally can be very strong motivations to take part in research, regardless of the method used. As Corbin and Morse state, sometimes there is no one else to whom a story can be told, and 'people just have a need to talk'. Rosenthal (2003), among others, has described the powerful healing effects of story telling in research, which can address a need to unburden oneself. Research projects are often also potentially educative. Researchers arrive with helpful information about services and insider knowledge that might be useful to participants. Some research participants have altruistic motives. They may want to help science or may hope that their participation contributes to improvements in society – perhaps even prevent other people or future generations from having the same adverse experiences as they had. They may want to contribute to changes in certain policies, often, but not necessarily, in a subject area that they feel strongly about, such as the protection of the environment, of community services, of citizen's rights, to give just three examples. Sometimes, people want to please other people, or find it difficult to say 'no' when asked to participate. Friends or neighbours may already participate. Occasionally researchers offer rewards for study participation, such as gift or shopping vouchers, money, which sometimes can be substituted for contributions to nominated charities, or access to goods or services. In health-related research, for example, free health checks or treatments may be undertaken in return for study participation (e.g. Townsend and Cox, 2013).

Reasons to participate or to decline participation in health-related research have been researched widely, especially in relation to clinical trials. The body of existing literature on these reasons is too large to reference here fully; however, it is interesting that some authors found motives not directly related to the respective trials or interventions. In their study on injecting drug users, for example, Fry and Dwyer (2001) found that study participants continued to take part in their research for reasons related to notions of active citizenship, altruism and drug-user activism. Altruistic motives for participation in research were also found among women in postnatal care by Baker, Lavender and Tincello (2005). Children and young people may perhaps also get out of school for a while in return for their participation in research, and for some this may present a welcome change to what they may see as a boring school day. This is not an exhaustive list of reasons and there are many more.

Therefore, there are a number of generic reasons that motivate people to participate in different kinds of research. The difference in participatory and collaborative study designs is that participants also carry a level of responsibility to complete the research, which may induce additional motivations to participate. Active participation and decision making in research may result in new skills, new knowledge and new friends. In the participatory research projects I have personally been involved in over the years with colleagues, we found that some volunteers for co-researcher positions came forward because they felt particularly passionate about, or were directly affected by, the topic under investigation, for example school bullying (Schubotz et al., 2006), attitudes to minority ethnic groups (McCartan, Schubotz and Murphy, 2012) or (lack of) employment opportunities in working-class neighbourhoods which experienced regeneration and gentrification (Schubotz and Devine, 2005). Other volunteers came forward because they wanted to gain experiences which they could use to apply for jobs or for further or higher education courses. Some people see active participation in research as an opportunity to practise active citizenship, including those who may feel disenfranchised.

To conclude, with Brodie et al.'s (2011) observations, active participation is generally a voluntary, action-based, purposeful and collective activity, which is connected to a worthwhile cause, has a sense of common purpose and intended consequences, namely the ambition to make an impact, or as Beresford and Carr (2012) put it: to make a difference!

Critically reviewing the promise of participation

The 'self-referential character' of participation literature (e.g. Tisdall and Davis, 2004) and the lack of rigorous appraisal (e.g. Koskinen, 2014) have been criticised. The core of the criticism is that the promise of change remains either unfulfilled or unevidenced. There is less doubt that those who are involved in participatory projects do indeed benefit, for example by gaining new skills or the strengthening of the social and cultural capital (Tisdall, 2008). However, the impact beyond the actual project participants is much less clear. The same applies to the impact and change that is targeted.

In order to test this criticism, Pratchett et al. (2009) conducted a systematic review of evidence on 'community empowerment', covering 3,600 articles and six distinct participatory mechanisms, including citizen governance, participatory budgeting and petitions. The authors concluded that involvement and participation had empowering effects on those directly participating, but that the evidence for empowering effects occurring at community level was less clear. This modest optimism about the effects of participation also translates to participatory research practice.

Eriksson et al. (2014) examined a number of academic–practice policy partnerships to explore the factors that led to effective collaboration between academics, practitioners and policy makers. The authors came to the conclusion that communication, collaboration, shared visions and objectives, and willingness of all stakeholders to learn from one another were key ingredients for a successful relationship. They also found that a mutual level of trust was one of the prerequisites for a successful project.

According to Carr (2012), a research synthesis on service user involvement in research showed that participation does not necessarily accommodate user voice nor does it lead to change. Carr found that the outcomes of the user participation were rarely evaluated, and the impact of the studies were seldom fed back to the participants. Carr notes 'a lack of organisational responsiveness to the issues identified by service users and a lack of clear commitment to change and its evaluation as a result of service user participation' (2012: 39).

Blair and Minkler (2009) systematically reviewed literature on participatory action research projects in gerontology. They concluded quite positively that the evidence from the studies suggested that although the involvement of older people in PAR projects could be challenging and labour-intensive, not only could these projects have positive effects in terms of skills building among those elders who were directly involved in these project, but it could also lead to positive outcomes for older people more generally. Littlechild, Tanner and Hall's (2015) assessment of the impact of research with older people as co-researchers is somewhat more critical. They found that, despite the growth of participatory research with older people, certain groups, such as those with dementia and those from black and minority ethnic backgrounds, remained largely excluded. The authors also found that there was a lack of critical evaluation and appraisal of the effects of the participation and a tendency to over-exaggerate the positives. Despite the existing limitations and the need to evaluate the impact of participatory research further, Littlechild, Tanner and Hall concluded that participatory research with marginalised older people has the potential to achieve meaningful change at both individual and social levels.

In order to explore the long-term effect of involvement in participatory research, Hampshire et al. (2012) returned to child researchers two years after their involvement in a project on children's mobility in Africa. Interviews were conducted to see whether the positive effects indicated at the time of the research, such as increased confidence, the gaining of new skills and expanded social networks, had prevailed over time. The authors found that tangible benefits from the research for education and employment had indeed been reported, although these were sometimes unpredictable. Negative effects experienced at the time of the project – for example on school work – had, however, been largely forgotten.

Fox (2013) describes her own difficulties in implementing a participatory approach in her PhD project – an ethnographic study with young people excluded from mainstream schooling. She reflects that she continued to attempt to control the research whilst her participants continued to resist this, thus duplicating the structures from the very institutional context from which these young people were excluded. Fox concludes that this made meaningful participation in her study difficult. This example highlights the lack of power researchers may have in settings like this. Fox points the finger at institutional research structures and requirements by institutional stakeholders and gatekeepers that in her view make meaningful voluntary involvement of young people difficult. In that conclusion, however, I disagree with Fox. As I pointed out above, participation can be meaningful at different levels, even as Lundy (2018) has argued, at the level of apparent tokenism. The 'gold standard' of participants leading the research is not always feasible or even desirable. Participatory research located in quite firm institutional settings, such as schools, prisons or care homes, will need to take account of these settings and work with them. Barriers to full participation do not mean that we should not try to be more inclusive, if there is a good rationale for this.

Summary

I attempted to demonstrate in this chapter that the move towards participatory and collaborative research practice was strongly influenced by the frustration and disillusionment with conventional research practice which too often served the researchers undertaking the research but had little or no tangible benefits for the research participants and their communities. This frustration was particularly felt among communities which were disadvantaged and disenfranchised.

Collaborative research practice is not uniform but rather diverse, and the level of involvement afforded to study participants can vary widely, as is demonstrated in Figure 1.1. People's motivations to participate actively in research and to take on the role of co- or peer researcher are equally diverse and range from altruistic convictions to quite vested interests in the respective research study, whether that is for change and improvement in the community or personal career motivations, for example among young people who may seek expertise and experiences that support a university career.

Finally, I made the point that participatory and collaborative approaches do not lead per se to superior research studies compared with conventional non-participatory approaches. Many contextual and individual factors determine the outcomes of participatory approaches, and despite the best intentions resistance among decision makers or other factors may result in promises of change remaining unfulfilled. This in itself is no argument against participatory approaches, but rather a reminder that alongside the aims and objectives of a collaborative research project the context factors and realistic expectations also ought to be explored and discussed routinely. This will be discussed in more detail in Chapter 3 of this book. However, first I turn my attention to more theoretical perspectives of participatory research practice.

FURTHER READING

Aldridge, J. (2015). *Participatory Research: Working with Vulnerable Groups in Research and Practice*. Bristol: Policy Press.

Cornwall, A. and Jewkes, R. (1995). What is participatory research? *Social Science & Medicine*, 41(12): 1667–1676.

EXERCISE 1.1

HOPES, FEARS AND EXPECTATIONS

One of the core questions in any participatory research project is to establish the rationale for a participatory approach. This is to make sure that the involvement of participants in the co-production of knowledge is genuine and not a tokenistic activity which is undertaken because it looks good from the outside. In every participatory project that I have been involved in we start the first meeting – mostly as part of a research training workshop – with volunteers and prospective co-researchers with a set of questions that everybody should think about.

- Why do we involve co-researchers in this project?
- What can co-researchers add to this project?
- What do co-researchers expect from this project, and what do we expect of them?
- What are the risks of involving co-researchers in this project?

Additional questions that could be explored could be questions around power – Who will make what decisions? – and stakeholders – Who is likely to be affected by the research? Who might lose or gain and what might they lose or gain?

   A related activity – often one that we undertake also at the very start – is to ask all participants, including professional researchers, about their hopes and fears. Sometimes we have done this via sticky notes that were anonymously pinned or stuck to a wall or a flip chart and then discussed. It is a good idea to keep these hopes and fears throughout the project and revisit them from time to time when decisions are being made about the progress of the project

---EXERCISE 1.2---

ASSESSING SKILLS AND CHARACTERISTICS REQUIRED FOR CO-PRODUCTION

At the start of each collaborative or participatory research project we need to gain clarity about the skills required for the completion of the project, but also need to understand what skills everybody brings and what tasks they are happy to complete. What skills and characteristics are you looking for in researchers and co-researchers for your project? Again this is an activity that can be undertaken just verbally, for example in a team meeting or group discussion, but also using pen or paper or flip chart and sticky notes. Both professional researchers and co-researchers should have an opportunity to express what they think they bring to the project, what their skills are, what areas of work they do not feel so comfortable with and what constraints there are, such as other responsibilities (e.g. caring, work, study). This activity will help in the distribution of particular roles for the research project and will help people from the start to develop a sense of ownership. Table 1.1 below is a good starting point, but other criteria can be added.

Table 1.1   Assessing skills and characteristics required for co-production

	Person 1	Person 2	Person 3	Person 4	Person 5
I am interested in...					
I am good at...					
I need help with...					
I want to learn...					
I don't want to do...					
I want to work with...					

2

THEORETICAL PERSPECTIVES ON PARTICIPATORY RESEARCH

What you will learn

This chapter is the most theoretical chapter in this book and reviews some of the more conceptual issues around participation. The chapter considers epistemological and ontological issues around participation and knowledge generation and how these affect the way we approach a research study. The chapter will discuss the main theoretical frameworks usually connected with collaborative research practice, but it will also explore how research frameworks less often associated with participatory research may contain positions and perspectives that can be used to warrant a more active inclusion of participants in the research.

Introduction

Whilst most chapters in this volume are concerned with the practical implementation of participatory research methods, here I will explore to what extent theoretical paradigms can underpin participatory approaches. Participatory research privileges inductive rather deductive theory-led approaches because the participants, their needs and expertise, have greater relevance than the theoretical paradigms that may underpin research methods. Whilst many social theories have been informed by the systematic collection of empirical data, theoretical paradigms may also in turn influence and inform the way data collection is planned and designed and they can offer a deeper understanding of the issue that we are researching. This, is something that McDonnell et al. (2009) have demonstrated for research in health and healthcare.

Epistemological and ontological underpinnings of research

According to Barnes and Cotterell (2012), social reality is subject to competing interpretations, meanings and significance and reality itself can be considered to be socially constructed. Whether or not one adopts a participatory approach can therefore depend on the ontological and epistemological position of a researcher. **Ontology** is concerned with 'the nature of existence, with the structure of reality as such' (Crotty, 1998: 10). It is closely related to epistemological issues which are concerned with our understanding of the nature of knowledge or, in other words, 'how we know what we know' (Crotty, 1998: 8). Epistemological stances are not mutually exclusive, and there may be a level of overlap, but the three main epistemological perspectives are objectivism, constructionism and subjectivism. Objectivism assumes that there is a meaningful reality which is independent 'from the operation of any consciousness' (Crotty, 1998: 8). **Constructivism** on the other hand rejects this idea of a meaningful reality and takes instead the view that meaning is constructed via human interaction and is therefore in a 'constant state of revision' (Bryman, 2012: 33). It follows that 'different people may construct meaning in different ways, even in relation to the same phenomenon' (Crotty, 1998: 9). Subjectivism also rejects the notion of an objective reality but, in contrast to constructivism, it holds that meaning is imposed on an object rather than arises from the interplay between object and subject (Crotty, 1998).

It is easy to see then how both ontology and **epistemology** connect various theoretical perspectives with different research strategies and ultimately research methods, techniques and specific data collection and analysis procedures. As Mason (2002) puts it, different interpretations of the nature and essence of social things and researchers' competing ontological views of these social things, which include different thoughts on how elements of the social world are connected with each other, not only say very different things about evidence, but produce their own rationale of how this evidence can and should be collected in the first place. According to Mason (2002: 16), there are 'principles and rules by which you [the researcher] decide whether and how social phenomena can be known, and how knowledge can be demonstrated'. Essentially, theoretical and methodological perspectives are informed by whether researchers believe that 'research can provide self-evidential proof of universally perceived objective realities'. This is often associated with macro-sociological, positivist approaches and utilises mainly quantitative research methods. Alternatively, one adopts 'more epistemologically modest concepts of perspective and argument', as Mason puts it (2002: 16), and this is regarded as a micro-sociological interpretative perspective and is seen as being linked to qualitative research methods. However, for Crotty (1998: 14) the 'great divide', as he calls it, is not between qualitative and quantitative methods, but rather objectivist methods on one side and constructivist/subjectivist ones on the other.

Crotty (1998) reminds us that, in practice, principal epistemological and methodological convictions rarely impact on a research project from the outset. Rather, the design of a research project often depends on practical considerations, namely the actual issue or problem that needs to addressed, the time frame available, the expectation of the funders or similar constraints, in other words a methodology which serves the particular purpose of the respective research project – and this can be either qualitative or quantitative. Nevertheless, even if we dismiss methodological and epistemological purism as impractical and idealistic, it is likely that theoretical persuasions or preferences play some part in the decision making about the research methods to be used, including participatory methods, and it is therefore meaningful to engage in a theoretical thought experiment to explore epistemological and ontological standpoints and how these might influence a research project (see Exercise 2.1 below).

Denzin (cited in Seale, 2000: 3) warns that 'by making qualitative research – and participatory approaches are predominantly qualitative in nature – "scientifically" respectable, researchers may impose schemes of interpretation on the social world that simply do not fit in the world as it is constructed and lived by interacting individuals'.

Even so, theoretical perspectives can influence the way participatory projects are run. Bryman's (2012) model on the influences on social research (Figure 2.1)

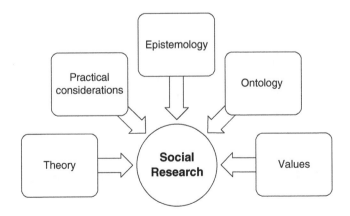

Figure 2.1   Influences on social research

Source: adapted from Bryman (2012: 39). Reproduced with permission of the Licensor through PLSclear.

represents how epistemological and ontological convictions inform social research practice, although other factors such as theory and practical considerations also determine the nature of research projects.

In relation to participatory approaches, Krueger and King (1998) name four reasons for the involvement of co-researchers, two of which are of a practical nature, whilst the others are connected to the value of the research. Their reasons are:

1   The ability of co-researchers to collect more in-depth data.
2   The ability to collect data in otherwise unfeasible settings.
3   The benefits that such research brings to the communities of the individuals involved in the research.
4   The fact that through participatory approaches the research itself becomes more meaningful to participants.

It is inevitable that researchers also bring their own values and personal research preferences to the table, as Figure 2.1 suggests. Unless researchers feel equipped to work and engage with marginalised and disadvantaged communities and garner personal satisfaction from these participatory research encounters, no epistemological or ontological argument alone is likely to convince them to adopt such research practice. However, personal preferences aside, there are some compelling micro- and macro-theoretical assumptions and paradigms that support participatory approaches. The first of these relates to PAR approaches, which are discussed in detail in Chapter 5, and the way knowledge is being conceptualised within these.

Ladkin (2007: 480) states that in the epistemological assumption of action research, 'knowing' is considered to be 'embedded within the cycles of action and reflection'. Namely, the theory purports that there are different ways of 'knowing', which include experiential and practical knowledge. Experiential knowledge can be gained from actual encounters with people or places. Practical knowledge, on the other hand, is obtained from engaging and actually doing things, and this results in new skills and competencies. This question of the relevance of experimental and practical knowledge is, in my view, a fundamental epistemological question not just for action research, but for all participatory approaches that involve people actively in the research process. Participatory researchers tend to believe that practical and experimental knowledge are not only important components of knowledge in general, but that they help us to access participants' world views.

Linking participatory approaches and social theories

Although Bryman (2012: 19) concedes that there is not always a definite link between theory and a specific form of data collection, research is not 'entirely dictated by theoretical concerns' as he puts it: 'methods of social research are closely tied to different versions of how social reality should be studied'. So, whilst data is not always collected for theory building or testing, this connection is often implicit.

An example for a very close link between method and *grand* (substantial) *theory* is ethnomethodology, which Garfinkel (1967, 2002) describes as studying practical and everyday activities, common-sense practices, practical circumstances and sociological reasoning, in other words 'how and by the use of what procedures and methods any particular world is produced and perceived' (ten Have, 2004: 139). Here it follows that a deep understanding of everyday talk and practice is core to ethnomethodological theory. Garfinkel's famous 'breaching experiments' (1967), in which he and his students and research assistants violated – or 'breached' – expectations in verbal communications in order to elicit information about common-sense communicative practices, show that even within very specific theoretical perspectives methodological variation and experimentation are possible. Generally speaking, however, ethnomethodological data collection is inextricably linked to the detailed analysis of everyday language, which would make a large-scale survey questionnaire, for example, an unsuitable instrument for data collection to inform theory formation. However, other theoretical paradigms or conceptual frameworks, which are less focused on particular and specific aspects of the social world, are also more flexible in terms of data collection methods.

Participation and the notion of *Verstehen*

As Flick (2014) puts it, the epistemological principle in qualitative social research is *Verstehen* – a term often associated with the work of the notable German sociologists Max Weber (1947) and Georg Simmel (Wolff, 1950). The academic Weberian meaning of this German word is perhaps best translated as 'deep understanding' or 'comprehending'. In the sociological context, *Verstehen* basically refers to a systematic interpretive process in which an outsider is trying to 'understand' or 'comprehend' a particular phenomenon, behaviour or action *from within*, at the level of the world of the individuals concerned, rather than from the outside looking in. This is done by the systematic, albeit subjective, interpretation of the context, motivation and meaning of this behaviour or phenomenon. In Weber's (1947) view, the individuals always attach subjective meaning to their actions, although this can be done overtly, covertly, via omission or compliance. Weber therefore concedes that all knowledge is necessarily always knowledge from a particular subjective point of view, and it is therefore potentially fallible. Nevertheless, he – unlike many participatory researchers today who dismiss the notion of 'objectivity' – still strongly believed in the value of an objective science and he felt that this was what social scientists should strive for. So, whilst Weber is credited for aiding the move away from positivistic approaches in the social sciences which aimed to follow a research logic typical in the natural sciences, for Weber an 'objective social science' remained the ultimate, albeit unattainable goal.

In my view, this notion of *Verstehen* can form one of the theoretical pillars of participatory approaches to undertaking social research: if we accept that the purpose of social research is the *deep understanding* of phenomena, behaviours, cultures, etc. then it is not so difficult to conclude that the inclusion of experts in the discovery and interpretation of these phenomena can potentially, albeit not automatically, aid this process. The key question for social researchers is therefore to what extent it is sensible to surrender some powers to the participants in social research projects and how this can support this process of 'deep understanding'. Whilst there is no definite answer to this question, and participation and co-production of knowledge can take different forms and approaches as the following chapters in Part II of this book demonstrate, in principle, participatory approaches and methods can aid systematic data collection and analysis and therefore potentially contribute to the Weberian concept of 'objective (social) science'.

To give just one example, it is quite sensible to believe that the active involvement of young people with care experiences in the planning and running of a research project on experiences of care leavers could potentially provide deeper insights into the lives of young people with such histories and backgrounds. Whilst young people in care can share their understanding as participants in interviews, focus groups or during ethnographic fieldwork, if care-experienced young people are also included in the design of the study (either as advisors or co-researchers) – they can also help to devise more appropriate questions, they can relate to the experiences of participants much better than perhaps an academic researcher can, and they can help to make better sense of the data collected, including contextual data, thus, aiding this process of deep understanding or *Verstehen*. This involvement can take place at different levels as Figure 2.1 illustrates and will be discussed in detail in Part II of this book.

Symbolic interactionism

A second theoretical pillar that can underpin participatory approaches is the framework of symbolic interactionism. Herbert Blumer was the sociologist who coined this term and one of the leading interactionist thinkers. Blumer was strongly influenced by Mead's (1934) theory and notion on how the self develops through interactions with others. At its core, symbolic interactionism holds that 'human beings act towards things on the basis of the meaning that these things have for them' (Blumer, 1986: 241); this is based on the interactions that people have with each other; and these meanings are mediated by an interpretive process used by people as they are dealing with actions and experiences. These meanings and interpretive actions become a central subject of investigation in social researchers' attempts to understand people and their feelings, experiences and actions. This principle is connected to the well-known *Thomas theorem*, which states: 'If men [people!] define situations as real, they are real in their consequences' (Thomas and Thomas, 1928: 571–572). In other words, people's actions depend mainly on their (subjective) interpretations of situations rather than on the (objective) situations themselves. So, if we agree with this theorem and its underlying meaning, personal and subjective interpretations of social situations become a major subject of social investigation. Interactionist theory also assumes that social meaning is not unique to individuals but is based on widely shared definitions which have their roots in symbols in their respective cultures. Nonetheless, symbols and meaning are learned and communicated through interaction with others, and they are fluid and flexible as a result of this. The Thomas theorem therefore provides social researchers with a principle that reminds them of the need to take a non-judgemental approach to their research practice and encourages them to see the world from the perspective of the people that they study – this is a fundamental principle for social interactionist approaches. Even though symbolic interactionism differs from Weber, if we accept these theoretical assumptions are valid (as with the concept of *Verstehen)*, we can then conclude that engaging the active participation of people close to the subject matter can help researchers access the interpretive and communicative structures that help construct meaning from the phenomenon under investigation.

Goffman's (1959) work on the dramaturgical and performative presentations of self and his theory of action has particular relevance to participatory group discussion methods, which are discussed in more detail in Chapter 7. His insight that people present images of themselves depending on the context they are in and the 'audience' they have also leads to the conclusion that the 'performance' that research participants give to outside (academic) researchers will be different from the one that they give to a research team that includes co-researchers or peer researchers who are more familiar with the research context that is being investigated.

Social constructivist theory

Social interactionism falls into the category of social constructivism, and constructivist theory in the tradition of Alfred Schütz (1962) and Peter Berger and Thomas Luckmann (1966) shall be discussed next. Constructivist theory assumes that people are born into existing meaningful social structures and a social reality that is then taken for granted; however, this social world is at the same time subject to human action and interaction. Academics in the tradition of social constructivism consider experiences as structured and understood through concepts and contexts which are constructed at an individual level. One of the central assumptions of social constructivism is that all knowledge – whether academic or everyday knowledge – is constructed by individuals via selection, structuring and idealisation. The extent and type of idealisation and structuring will depend on the context in which this takes place. So, for example, academic knowledge constructions will have a higher level of abstraction and can be potentially related to, or lead to, the formation of academic theory. This will not be the case for everyday and common-sense-type knowledge constructions; nonetheless these are theories of sorts too and, as Schütz (1962) maintains, they are equally constructed using a process of active knowledge production. Reason (1993: 1259) alludes to 'different kinds of knowing' which have to be integrated during research utilising self-study – an important aspect of reflective practice in participatory projects. Crucially, whether it is academic or everyday knowledge construction, they are mediated and aided by social interaction and interchange and are based on the everyday language that we use. This means that social interactions should be studied from the point of view of the meaning given to them by individual actors. As Fulcher and Scott (2003: 55–56) put it:

> People continually create and recreate their social world. [...] People rely on their audiences sharing a background of assumptions that allow them to fill in the gaps for themselves and so to understand what is being said.

Again, this can be a good reason for a more participatory approach to social research as the access to the interpretations and the meaning that social actors give to phenomena is ultimately mediated via the spoken word and via symbols which are unique to each social context and to which outside researchers only have limited access. As Flick (2014: 71) states: 'Research acts [themselves] are also part of the social construction of what we can address and find in social research.'

Psychological frameworks

Social psychology offers another useful framework which potentially provides a theoretical backing for participatory approaches. There are a number of theories in social psychology which have been discussed in relation to participatory research, such as transformative learning theory (Mezirow, 1991; Percy, 2005), but here I want to focus on the notion of 'subjective theories', which is based on George Kelly's (1955) claim that ordinary people develop their own theories (or personal constructs) of how the world around them functions. Kelly argues that ordinary people, just like scientists, test and revise these constructs or theories, if necessary. According to Groeben (1990: 20) 'subjective theories' can be defined as:

> cognitions relating to the self and the world constituting a complex aggregate with an (at least implicit) argumentational structure; these cognitions fulfil functions parallel to those of objective 'scientific' theories, namely those of explanation, prediction and technology.

This insight has significantly influenced participatory research approaches, namely action science and citizen science (see Chapter 3).

Psychology is somewhat more concerned with personal and individual transformations than with change at societal level, so the personal relational aspect of undertaking collaborative research projects with participants is of particular interest. As Tolman and Brydon-Miller (2001: 5) state:

> Participatory and interpretive methods are relational, i.e. they acknowledge and actively involve relationships between researchers and participants, as well as their respective subjectivities.

The notable and practical consequence of this notion of subjective theories is that psychological collaborative researchers are particularly concerned with the creation of an even power balance between academic researchers and co-researchers on the basis of the assumption that there is really not very much difference between the way academic researchers and ordinary people/research participants make sense of the world around them and attribute meaning to phenomena. So, one of the implications of this argument is that co-researchers are regarded as full members of the research team and their voices are given equal value to those of the academic researchers – at least this is the aim/theory.

Feminism

Feminism's main contribution to participatory and emancipatory research practice is to expose the failure of conventional methods to capture the voice of women and other disadvantaged groups of people. Hesse-Biber (2007: 10) summarises the overarching feminist perspective on research:

> It is a woman's oppressed location within society that provides fuller insights into society as a whole; women have access to an enhanced and more nuanced understanding of social reality than men do precisely because of their structurally oppressed location vis-à-vis the dominant group, or men.

Feminism has a plurality, reflecting the diversity of feminist perspectives – liberal feminism, Marxist feminism, radical feminism, to name just three – see Tong (1995) for a more comprehensive categorisation. These feminisms 'make sense of the world in a myriad of ways', as Crotty (1998: 160–161) puts it; however, the shared experience of oppressive patriarchy and the desire to change it is shared among the different strands of feminism.

One of the significant early contributions of feminist scholars to the field of participatory research methods is Maguire's 1987 publication *Doing Participatory Research: A Feminist Approach*. In this volume she describes how the three-part process of knowledge creation used in participatory research – 1) investigation, 2) education and 3) action – is not just 'a new set of research techniques', but 'a systematic approach to personal and social transformation' (1987: 3).

Morawski (2001: 59) reminds us of one of the principal assumptions of feminism, namely that science is 'constituted through a complex set of sustained consensual practices' and is not 'independent of its practitioners, their actions, their aspirations, and their culture; nor is it always separate from the actions of non-scientific actors or institutions'. According to Morawski (2001: 59), the feminist agenda is not just the study of gender experience, but it rather 'entails multiple strategies to revise or transform the dominant practices of science that have found to be androcentric or sexist'. By doing so, it not only aims to show the reality of women's experiences who for many decades have been marginalised in academic research, but feminist research strategies have the capacity and ability to identify and address bias against disadvantaged and marginalised groups in general. Morawski argues that a focus on narrative research methods as a 'cognitive research instrument' alongside an extensive analysis of the context in which a research project takes place will help us to explore and understand the subjectivities in the field. In the view of most feminist scholars, such context data form an integral part of a research project and must not be ignored or downplayed as is often the case in positivist approaches. However, Morwaski proposes that a transformation of the research relationships into more participatory and collaborative practice, which sees participants involved in the data collection, analysis, interpretation and evaluation, will also help us address subjectivity and potentially lay bare multiple power relations in a research project. Participatory and collaborative practice then provides a useful framework and prism to view research with all marginalised or minority groups.

Morawski refers in her writing to the classic study by Harding (1986) in which she outlines a five-tier feminist research programme. One of these tiers is particularly relevant to this book as it is concerned with the exploration of feminist research epistemologies. The core principles are that there can be no strict boundaries between the academic scientist and the practice context and the links between science, practice and action are, in fact, substantial. In consequence, there is no such thing as a factual or 'valid' representation of 'reality'. Rather feminism positions itself in the constructivist camp and argues that what is required are plural methods which explicitly incorporate an analysis of contextual factors and relationships in the research findings.

Hoff's study (1988) with women who have experienced domestic violence provides a perfect example of the importance of applying sensitivity to the research context. Hoff argues strongly that her study highlights the need to undertake research projects on sensitive subject areas and with vulnerable participants in a way that protects the participants, whilst at the same complying with the principles of academic rigour. Hoff claims that these context factors essentially generate secondary effects of the research process. She argues that these have to be taken into consideration and the potentially harmful political and ethical ramifications for study participants have to be made explicit from the onset of a study.

Whilst feminism has diversified into various approaches and forms, understanding that researcher–participant relationships are central parts of research projects paves the way for researchers not just to reflect on these relationships, but also to actively engage in collaborative approaches. Morawski (2001: 69) refers to Lather (1991) when she concludes that a challenge for feminist researchers is the 'commitment to producing knowledge that leads to positive change in the world'. This principal desire for positive change has influenced action research methodologies that are discussed in more detail in Chapter 5.

Is there a unique feminist epistemology – a special feminist or female way of knowing? Crotty (1998) draws on feminist writers' own scepticism about the notion that 'women know in a fundamentally different way from men' (1998: 174). He refers to Fonow and Cook (1991) who reject this notion postulated by others that quantitative research is a somehow a 'male' form of research whilst qualitative research is somehow 'female'. Nevertheless, Crotty (1998: 175) agrees that one of 'the characteristic features of feminist epistemology is the attention to the affective components of the research act', and he quotes Fonow and Cook (1991: 9–11) who see in this 'an attempt among feminist scholars to restore the emotional dimension to the current concepts of rationality'.

Marxism, critical theory and participatory approaches

Few social theories have had such a considerable societal impact as *Marxism*, and arguably no other theory has been as closely connected to the ambition to achieve social change and social action. If there was a model for a socially active and engaged, but equally theoretically influential academic, it would probably have to be Karl Marx (1818–1883). For Marx, the whole purpose of his interdisciplinary academic work and the resulting theory of political economy, which heavily influenced various social science disciplines, was to provoke and initiate social change on a macro-societal level. The starting point for Marx's theory was the social reality of people, namely of the people who lived in desperate squalor during the time of the industrial revolution – the proletariat. At the core of Marxist theory is the notion that people's lives are determined by societal structures or, more specifically, the economic system in which they live. This gives them limited life choices. What is central to the capitalist system, according to Marx, is the private ownership of the means of production, which is the cause of social inequality between classes. In Marx's thinking, this economic infrastructure also determines the way religious, political and educational spheres, but also family structures, are organised in society, creating essentially a superstructure. Marx believed that there was an inevitability in the way societal change would occur via a social revolution, although this required the development of a class consciousness, or in other words, an awareness of the exploitative structures of society. Marx's political activism was directed at making a contribution to this consciousness raising, and it is no coincidence that he is the co-author of the *Manifesto of the Communist Party* (Marx and Engels, 1848), one of the most influential and analytical political manuscripts ever written, first printed in the print shop of the Workers' Educational Society in London.

The aim to create a fairer and more equal society, which is at the core of Marx's theory and his political activism, made it almost inevitable that Marxism and critical social theory, which developed and diversified on the basis of his work, became the building blocks of participatory and action research practice, sharing, with Marx, the action-focus and ambition to improve the lives of disadvantaged people. The misappropriation of scientific Marxist theory and the distortion of Marxist ideals by would-be socialist and communist leaders in Eastern Europe and elsewhere after the Second World War has to some extent contributed to the discrediting of Marxism, certainly in the public eye. However, Marxist science enjoys continued influence in the academic world, and his vision of a fairer society has inspired researchers in their attempts to bring about social change for those most disadvantaged by society, including participatory and action researchers.

Marxist thinking influenced many early sociologists, such as Durkheim, Simmel, Weber and Tönnies, as well as other theorists such as Lukács, Gramsci and Althusser. However, it is the emergence of the Frankfurt School with the establishment of the Institute of Social Research at the J. W. Goethe University Frankfurt/Main in 1924 that is of particular relevance to this book. Over the years, the Institute has been a home for notable social scientists such as Adorno, Horkheimer, Marcuse, Fromm and Habermas, and they jointly have been connected to the emergence and development of one of the most influential theoretical developments in social science, namely critical theory. Academics connected with the Frankfurt School never represented a homogeneous group, yet, like Marx, whose work was the main founding pillar of the Institute, they were all concerned with conditions that enable social change. Richard Bernstein's (1976: 235) appeal that 'an adequate social and political theory must be empirical, interpretive and critical' has been quoted many times, and it reflects the ambitions of the researchers in the Frankfurt School. Brydon-Miller (2001: 79) points to the dialectical process of action and reflection that critical theory advocates and which has, in turn, influenced participatory research practice:

> Critically informed inquiry generates a form of knowledge that results in and grows out of the liberation of those generating the knowledge; it is simultaneously knowledge based in action and action based in knowledge.

One of the most influential envoys of critical theory is Jürgen Habermas (1972, 1984, 1985), whose work on social interaction as communicative action has influenced the work of participatory research practice (Kemmis, 2001). According to Habermas, language and communication are central to critical social theory, and human language and action are structured linguistically. For Habermas, 'ideal speech situations' are the vision of emancipation, and these 'are characterised by mutuality of expectation rather than one-sided norms' (Crotty, 1998: 143).

Brydon-Miller (2001: 79) observes that Habermas identifies three distinct processes of enquiry:

1 *Empirical analytical knowledge.*
2 *Practical interests of humankind,* expressed through human communication and language.
3 *Critical knowledge,* which is knowledge born out of social action that supports the emancipatory interests of humankind.

Godin et al.'s (2007) publication directly references Habermas' notion of 'communicative space', in relation to a participatory, user-led research project on forensic mental health care. Habermas' model of 'strategic action' versus 'communicative action' is used to analyse accounts of interactions that participants in this research, who were users of the mental health services, had with service providers.

Kemmis (2001: 100–101) reminds us that critical theory has been developed and advanced over a period of some years. Applying Habermas' theoretical body of literature,

Kemmis describes action research from different perspectives: (1) an action research group as a 'critical community'; (2) action research as 'shared engagement in communicative action'; and (3) action researchers 'as engaged citizens committed to local action but with a wider critical and emancipatory vision for their work'. This last point is reiterated by Brydon-Miller (2001) who emphasises that critical social science involves a process of self-understanding and collective self-formation, as well as the desire for social action. Perhaps the main contribution of critical theory and Marxism to participatory and emancipatory research approaches is that it provides a vision for macro-social change, which is maybe what Chevalier and Buckles (2013) allude to when they speak about the need to up-scale participatory work.

Systems theory

Whilst most theoretical work in relation to participation is more comfortably embedded in interaction theory approaches, there have also been some attempts to locate participatory practice in theoretical frameworks which have their basis in systems theory. Baraldi's work on children's and young people's participation is one example of this (Baraldi and Ieverse, 2012; Baraldi, 2014). Baraldi uses Luhmann's social systems theory (Luhmann, 1995), specifically in relation to communication systems (Luhmann, 2002), to make sense of children's and young people's active involvement in research. Even though Baraldi's focus is on children and young people specifically, his theoretical models have some appeal to the conceptualisation of participation more broadly.

Baraldi attempts to better clarify the meanings attached to the concept of (children's) 'agency' which has been very central to the development of childhood studies (James, 2009). Agency is here defined via three core aspects, namely 'action', 'perspective' and 'social conditions'. The argument is that children and young people hold views ('perspective'), and that they have the capacity to respond to, mitigate or resist 'action'. Finally, all of this takes place in particular 'social conditions' within which children and young people interact. Baraldi (2014: 65) argues further that the realisation that children and young people *do* have 'agency' and are 'social beings' rather than 'social becomings' is important for a better understanding of children and young people as competent participants in their own socialisation and in the creation of meaning within this process. However, in Baraldi's view, this does not sufficiently explain participation as 'doing'. The point that Baraldi is trying to make is that a focus on the notion of 'agency' potentially results in a tendency to *over*estimate the capacity of actors to act independently whilst at the same time *under*estimating the potential constraints that actors – here children and young people – face in their desire and attempt to participate and to take actions. In my view this is a valid point not just in relation to the participation of children and young people, but in regard to participation and action more generally. (Enabling and disabling factors and power relations that affect participatory research approaches are discussed in more detail later in this book.)

Baraldi (2014: 66) sets out to 'describe and explain the interplay' between partic-ipation and social structures, repeating the central question from childhood studies, namely to what extent children *can* and *do* contribute to social change. Extending and generalising this question beyond the immediate issue of the involvement of children and young people, it arguably has particular relevance for action research methods which are aimed at social change.

Warming (2012: 31) adds here that maintaining the view that children should have the same rights as enjoyed by adults 'is almost as problematic as the "not-yet-citizen" approach, as it overlooks the bodily and socially constructed differences that character-ise childhood'. Warming follows Alanen and Mayall's (2001) argument that there is a 'generational order' which determines that children and adults occupy different social positions which in turn determine the different motivations, entitlements and formal rights for participation for both adults and children (Warming, 2012: 32). She proposes that a useful theoretical framework for the facilitation of participation of children is that by Axel Honneth (1995) on social recognition. The application of this framework would lead to the conclusion that:

> an important task in adults' facilitation of children's citizenship is to re-define the social construction of what it means to be 'a person possessing the same moral sanity as all other people' in a way that includes children rather than defining them as 'less than' and thus 'not yet' adults. (Warming, 2012: 39)

Applying Luhmann's theoretical framework, Baraldi (2014) argues that social struc-tures condition active participation. He states that the notion of 'agency' implies the availability of choices of action and participation. The author further argues that 'all [children's] actions can modify chains of actions' (Baraldi, 2014: 73), but he also stresses that there are 'important limitations for [children's] contributions to structural change' (2014: 74). Baraldi particularly refers to existing hierarchical social structures which can limit or block both participation and action and therefore can also potentially block a display of agency. This relates well to Warming's insights on social recognition and the facilitation of this process based on Honneth's theoretical framework. Again, we can reasonably extend these insights beyond the issue of children's and young people's role as active participants in research.

Baraldi proposes that 'promotional communication systems' (2014: 74) could be used to overcome existing hierarchical structures, and this is a very useful concept which should be considered when designing participatory research projects that involve peo-ple as co-researchers. Baraldi points out that such promotional communication systems in fact create a paradox, namely that effective participation and action for social change often depend on the creation of such enabling conditions for this change and partici-pation to take place in the first place. Again, he refers particularly to the positioning of children in an adult world where often adults have to create the conditions where children can participate and initiate changes (for example the legal framework for par-ticipation and action, i.e. the United Nations Convention for the Rights of the Child

(UNCRC), government-appointed Children's Commissioners and participatory structures such as Youth Councils, advisory groups, rights-respecting schools, etc.). However, similar arguments could be made about the creation of conditions for marginalised or hard-to-reach groups, such as people with disabilities, vulnerable older people, minority ethnic groups, indigenous communities, and so forth. Finally, Baraldi argues that participation therefore has to be seen as embedded within the 'system' – again he is using Luhmann's terminology – of 'facilitation'.

To summarise, whilst systems theoretical approaches are not the most cited frameworks when it comes to participatory research methods, they can still provide useful theoretical insights that can inform the design of participatory research projects. Systems theory is particularly useful in understanding the necessity of the creation and use of promotional communication systems that facilitate and enable participation and the creation of new narratives that can eventually lead to action and social change. Participation is influenced by these communication systems. Paradoxically this facilitation process depends on the willingness of those in powerful positions who are often the same groups of people in the structures and powerful positions which social action often targets. Yet, in systems theory, the powerful themselves are unable to produce structural change, all they can do is provide the conditions in which change can occur. In the words of Baraldi – again focused specifically on children's participation, but with a much broader scope:

> Structural change and new narratives can only be produced in communication systems. They cannot be produced by adults' actions that enhance children's agency, or by children's actions, displaying agency; they are produced in communication processes, on the basis of specific structures of epistemic status and authority, coding, positioning, and forms of expectations. Only the ongoing production of communication can promote new structures and narratives, both in the specific interactions and in complex social systems that include interactions. (Baraldi, 2014: 76)

So whilst systems theory does not deny the role of agency in participation and social change, it argues that there must be an initial external impetus to create the conditions that can facilitate participation and change. With regard to the subject matter of this book, this claim has strong resonance in relation to the design and planning of participatory projects and the power relations within such projects.

Structural functionalism

As with systems theory, structural functionalism (associated with Talcott Parsons and Emile Durkheim, some of the central figures in social science theory) is not usually connected to participatory and collaborative research approaches. Structural functionalism assumes that people's behaviour is determined by a set of social facts, or constraints or rules (Durkheim, 1982 [1938]). For Durkheim, these social facts or constraints are certain established ways of thinking, feeling or acting, that are passed down from generation to generation, as he has shown, for example, in relation to religious life (Durkheim, 1995 [1912]). Parsons (1949) sees these norms, social facts, constraints or rules as having some purpose or function; they make society work smoothly and create order. Micro-sociologists (for example symbolic interactionists) have criticised this system-orientation, as it neglects the agency that individuals have and their role in maintaining and changing these structures. Whilst Parsons is still concerned with individual action, it is from the perspective of how the environment determines the organisation and character of this social action. This does not dismiss agency entirely, but the lack of focus on agency is one of the main reasons why structural functionalism as a theoretical framework is rarely connected to participatory research methods that, as we have seen, privilege agency as a factor for change and action.

When discussing the move towards patient-centred care and research, McDonnell et al. (2009: 32) identify 'Parsons' blind spot', the fact that:

> he ignores the possibility of conflict between the doctor's belief system, which informs clinical decision making, and the values and beliefs that the patient brings to the medical encounter.

The authors argue that the public trust in medical, paternalistic authority can no longer be assumed. Their criticism can be applied to a range of other 'systems' in society, such as education, government and the built environment to name just three, where increasingly participatory approaches are being used to involve ordinary people as service users in policy decision making.

However, functionalist and structuralist frameworks still have something to offer when it comes to the interpretation of action or lack of action and in contextualising and understanding people's behaviour or their disadvantaged social situations. If Parsons' 'blind spot' is his ignorance of the conflict between belief systems, then arguably the 'blind spot' of some participatory and action researchers is that individual agency is often limited by the social environment and the way people are socialised. Arguably, recognising and addressing potential social constraints when discussing expectations in relation to potential social change and action as a result of a participatory, collaborative project is good practice. One of the main ethical issues in participatory research is to negotiate participants' own expectations with regard to change and action and in some cases this means to deal with the disappointment of anticipated and awaited social action simply not occurring at all – see Chapter 4.

On an academic and theoretical level, Durkheim's and Parsons' theories have useful contributions to make in terms of contextualising constraints to social action and

The sociological tradition of *Verstehen*

- **Theoretical Standpoint**: Deep understanding, comprehending and explaining of the meaning that social actors give to their world and actions. Attempts to interpret this from the social actors' points of view.
- **Participatory Rationale**: Involvement of community representatives and co-researchers can help us to get closer to an understanding of their worldview.

Symbolic Interactionism

- **Theoretical Standpoint**: Social meaning is based on widely shared definitions which have their roots in symbols in their respective cultures. Symbols and meaning are learned and communicated through interaction with others and are fluid and flexible.
- **Participatory Rationale**: Active participation of people close to the subject matter of the study can help researchers access the interpretive and communicative structures and help construct meaning.

Social Constructivist Theory

- **Theoretical Standpoint**: All knowledge is constructed by individuals via selection, structuring and idealisation. Thus, social interactions should be studied from the point of view of the meaning given to them by individual actors.
- **Participatory Rationale**: Involvement of community and co-researchers can give us access to the interpretations and the meanings which are unique to social contexts that outside researchers do not normally have easy access to.

Feminism

- **Theoretical Standpoint**: Fostering of personal and social transformation. Bringing to the fore voices of disadvantaged and disenfranchised groups and communities.
- **Participatory Rationale**: Dismantling of the strict boundaries between the academic scientist and the practice context and the links between science, practice and action with a view to bring about positive change.

Marxism

- **Theoretical Standpoint**: Critically informed enquiry. Not just describing the world, but changing it. Creating a fairer more equal society.
- **Participatory Rationale**: Providing a vision for social change. Creation of non-hierarchical communicative spaces for communities to come together to discuss and address desired social change.

Systems Theory

- **Theoretical Standpoint**: The social structures in which we operate are enabling or disabling factors in relation to our agency to participate and bring about change.
- **Participatory Rationale**: Using participatory research designs to proactively create promotional 'communication systems' to overcome hierarchical social structures.

Structural Functionalism

- **Theoretical Standpoint**: People's behaviour is determined by social facts, constraints and rules, i.e. established ways of thinking, feeling or acting, which are passed down through generations and make society work smoothly and create order.
- **Participatory Rationale**: Using established belief systems and stereotypes that participants may bring to a research project. Through participatory practice, to overcome existing taken-for-granted norms and perceived limitations to social agency and social actions.

Figure 2.2 Connection between theoretical perspectives and participatory approaches

change. They also offer a link to Fiske and Taylor's (2016) notion of people as 'cognitive misers', which connects to cognitive psychology. In their research, Fiske and Taylor were able to show that people take mental shortcuts to process new information because it is impossible for the human brain to process all new information thoroughly and repeatedly. This can lead to established beliefs and stereotypes being reproduced. Similarly, individual agency has limitations, and people can accept and take for granted structures, norms, social actions and systems that they grow up with, as Durkheim (1995 [1912]) showed in his iconic study on religious life. It is this 'reality check' that may help researchers in collaborative and participatory projects to negotiate and contextualise expectations among participants and communities. After all, regardless of how well a collaborative project is undertaken, there can never be the promise of change, and it may well be the same macro-structures that are at the root of disadvantage or discrimination which prevent action from taking place.

In Figure 2.2. I have summarised the main theoretical standpoints discussed in this chapter and how they in my view can connect to participatory research practice.

Summary

As we have seen, from a theoretical point of view participatory approaches are clearly suited to theoretical frameworks that privilege individual agency and connect this with a vison of social change. However, what this chapter has demonstrated is that the rationale for co-production approaches is by no means limited to feminist or Marxist frameworks, to mention just two. Many participatory projects are actually not starting out from a theoretical perspective, but rather from an identified issue or need. Social theory is very secondary in that respect. Nevertheless, consciously or unconsciously, theory influences our thinking and actions – and not just the thinking of professional or academic researchers, but of co-researchers as well, as we have seen in this chapter. It is therefore important in collaborative research practice to be aware and reflective of the subject standpoints that researchers and co-researchers bring to a project, as this potentially determines the study design and will ultimately have an impact on its outcome. Whilst on a more theoretical and less practical level, the exercise at the end of this chapter is therefore a good activity to raise self-awareness about how we approach a study.

FURTHER READING

Barnes, M. and Cotterell, P. (eds) (2012). *Critical Perspectives on User Involvement*. Bristol: Policy Press.

Crotty, M. (1998). *The Foundations of Social Research: Meaning and Perspective in the Research Process*. London: Sage.

EXERCISE 2.1

RESEARCH AND EPISTEMOLOGICAL PERSPECTIVES

In this chapter we discussed different epistemological perspectives and their applicability in relation to participatory approaches. The three main ones discussed were: objectivism, constructivism and subjectivism. All have different theoretical assumptions and underpinnings. Imagine you have to design a research project which aims to study everyday life in a post-primary school. (You can pick another topic if you like.) Try to design a research project, including data collection methods and means of analysis, from the standpoint of all three epistemological perspectives. How differently might they look? You can use Table 2.1 below as guidance on what aspects to include. This activity is about understanding ideal-typical perspectives and locating personal perspectives. There is no right or wrong in this, and there are different reasons why some research methods might be suitable or unsuitable to produce the outcomes we require.

This exercise can also be adapted by considering what a feminist or Marxist project or one in the tradition of Freire could look like, and what elements this would need to contain.

Table 2.1 Research design and epistemological perspectives

	Objectivism	Constructivism	Subjectivism
Methods of data collection (e.g. survey questionnaire, participant observation, interviews)			
Sampling (e.g. probability or non-probability, random, opportunistic, snowball)			
Number of participants required			
Data analysis techniques (e.g. statistical, thematic analysis)			
Any other features			

3

APPROACHES AND POPULATIONS IN PARTICIPATORY RESEARCH

What you will learn

This chapter will discuss some of the main approaches of participatory research that have developed over the years and their unique features. The focus here is on demonstrating the diversity of collaborative research practice. I will showcase the research areas in which participatory methods have been employed and the population groups which have been the main focus of these approaches and applications. The purpose of this chapter is really to give stimulus and impetus to those who think about the development of their own research projects.

Introduction

As participatory approaches have proliferated and diversified over time, some have become closely associated with specific subject areas, study fields or population groups, or are organised in unique ways. Often the approaches and applications discussed in this chapter share similar methodological and epistemological principles and they utilise broadly the same means of data collection, but focus on unique issues or arenas. One example is the rapid growth of the use of participatory and collaborative approaches in professional research fields, such as education, health and social work, where advances have been made in the active inclusion of service users and clients in research practice.

This overview is not exhaustive, and does not include action research (AR) and participatory action research (PAR), as Chapter 5 is dedicated to this. However, this chapter may help to systematically categorise many current collaborative and participatory approaches and stress the breadth of participatory research undertaken. The chapter starts with an overview of specific approaches followed by a discussion of topics and themes covered.

Participatory approaches

Community-based participatory research (CBPR)

One of the most well-known participatory approaches closely connected to, and frequently used in, health research is community-based participatory research (CBPR). CBPR is a collaborative approach to research which, when undertaken well, promotes equitable partnerships in all aspects of a project from the design stage to the interpretation of results and implementation of findings and outcomes. According to Minkler and Wallerstein (2011: 2):

> In contrast to more traditional investigator-driven research, CBPR begins with an issue selected by, or of real importance to, the community, and involves community members and other stakeholders throughout the research process, including its culmination in education and action for social change.

CBPR projects start with the identification of a research topic which is of importance to the community. CBPR is action-focused, addressing health inequalities. Leung, Yen and Minkler (2004) note that, despite significant advances in epidemiology, it remains unclear why certain health outcomes occur, and they argue that CBPR can be used to gain a better understanding of the *social* context of ill-health and complex community health problems, and to promote action including structural changes as an integral part of medical research.

In one of the most frequently cited articles on participatory research methods, Cornwall and Jewkes (1995) contend that the motivations for the use of participatory methods in medical research are (1) of a pragmatic nature and (2) about equity. Evidence suggests that the involvement of local people in research and research planning can enhance effectiveness and save time and money in the long term. However, participatory research is also about action and the reduction of health inequalities.

CBPR projects are therefore designed as power-sharing, mutually empowering processes for both the researcher(s) and the respective community involved. They are undertaken with the principle of mutual respect and the mutual recognition of the knowledge, expertise and resource capacities, and in Minkler et al.'s (2003) view this is consistent with the aims of 'results oriented philanthropy'.

Like many other participatory approaches, CBPR aims to integrate the researchers' theoretical and methodological expertise with the real-world knowledge and experiences of non-academic participants (Cargo and Mercer, 2008). Community members, organisational representatives and researchers collaborate in all aspects of the research process (Becker, 2001). According to O'Fallon and Dearry (2002) the six common principles of CBPR are that it:

1 Promotes active collaboration and participation at every stage of research.
2 Fosters co-learning.
3 Ensures projects are community-driven.
4 Disseminates results in useful terms.
5 Ensures research and intervention strategies are culturally appropriate.
6 Defines community as a unit of identity.

These core principles of CBPR are subject to further development, and more recent publications (Burke et al., 2014) even name nine principles, which also include:

• Building on strengths and resources within the community.
• Collaborative equitable partnerships.
• The balance of action and research for mutual benefit.
• Local relevance of the research.
• An inclusive dissemination process.
• A long-term commitment to the engagement process.

As discussed in Chapters 1 and 2, it is not uncommon for collaborative participatory research projects to be undertaken in disadvantaged communities, and CBPR often addresses health inequalities in these contexts. Mosavel et al.'s (2005) study in South Africa used a CBPR approach to explore the need for cancer screening in a disadvantaged community in Cape Town. This was done in light of a more general need to understand, and raise awareness for, health promotion programmes in this community. However, examples of CBPR approaches are very diverse and also include: projects following natural disasters (Farquhar and Dobson, 2005); issues of food safety around food banks for homeless people (Jacobson and Rugeley, 2007); sexual health projects, including research on HIV/Aids (Marcus et al., 2004; Gleason-Comstock et al., 2006; Pinto et al., 2007) and the development of interventions for sexual abuse victims (Williams and Nelson-Gardell, 2014); elderly and palliative care (Jones, Pomeroy and Sampson, 2009; Scharlach and Sanchez, 2011); substance abuse interventions (Poupart, Baker and Horse, 2009; Windsor and Murugan, 2012); mental health programme evaluation tools for indigenous populations (Gowen et al., 2012; Kendall and Barnett, 2015); and minority ethnic groups (de Freitas and Martin, 2015).

It is no coincidence that journals like *Social Science and Medicine* and *Action Research and Healthcare* published special issues focusing on participatory research practice in their fields in 1995 and 2015 respectively. Macaulay et al. (1999) reviewed a number of health-related participatory research projects and found that their results can be transferable and may contribute to the development of new theoretical models. The studies can not only increase local knowledge, but also capacity, self-empowerment, and they can lead to improved health outcomes and better community planning.

User-led research

User-led research is primarily concerned with the research involvement of service users in the field of health and social care although the boundaries of what constitutes social care can be reasonably fluid. User-led research projects can be diverse and have ranged from youth work and youth services, LGBT issues in health services, to service evaluations and quality assurances – all are covered in chapters in the edited volume by Beresford and Carr (2012). According to the authors, user involvement emerged in the 1980s to redress paternalistic top-down approaches to welfare state service delivery. Service user movements such as the disabled people's movement were instrumental in challenging the research agenda which is now much more focused on positive outcomes for users. In some countries, service user involvement in the running and development of welfare services is now not only seen as good practice, but is a statutory requirement (Barnes and Cotterell, 2012). Since its emergence, user-led research practice has become increasingly concerned with assuring that service user participation is not just a tokenistic undertaking but leads to improved service delivery (Ormrod and Norton, 2003). Service user involvement research covers a wide range of different areas, covering broad areas such as mental health services (Pelletier et al., 2011), the establishment of priorities in order to assist the planning process for a large regional health system (Patten, Mitton and Donaldson, 2006) but also specific remote aboriginal communities (Minore et al., 2004), or social care services, such as social care management (Carpenter, 1995), the challenges of leaving care and starting an independent life (Torronen and Vormanen, 2014) and carer representation (Fox, 2009). User-led research can also be used to examine specific issues and everyday concerns, such as helping older people avoiding falls (Ross et al., 2005).

Participatory rural appraisal (PRA) or participatory learning and action (PLA)

Participatory rural appraisal (PRA) or participatory learning and action (PLA), as it is also known, belongs to a group of closely related participatory approaches which are focused on efforts to 'engage poor and marginalized communities in self-directed analysis, problem-solving and emancipatory action' (Chevalier and Buckles, 2013: 22). Chambers (1997: 102) calls PRA a 'family of approaches and methods to enable local people to share, enhance and analyze their knowledge of life and conditions, and to plan, act, monitor and evaluate'. The other approaches in this group include community-based or participatory planning; geographic or community mapping; participatory poverty assessment (PPA) and collaborative ethnography (Lassiter, 2005 – see also Chapter 6). These are methods which are widely applied in the field of international development including areas such as agro-ecosystem analysis, applied anthropology, field research on farming systems and rapid rural appraisal (Chambers, 1994). A common feature is their aim to enable local people to share, enhance and analyse their knowledge of life and conditions with a view to improve these.

According to Chevalier and Buckles (2013: 23), the main contribution of these approaches is 'the creative, pluralistic and dynamic use of visual and tangible forms of expression and analysis addressing issues of livelihood and natural resource management'. The participatory activities used in these approaches include mapping, creating models and diagrams, using sorting, ranking and rating techniques, but also story telling and role play in order to capture the experiences and lives of disadvantaged native communities who experience decreasing access to their natural resources and suffer from the effects of increasing urbanisation, affecting their traditional lifestyles. Issues such as low literacy levels and socio-economic status mean they can find it difficult to verbalise their needs and rights. PRA and PLA utilise traditional ways of thinking, learning and decision-making processes to voice the concerns of these communities and draw on their expertise. However, among all participatory approaches discussed in this volume, PRA and PLA approaches are perhaps most likely to utilise survey and other quantitative research methods.

Chevalier and Buckles (2013: 24) argue that PRA and PLA have 'contributed an important body of literature and research that acknowledges and promotes long-standing indigenous, traditional or local knowledge systems (IKS, TKS, LKS) that can be mobilized in support of endogenous development'. Researchers involved in PRA and PLA assert that Western science can also learn from the knowledge that

is built into the cumulative wisdom, practical knowledge and oral teachings of place-based communities, [such as] the wisdom [that] is embedded in stories, legends, folklore, songs, rituals and norms of conduct and technical practices that are part of day-to-day livelihood activities and interactions with nature. (Chevalier and Buckles, 2013: 24)

McGee's (2004) study on poverty trends in Uganda lays bare the different outcomes of a conventional household survey compared to a PPA project. The author argues that the household survey results reported a continuous drop in poverty, this contradicting the results reported by a non-governmental organisation (NGO) in the affected communities. From the author's point of view, one of the reasons for the conflicting results was that different measures of poverty were being used by the researchers running the household survey and the communities living in poverty. For them, the notion of poverty was a multi-dimensional experience of deprivation rather than a survey measure based on income, consumption and a lack of material goods. McGee argues that the active participation of the affected communities in capturing the experiences of poverty demonstrates a much better understanding of the issue and can potentially lead to more appropriate policy interventions. This is also the view of Smucker et al. (2007) who found that participatory feedback workshops that facilitated a dialogical process with local communities allowed researchers to develop a better understanding of how social and environmental changes affected land use in Kenya. The participatory workshops allowed the participants themselves to frame the change processes required.

Temu and Due (2000) also compared conventional survey results and a PRA approach in relation to establishing deprivation rankings in Tanzania. They argue that the wellbeing ranks established using their PRA approach were valid and reliable, and, in fact, the participatory approach involving the communities could save costs and improve the quality of the collected information. The overall goal of the PRA project was to help rural communities in sub-Sahara Africa to develop environmentally sustainable crop and livestock practices.

Ghaffar, Khan and Ullah's (2007) study on dairy farming, which also used a PRA approach, was based on surveys conducted in two very different ecological zones in Pakistan. Their aim was to help the local communities to maximise productivity of their livestock and therefore the income from farming. Again, this study showed that participatory approaches such as PAR or community planning address very specific issues that are of particular relevance to local communities. The study also shows that PAR approaches cross disciplinary boundaries and are not necessarily social science-based methods.

Bock (2001) discusses how PRA approaches can be effectively used by international aid organisations to manage their programmes in areas of conflict and ethnic division. He argues that the involvement of the respective communities in areas of need can actually contribute to a harmonisation of tensions, which he argues is more consistent with best practice in international development. With the intention to aid the design of more effective and sustainable community development projects, Dorsner (2004) investigated the mechanisms and complexity of community participation in a study in Senegal.

Goodfellow-Baikie and English (2006) ran a training project in a First Nations community in Northern Canada to explore the meaning of work after an unsuccessful community economic development programme. The lack of support from community leaders was found to be one of the factors that determined the failure or success of programmes like this.

However, PRA approaches are not exclusively used in developing countries or with native/indigenous communities. Ashwood et al. (2014), for example, undertook a project to address the issue of water pollution, whilst Franz et al. (2010) used a PRA approach to investigate how farmers learn, in order to inform agricultural educative practice. In support of participatory and peer-to-peer approaches, the project concluded that farmers enjoyed peer teaching and valued participatory approaches to research. The authors also found that farmers mainly learn from each other at grassroots level, all findings that support participatory approaches to research and learning. Misgav (2014) explored the role of memory and multiple meanings of place in the development of a renewal plan in a local community in Israel. Using a participatory mixed methods approach, during a three-year project the author explored residents' sense of place and their wishes for their neighbourhood.

Despite all of this evidence, according to Chevalier and Buckles (2013), many PRA and PLA researchers have so far failed to pay sufficient attention to theorising strategies for social transformation, which in their view explains that PRA and PLA is still a reasonably marginal approach in academic research and training. The need to up-scale participatory efforts is discussed in more detail in Chapter 5.

Participatory organisational research (POR)

Participatory organisational research (POR) follows the principles of PAR but is commonly used as a term and approach in management research. Its applications include studies in a range of areas such as the management of the environment, but also the organisation of processes in the workplace. Burns et al. (2014) argue that POR has great potential as a means for co-production of knowledge in the context of management research as it can help to elicit the unheard voices of members in organisations, such as users or clients – in Burns et al.'s case, elder care users in care homes. Puente-Rodríguez et al. (2016) used a POR approach in a study to explore the coastal zone management and environmental management systems (EMSs) within port communities in the Netherlands. They argue that participatory approaches involving a range of stakeholders could become mandatory in order to manage and protect eco-systems effectively. Collins (1997) used a participatory approach with leading professional social workers to study the management of change in welfare organisations in South Africa.

Action science, citizen science and Science Shops

A methodological approach which is directly concerned with spontaneous tacit theories that inform the practical knowledge and behaviour has become known as *action science* (Friedman, 2008). Action science concerns itself with the gap between social theory and social practice, or in the words of Argyris and Schön (1991: 85) with the 'dilemma of rigor or relevance'. The ambition of action science is to 'bridge this gap between social research and social practice by building theories which explain social phenomena, inform practice and adhere to the fundamental criteria of science' (Friedman, 2008: 132). This is done by forming so-called 'communities of inquiry' within 'communities of practice'. Despite the fact that the focus in action science is on theory building, Argyris and Schön (1991) argue strongly that action science should be seen as a member of the PAR family. *Citizen science* is a closely related term. Chevalier and Buckles (2013: 30) note:

> Citizen Science is another recent move to broaden the concept of social engagement in scientific work, to include broader 'communities of interest' and citizens committed to enhancing knowledge in particular fields. In this approach to collaborative inquiry, research is actively assisted by volunteers who form an active public or network of contributing individuals. Participants may or may

not have scientific expertise or share the same geographic, occupational, cultural or educational background.

Examples of citizen science span a variety of academic disciplines, from the social, natural to the medical sciences. They have many different aims and objectives, different levels of collaboration in the actual research and with different dynamics, i.e. initiated and led by academic or non-academic organisations, and even by the public.

Chevalier and Buckles (2013) view collaborative citizen science projects as particularly promising in relation to what they see as the need to up-scale participatory scientific programmes, especially in the natural and environmental sciences and conservation (Bela et al., 2016), for example by involving volunteers and the public in the monitoring of phenomena in the natural world. Recent star-gazing projects involving the public and amateur astronomers are a good example for this, as are the popular annual garden bird-watching events, organised by the Royal Society for the Protection of Birds (RSPB) in the UK or the Naturschutzbund (NABU) in Germany, all of which attract tens of thousands of participants. Advances in information and communication technology, including social media applications, have facilitated some of these activities such as the mapping of the night sky, and have also made the collection and processing of data considerably easier.

However, the advances in collaborative efforts also extend to the political and social sciences with experiments in e-democracy. Citizen science also provides a financial dimension to research via crowd sourcing and crowd funding initiatives that many other collaborative projects do not benefit from.

Science Shops also encourage the collaboration of the academic and non-academic community, but their focus is broader than that of action science. Science Shops have developed over the last 40 years or so with the ambition to tackle real-life questions and societal challenges using the co-production of knowledge approaches involving civil society organisations, researchers and university students (Hall et al., 2013; Steinhaus, 2014; Hall, Tandon and Tremblay, 2015). They are a particular variety of citizen science where people, via community or third sector organisations, express a need for research.

Mulder and de Bok (2006: 285) summarise the Science Shop approach as follows:

Science Shops provide independent, participatory research support to civil society. They both use traditional science communication techniques to produce usable results, and they are part of an interactive science communication system. They work from the democratic motive for science and technology (S&T) communication, helping to articulate civil society issues, putting citizens' requests on the research agenda, and supporting citizens in the subsequent use of research results.

Science Shops act as intermediaries between the different partners in the knowledge co-production. They are often part of a university infrastructure, but can also be independent structures maintained with public funds. Their distinct feature is that they operate in the realm of public engagement, responding to research needs identified by the public. Normally, once a civil organisation, community or not-for-profit organisation approaches a Science Shop with their perceived research need, they will offer mostly free advice and consultation. A project or topic is then agreed and, in most cases, a higher education institution or university will be contacted in order to find appropriate academic research support. Often the research lead is then assumed by either students, under staff guidance, or by junior research staff. Usually this happens free of charge as part of the students' qualification, or as part of *pro-bono* support given by academic staff as part of their community engagement or outreach. So, ideally Science Shop projects are of mutual benefit; whilst the communities' research needs are met, students engage in practical real-life research which contributes to their education and the universities fulfil their obligations to foster positive engagement in the communities around them (Tandon et al., 2016). This makes Science Shops a participatory research method which is particularly good value for money and has the potential to generate good quality research.

Participatory arts-based research and extended participatory theatre methods

The use of visual and performing arts and music in research is not new, and there is some evidence that participatory arts-based projects can have positive effects and result in empowerment, improved mental health and greater social inclusion (Hacking et al., 2008). The participatory turn in research has seen a diversification of collaborative research projects that engage people in arts-based activities. Music, theatre or visual arts, including photography, can be used in all parts of a research project, from the defining of the research question, the support of data collection and analysis, to the dissemination of findings.

Art can be used as a form, a process or a context to explore a large variety of topics and issues, such as norms, values and relationships (Grassau, 2009) and it can help to cross disciplinary boundaries. Similarly to Photovoice, which is discussed below, art-based approaches provide really valuable mechanisms to engage with vulnerable and hard-to-reach populations.

In a recent study Gitonga and Delport (2014) explored the use of hip hop in participatory research projects on the identity construction of young women. In their study, music was used to encourage participation and to elicit self-narratives. The authors discovered that music can be used as what they call 'data-generation stimulus' in participatory research and particularly for young people where music can play a central role in the formation of their identity.

Foster (2007) used visual art, poetry and short film-making in a similar vein to encourage self-reflection among research participants but also as method of data collection and dissemination in a project undertaken from a feminist perspective. Little and Froggett (2010) worked with story telling as a participatory art form with older people in a community development project and in a community and healthy living centre. The authors found that the psychosocial processes involved in participatory story telling can contribute to the authentic representation of individual and community voices. Bernard et al. (2015) used theatre as a venue for an interdisciplinary project to address and tackle ageism, which emphasised the important role for theatre and drama as a medium for intergenerational work with both older and younger people.

Bicknell (2014) explored the social and emotional wellbeing benefits for older people who took part in participatory dance-theatre performances. She found that apart from the health benefits for participants, participatory dance-theatre can contribute to confidence building, give a sense of purpose and extend social networks as well as challenge ageist perceptions among those who attend such performances. Salmon and Rickaby (2014) reported similarly positive effects, such as the development of new skills, improved mental health, increased confidence and resilience and an improved sense of social connectedness among young people in care who were involved in the development of a musical play exploring life in the care system. Zeitlyn and Mand (2012) and Gardner and Mand (2012) undertook research with 9–10-year-old children from transnational British Bangladeshi backgrounds using participatory ethnographic methods and arts-based participatory methodologies to explore children's constructions and conceptualisations of particular places in both Britain and Bangladesh. Wrentschur (2014) concluded that his extended participatory theatre approach with disadvantaged young people not only increased their capabilities to manage their own lives, but also raised awareness for systemic and concrete policy changes that were needed to improve their lives. Daniel et al. (2014) worked with disabled young people in Scotland using a collaborative participatory Forum Theatre methodology as a medium to explore and improve support and protection mechanisms for adults with disabilities.

Carey and Sutton (2004) reported the findings of a large-scale community arts programme in Liverpool which used participatory arts initiatives to increase community involvement.

Photovoice

Visual and online approaches, especially visual ethnography, will be discussed in more detail in Chapter 7. Photovoice is one of the examples which has utilised and developed visual methods for participatory approaches – especially but not exclusively – for studies with impaired participants. Because Photovoice has had such an impact on participatory approaches it ought to be mentioned here as a separate entry. Photovoice is a participatory photography method which is used to assist dialogue with the aim to initiate social change. The term 'Photovoice' alludes to the two key points in this research method. Firstly, participants are (usually) equipped with a camera to take photos as part of the research project, and, secondly, the pictures 'are used to give respondents a "voice" or to provide a somewhat "objective" record of participant experience' (Gotschi, Delve and Freyer, 2009: 293).

Perhaps more than most other participatory approaches, Photovoice is designed for collaborative and emancipatory studies with people with whom the use of conventional research methods involving verbal or written skills is particularly challenging, such as people with intellectual disabilities, adults with little reading or writing skills, indigenous/First Nation communities and children, as some of the following examples show.

In their article, Povee, Bishop and Roberts (2014) describe Photovoice as an accessible method that has the potential to provide people with intellectual disabilities the experience of inclusiveness and the opportunity to develop new skills, and ultimately confidence. The authors warn, however, that researchers need to be prepared to invest time and money, to share power with their participants, and to tolerate uncertainty.

In Novek and Menec's (2014) study undertaken in a remote rural area in Canada with indigenous communities, participants took pictures of their environment to explore how age-friendly their communities were. The pictures were discussed, sorted and categorised in participatory group discussions. Another study using Photovoice with an indigenous community in Canada was that of Castleden, Garvin and Huu-Ay-Aht First Nation (2008). The authors report that Photovoice as a method balanced power between the researchers and a First Nation community that has been sceptical and reluctant to take part in research in the past. They found that participatory approaches can create a sense of ownership, foster trust, build capacity and respond to cultural preferences. Adams et al. (2012) undertook a study focusing on healthy eating with an Aboriginal community in Australia. Over a short period of time, the participants in that study took photos relating to their food and met afterwards to discuss their food selections. The aim of the study was to raise awareness of healthy eating options, taking into account the particular heritage and history of this Aboriginal community.

Streng et al. (2004) conducted a project with recently immigrated Latino adolescents in the USA which involved 'photo-assignments' and 'photo-discussions'. They organised exhibitions of the participants' work to raise awareness among the local population, and explored issues including quality of life, education experiences and adolescent health. Sutherland and Cheng (2009) also explored experiences of immigrants using Photovoice, in this case of women who had migrated to Canada. Similar to Streng et al. (2004), the authors argue that Photovoice as a methodology facilitated the empowerment of their project participants.

Critical pedagogy and participatory approaches in teaching and learning

Critical pedagogy originates in Freire's (1971) work and is the best-known participatory method among a range of participatory approaches in teaching and learning, predominantly used in professional subject areas, such as social work and nursing and education. Critical pedagogy represents 'one of the most critical perspectives on the twin issue of knowledge and grassroots, community-based development' (Chevalier and Buckles, 2013: 26). Freire's work is regarded as one of the key pillars of PAR, as is discussed in detail in Chapter 4. Critical pedagogy regards critical research as a tool to promote radical democracy and liberation. Unlike other participatory methods, it is primarily concerned with rethinking and restructuring adult education and only indirectly with stimulating social change. As Chevalier and Buckles put it:

> Freire views the transmission of mere facts and existing bodies of knowledge to be futile as a learning strategy and as a way to promote well-being in a just and equal society. He challenges the teacher–student dichotomy itself, advocating a relationship of deep reciprocity that takes its inspiration from the dialectics of Socratic teaching. Critical pedagogy [...] subverts oppressive regimes of knowledge and power through the exercise of critical consciousness, inviting people on the margins of society to interrogate and question dominant thinking and systems of power, and take action against them. (2013: 26)

Pure, radical, critical pedagogy projects in Freire's tradition are perhaps less common today, certainly in the Western world. However, there is no lack of collaborative studies which attempt to change traditional hierarchical educational structures, in order to develop more appropriate and empowering ways of learning, for example in areas of community development (Messerli and Abdykaparov, 2008), but also in teaching and service learning (Hyde and Meyer, 2004; Stickley et al., 2009; Johnson, 2010).

Participatory evaluations

One of the areas where participatory approaches are increasingly being used are evaluations. Stakeholder involvement in evaluations first occurred in the 1970s when doubts emerged about the practice relevance of 'objective' and 'scientific' evaluations. Participatory evaluations as a term and approach was more frequently used from the 1990s onwards, for example under the umbrella of 'developmental evaluations' (Patton, 2011) or 'empowerment evaluations' (Fetterman, Kaftarian and Wandersman, 2014). The idea is that professional researchers teach evaluation techniques to practitioners over time with the aim of generating organisational learning for institutions and their stakeholders (Cousins and Earl, 1995; Stake, 2004), which creates enabling conditions for project and organisational development and to facilitate empowerment and social change.

Using examples of social development projects in Asia, Crishna (2007) argues that participatory evaluations of such projects are crucial tools for providing evidence that claims made by participatory researchers about the projects' impact and outcomes are credible, reliable and valid in order to encourage the intended changes in thinking. They regard the role of the external evaluator in these processes as that of a facilitator, encouraging participation from everyone using imaginative and alternative strategies.

Participatory evaluation approaches have been used to critically assess whole programmes of participatory action research (EKOS, 2007), but also individual projects and interventions. The range of these is broad and includes: collaborative community partnerships, for example between education institutions and community organisations (Kim, Calloway and Selz-Campbell, 2004); medical services and interventions, including service commissioning (Niba and Green, 2005; Evans et al., 2015); government programmes and pilot projects (Biott and Cook, 2000; Malik, Ward and Janczewski, 2008); leadership and capacity-building programmes (Lennie, 2005); and community organisation and NGO development (Andrews et al., 2005; Lennie et al. 2015). Participatory evaluations were also used to assess projects with indigenous (Letiecq and Bailey, 2004; Gowen et al., 2012) and minority ethnic communities (Thomas et al., 2006). Gilchrist et al. (2013) reported on their experiences of working with children and young people as co-evaluators. This related, for example, to the Youth4U programme which was run by the Department of Education in England from 2009 to 2011. The purpose of this programme was to involve young people from marginalised communities in the evaluation of services in their areas. One of the findings of the programme was that the involvement of the young people as Young Inspectors led to the improvement of services within six months of the initial visit.

Rights-based participatory approaches

The rationale of rights-based approaches to research is based on human rights law and international conventions, for example the UN Convention on the Rights of the Child (UNCRC) or the UN Convention on the Rights of Persons with Disabilities (UNCRPD). In a nutshell, these essentially state that people have the right to be consulted on and have a say in all matters that affect their lives, they have the right that their views are given due weight and that decisions should be taken with their best interest in mind. Using children's rights as an example, the underlying assumption here is 'that the state of childhood will be improved if we are prepared to take children's rights more seriously' (Freeman, 1992: 53). Rights-based approaches use this rationale to argue that research is one of the issues that can arguably affect people's lives and therefore should be inclusive. Staying with children's rights and children's participation, Brady et al. (2012), but also Borland et al. (2001), report a shift from children and young people being mainly objects of research to being increasingly regarded as social actors whose unique perspective needs to be taken into consideration. As Borland et al. put it, this has moved from research *on* children to research *with* children and research that has the potential to empower children. Lundy and McEvoy (Emerson) (2012) and Emerson and Lloyd (2014) argue that the right to be heard is closely related to the right to information which is 'a prerequisite for the effective realization of the right to express views' (United Nations, 2009: para. 82) and the right to freedom of expression. Inclusivity and research participation is usually achieved by initially educating and informing participants first about the respective research topic. This is increasingly done using creative means and arts-based means, but also means using visual and online methods.

With regard to people with disabilities, a group often excluded from mainstream research, Ollerton and Horsfall (2013) discuss their rights to be actively involved in research to facilitate not just accessible research, but to promote social change, whilst

Community-based participatory research (CBPR)

- **Key Features**: Involves participants in all aspects of a research study. Promotes co-learning.
- **Fields of Application**: Often used in health research, but truly cross-disciplinary.

User-led research

- **Key Features**: Evolves around service user involvement with a view to improve welfare state services.
- **Fields of Application**: Mainly health and social care sector, but applicable to other services, such as education and youth services.

Participatory rural appraisal (PRA) & participatory learning and action (PLA)

- **Key Features**: Engages marginalised communities in self-directed problem solving and emancipatory action.
- **Fields of Application**: Most common in the field of international development.

Participatory organisational research (POR)

- **Key Features**: Co-production approach used to elicit unheard voices in organisations.
- **Fields of Application**: Most commonly used in management research and to improve organisational processes.

Action Science/Citizen Science/Science Shops

- **Key Features**: Ordinary citizens involved in 'communities of inquiry' or 'communities of practice' in order to close the gap between theory and practice. Democratisation of science approaches.
- **Fields of Application**: Any field of natural or social sciences where ordinary people can engage with sciences. Also Science Shops, which connect academic researchers and students with NGOs and their communities.

Participatory arts-based approaches and Photovoice

- **Key Features**: Use of creative methods or photography to engage with communities about their lives.
- **Fields of Application**: Where verbal or written data collection methods are challenging, e.g. research with children, older people, people with disabilities, migrant communities, prisoners. Any topic or field of study.

Critical pedagogy

- **Key Features**: Aims to promote radical democracy and liberation from the grassroots via critical adult education and tackling hierarchical educational structures. Based on Freire's work on conscientisation.
- **Fields of Application**: Mainly used in professional fields such as social work, nursing and education.

Participatory evaluations

- **Key Features**: Grassroots and stakeholder involvement in evaluations to generate empowering organisational learning.
- **Fields of Application**: Any kind of programme evaluations, e.g. in NGOs and in social development projects.

Rights-based approaches

- **Key Features**: Emphasises the right of people to be consulted in matters that affect their lives.
- **Fields of Application**: Mainly, but not exclusively, focused on children and young people (via UNCRC) and people with disabilities (via UNCRPD).

Figure 3.1 Key features of participatory research approaches

Stevenson (2010) used the Emancipatory Disability Research (EDR) paradigm to conduct inclusive rights-based research with a group of young people with Down Syndrome involved as co-researchers.

From the perspective of rights-based participatory research, participation should ideally be facilitated in as many aspects of the respective projects as possible but, as Brady et al. (2012) remind us, often it is the context and circumstances where research takes place that determine the level of participation and, as Franks (2011) puts it, 'pockets' of meaningful participation are preferable to no or tokenistic partici-pation. Rights-based approaches therefore do not necessarily involve people actively as co-researchers in the research process, as in Stevenson's case or in Winter's (2012) study, which explored the participation rights with very young children (4–7-year-olds) in care, using arts-based methods. Rather, the emphasis is on a rights-respecting approach to research. Stevenson (2010) stresses that this requires academic researchers to embrace a position as human rights activists and facilitators to ensure that partici-pants' voices are heard within the research process and in the outputs arising from it.

Topics addressed using participatory methods

As discussed in Chapter 1, participatory research methods developed, to a significant degree, as a response to the frustration of the failure of conventional, often positivist and objectivist, research practice to capture the experiences of those living in disadvantaged or marginalised communities and to address existing shortcomings. It is therefore no coincidence that collaborative and participatory approaches to research have been dispro-portionately concerned with issues that conventional projects would often find too hard to handle. For example, a randomised household survey may not be a suitable instrument to capture the experiences of transgender people, simply because the sampling mechanism would not allow this to happen in sufficient detail or depth. Other population groups may also be excluded from mainstream conventional research – either because the topic may be regarded as too sensitive (sex work would be an example of this) or because mainstream instruments are unsuitable for certain population groups who may not have the verbal or written skills to respond (people with severe learning disabilities come to mind).

As participatory methods have diversified throughout the last decades, so has the range of topics addressed and population groups involved in participatory research. By way of example, two of these topics are discussed below – sexual health and sexuality-related topics, and abuse and violence.

Sexuality, sexual health, sexual exploitation, sexual identity, sex work

Although there is somewhat greater openness now, sexuality, sexual health and sex-ual identity remain subject areas which are regarded and treated as sensitive by many.

Sexuality and sexual health also remain heavily policed by social norms, often connected to religious beliefs and conventions. The apparent emergence of 'increasingly "sex-saturated" societies' (Renold, 2013) offers little more than pseudo-openness. It is therefore no coincidence that a range of sexual health issues has been addressed using explorative participatory means. One of these areas is sex work. Sex workers are a particularly vulnerable group of people because existing social norms and expectations almost universally marginalise them and put them at risk not only of exploitation, but also poor health.

Cornish and Ghosh (2007) undertook an ethnographic study to explore community involvement in HIV prevention programmes as part of health promotion initiatives with sex workers in India. The research was undertaken jointly with the Sonagachi Project, a sex-worker-led HIV prevention project. The sex workers became co-investigators in the project. Cornish and Ghosh state that the nature of the topic meant that the researchers had to engage with the wider community, including local men's clubs and brothel managers, some of whom arguably contribute to the exploitation of the sex workers. However, the authors argue strongly that ultimately, in order to have a positive impact on the lives of the sex workers, it was important not only to acknowledge these power relations but to actively plan for them.

Abel and Fitzgerald's (2008) explorative study into street-based sex work among young people under 18 years of age in New Zealand was published around the same time as Cornish and Gosh's article. This mixed methods participatory project, which included a survey and interviews with young sex workers, was also primarily concerned with the health and safety practices of sex workers.

Shannon and her colleagues (2008) undertook a PAR project to explore the role of social and structural violence experienced by women engaged in survival sex work in Canada. Many of the 46 women involved in this study were also injecting drug users and were therefore at elevated risk of contracting HIV and other sexually transmitted or blood-born infections. As with the previous two studies, sex workers were actively involved in this project as co-researchers. The focus groups and interviews conducted highlighted the need for improved HIV prevention strategies that took account of the structural exploitative conditions that the sex workers were faced with.

Sexual health and safe sex are issues that affect the population more generally, and Weiss et al. (2010) undertook a CBPR project to tackle the spread of HIV/AIDS in a community in the USA. The project was initiated by a group of citizens in Florida concerned about high rates of HIV/AIDS and teenage pregnancy in their community. The community activists conducted a phone survey before developing an educative DVD in co-operation with a local school.

In order to inform sexual health policy making, Renold (2013) undertook an explorative participatory research project with 10–12-year-olds on behalf of the Cross-Party Group on Children, Sexualities, 'Sexualisation' and Equalities in the Welsh National Assembly. The authors engaged with the children in order to explore how they experienced and negotiated their sexual and gender cultures and how peer cultures shaped their everyday social worlds.

Another area frequently researched using participatory methods is gender and sexual identity. McAlister and Neill (2009) worked with a group of young women in Northern Ireland who identified as lesbian or bisexual to produce a resource pack that addressed their specific sexual health needs. Whilst some progress has been made in relation to legislations for the equal treatment of people with different genders and sexualities in a number of societies, LGBT people continue to be disproportionately the target of homophobic and transphobic hate crimes. Browne, Bakshi and Lim's (2011) study explored LGBT safety issues in Brighton in southern England, a city with the reputation of being one of the most welcoming and safest for LGBT people in the UK. The study found that participatory approaches with LGBT communities may empower them to work towards better social integration. Fenge et al. (2009) undertook a PAR project which used narrative research methods to explore the needs, experiences and aspirations of older lesbian women and gay men in England, who grew up in much less sympathetic contexts regarding homosexuality.

Abuse/violence

Sexual abuse, sexual exploitation and violence against children but also adults have been areas which have gained greater public prominence due to very high-profile cases involving celebrities in creative industries, religious institutions, care homes, schools, sports clubs and political parties, among others. What is common to these cases is the abuse of power relations. Little research had been undertaken in the field of sexual exploitation until the 2000s due to the undercover nature of the exploitative situations. Some of the pioneering researchers in the field of child sexual exploitation (CSE) include Beckett and Warrington who in 2015 published a report on a participatory project that was undertaken by the International Centre for the Researching of Child Sexual Exploitation, Violence and Trafficking at the University of Bedfordshire in the UK. The research explored the experiences of young people who had been victims of CSE and the criminal justice system (CJS). The aim of the project was to highlight the disempowering effects that the CJS can have on young victims of CSE, and to change and improve the system in order for it to work in the best interests of children and young people.

Spinney's (2013) Australian-based study was concerned with the experiences of, and service provision for, children and young people who had become homeless as a result of domestic and family violence. This action research project included the development of a participatory evaluation tool to assess early intervention mechanisms to deal with homelessness as a result of family and domestic violence.

Roberto, Brossoie and McPherson's (2013) study was concerned with intimate partner violence against older women in a rural area in the USA. The study emerged from a collaborative academic–community partnership and, as with other related intimate violence cases, one of the main issues that study participants identified was the extent to which the issue was hidden and under-reported. Older victims highlighted the need for improved awareness of, and professional sensitivity towards, the issue as well as improved service options.

People and communities involved in participatory research

Many participatory and collaborative research projects not only address potentially sensitive and often under-researched topics, but also involve populations that are particularly disadvantaged and marginalised, as I will show in this following section. Examples include projects with children and older people affected by sexual or domestic abuse and violence. This is not to say that children, people with disabilities or older people are per se 'vulnerable' populations, but in certain circumstances their voices are less likely to be heard and they can be left behind when it comes to service delivery.

People in poverty or on low income

People who experience social disadvantage or who live in poverty have traditionally found it particularly hard to see their needs met. Often this is to do with the stigma attached to poverty and perceptions that they are somehow to blame for the adverse circumstances in which they live, for example, because they don't work hard enough in school, they don't try hard enough to get a job, they drink or take drugs, do not budget sensibly and so forth.

Braithwaite et al. (2007) undertook a CBPR project to capture the experiences of people in a disadvantaged community during a process of community regeneration. Community generation often invokes gentrification processes which can lead to further segregation by socio-economic background and the well-intentioned regeneration programmes can further disadvantage those at the bottom end of the income scale. Braithwaite and colleagues trained and employed community members who had no formal research training but had insider knowledge of the local community to explore the risks and experiences related to community regeneration. The authors found that positive perceptions of co-researchers by other community members are important in order to conduct successful participatory action research in disadvantaged communities that have previously been disappointed or felt let down by researchers.

Rimmer (1998) undertook a participatory research project with a group of very poor women in England to raise awareness about credit unions and to increase the power of women in the credit union. A Joseph Rowntree Foundation report published in 2008 was also concerned with women in poverty and attempts to contribute to capacity building among these women in order to equip them to lobby their interests to policy makers. After the project the women presented policy makers with three recommendations. The participatory workshops with the women were found to build confidence among the participants and to expand their knowledge of government policy-making processes.

Gough, Langevang and Namatovu (2014) and Adato, Lund and Mhlongo (2007) undertook studies in low-income settlements in Uganda and South Africa respectively. The authors of both studies came to the conclusion that the participatory methods they used to engage the respective communities led to a better, more nuanced and contextualised understanding faced by the communities they investigated.

Buettgen et al. (2012) explored the connection between disability and poverty in a PAR project in Ontario, Canada, in which both non-disabled and developmentally disabled people were engaged as co-researchers. Whilst acknowledging some of the challenges, namely in the delivery of change (reduction of poverty in this case), the researchers concluded that the PAR approach allowed the disabled co-researchers to provide positive role models for other people with disabilities in relation to meaningful participation and inclusion. The authors also concluded that the project provided an opportunity for disabled people to have their voices heard and to empower those who want to 'advocate for social change in the context of the rights and responsibilities of civic life and citizenship' (2012: 614).

Disabled people

A large body of literature spanning an enormous range of topics exists when it comes to participatory research approaches with people who have either physical or learning disabilities. There are two main reasons for this: firstly, alongside feminist movements, disabled people's movements and disability rights movements were at the forefront of demanding positive social change and equality for disabled people who were often at the receiving end of social exclusion and poorer services, e.g. in housing, education or employment; secondly, conventional research practice often failed to include the voices of people with disabilities and represent their lives adequately. Participatory research approaches provided the necessary evidence base to make positive changes but also facilitated processes that afforded people with disabilities to have their voices heard.

Erdtman (2012), for example, reports on a method he calls 'idea circles', which was used during a three-year research project run by the Swedish Disability Federation in order to identify ideas and issue for research projects. These idea circles were led by people with disabilities and enabled them to have a say in the identification of issues that they felt needed to be researched rather than being brought into a project which was designed by someone else on their behalf. According to Erdtman, the key research needs identified in the idea circles were: identity, society/politics, attitudes towards people with disabilities and their inclusion in the labour market.

One of the groups most excluded from research and decision making is people with intellectual or learning disabilities. Often they are deemed to be unable to make informed decisions, including giving consent to taking part in research. Many researchers working with people with intellectual or learning disabilities focused on the exploration of their capacity to make, or contribute to, decisions that affect their lives. In one of the earlier studies in this field, Sample (1996) explored the feasibility of the use of PAR approaches with individuals with cognitive disabilities whilst also reporting on a three-year research project he undertook with the aim to increase participation in the community by adults with developmental disabilities. McConnell et al. (2018) tested the feasibility of a co-production approach as part of a randomised controlled trial (RCT) to develop a new online service for people with depression. The authors concluded that it is important that all parties recognise and value their assets and contributions in such a research project.

Jones et al.'s (2010) study explored the issue of learning disability and the perceptions of vulnerability and abuse associated with the disability. Jones argues that one in three to one in two people with learning disabilities are estimated to have experienced different kinds of abuse, but research has failed to explore this issue. Jones et al. addressed this gap using a co-production approach to explore how people with learning disabilities understand abuse and what help-seeking behaviour they employed. The study results were used to inform the development of counselling services for people with learning disabilities. The University of Glamorgan in Wales also explored the abuse of people with learning disabilities (Looking into Abuse Research Team, 2014) and involved people with lived experience as part of the Research Advisory Group, but also as co-researchers. The authors then reflected on some of the issues relating to power relations when working with people with disabilities as co-researchers.

Milner and Kelly (2009) used a PAR design around disabled people's narratives to explore the identification with their communities, the services it provided and participation in the community. The aim of the project was to draw conclusions about creating less disabling and more inclusive communities.

The VIPER (Voice, Inclusion, Participation, Empowerment, Research) project was undertaken by the Council for Disabled Children in England between 2011 and 2014. Its aim was to explore the level of involvement and barriers experienced by young people with disabilities in decision making by service providers. The project also aimed to support young disabled people in relation to their participation and to produce resources that aid this. In their *How We Did the Qualitative Research* report (2012) the Council reflects on the participatory nature of the study, which featured a group of young people with disabilities working as co-researchers on the qualitative element of this project. The young people were involved in all stages of this project which included the development of the thematic framework for the study as well as the data analysis and dissemination, including the drafting of policy recommendations, which are published in a separate report (Council for Disabled Children, 2013).

Burke's (2012) participatory photographic project of playground interaction among disabled and non-disabled children in Australia challenges the very notion that children with impairments are ultimately 'socially disabled'. The authors found that children with disabilities were just as much creative agents in their play as the non-disabled children, dismissing the notion of social disability.

Kramer et al. (2011) undertook a PAR project – utilising visual methods – with a group of people with intellectual disabilities. The main aim was to increase the group's capacity for self-advocacy. The researchers concluded that the project led to an increased sense of empowerment and greater awareness among the group members as well as an increased capacity to take an active role in the PAR project. Kramer and colleagues also found the inclusive research process to be beneficial beyond the actual project. Garcia-Iriarte et al.'s (2009) project had a similar aim to help build capacity among a self-advocacy group of people with intellectual disabilities. The authors concluded that their PAR approach led to an increase in the group's capacity for advocacy that could potentially lead to change but warned that increased control did not automatically achieve this.

Morgan, Moni and Cuskelly (2015) also noted that their participatory research approach with young people with intellectual disabilities trained to be collaborative researchers on their project led to positive developments in the knowledge, conceptual understandings and the skills that their research participants had. Similarly, Hogg and Schur (1998) reported that their participatory research project in a residential care home for people with learning difficulties informed the administrative processes in the care home and engaged residents in decision-making processes.

Conder, Milner and Mirfin-Veitch (2011) researched quality of life and developed a tool with a group of people with intellectual disabilities, engaging them as co-researchers. Whilst again reporting positive changes for the participants in the project, especially the co-researchers with intellectual disabilities, the authors also note a range of limitations, which include 'the very nature of some of the participants' disabilities' and the researchers' 'ethical dilemma' of 'providing the vehicle for greater insight into how an individual's life might improve whilst not being in a position to effect change' (2011: 46).

Acknowledging the fact that most adults with intellectual disabilities live at home with their parents or carers rather than independently, Walmsley and Mannan (2009) undertook a PAR project with parents of adults with intellectual disabilities in Ireland. Whilst this could attract a level of criticism for not directly giving people with disabilities themselves an opportunity to have their voices heard and taken into consideration, clearly the concerns of carers are of interest. The aim of the project was to improve the connection between carers of adults with learning disabilities and service providers and the authors concluded that their participatory research approach had the potential to increase the understanding of the realities of family life for people caring for adults with intellectual disabilities.

As we can see, many of the participatory research projects with people with disabilities are more generally concerned with the agency of disabled people, their voice, creating opportunities for advocacy, representation in the community and so forth. However, some research also explored the impact of assistive technical equipment that people with disabilities use on the power relations, for example in higher education settings (Seale, Ward and Draffan, 2008).

Older people – ageing populations

Older people have increasingly become the focus of research due to the demographic changes that many societies experience. People are living longer, and society is waking up slowly to the demands and needs of an ageing population. Increased longevity requires the development of appropriate services for older people to tackle health- and care-related issues, but also issues such as social isolation. Using a user-participatory approach, including the employment of retired citizens as interviewers, Dwyer and Hardill (2012) examined the extent to which rural services in England promoted the social inclusion of older people living in remote rural communities in three regions. Another PAR project with older people in a community in South Africa was undertaken by Strydom (2003) with the aim of improving needs assessments and developing intervention programmes to address the ageing population in remote communities. User-led research approaches have included older people in researching quite specific issues, such as avoiding falls (Ross et al., 2005), but also more general adult social care planning and evaluation projects (Bowers and Wilkins, 2012).

Minority ethnic groups and indigenous communities

Participatory research practice has regularly addressed disadvantage experienced by minority ethnic groups in developed countries, but also the living conditions by indigenous communities across the world. Some of this research falls within the tradition of development studies, which Edwards (1989: 118) criticised so heavily for treating participants as objects of investigation rather than 'subjects of their own development', being largely irrelevant to their lives. Arguably, Edwards' contribution has had the effect of a wake-up call and much of research practice has changed since then. Booth (1994) names the greater involvement of NGOs but also of what he calls 'grassroots researchers' (1994: 11) in development studies. These have been important factors of change towards more research-orientated empowerment of disadvantaged communities with the aim to improve their lives.

For Braun et al. (2014) this change from positivist to empowering decolonising methods was central to their participatory research project. The subject of their research was ageing in indigenous populations, and the researchers utilised the story-telling tradition of indigenous elders to voice and collect stories that challenged non-indigenous investigators and stressed different values and worldviews. Newbigging et al. (2012) equally acknowledge the need to value different forms of knowledge in social care and mental health service design and delivery in order to meet the needs of different ethnic groups. In their specific example they report on a review of mental health literature and services in which African Caribbean men participated as co-researchers; African Caribbean men are over-represented in terms of admission to acute mental health services, but under-represented in terms of service user involvement.

Prisoners and their families

In prisons, disempowerment is often not a by-product, but part of the institutional design, as prisons are per se hierarchical institutions which are set up to punish offenders. The ongoing failure of the prison system in relation to the health and safety of people in custody (self-injury and suicide, drug abuse and violence) and the very low rate of successful transfers from prison back into society has become a growing issue, and it is increasingly accepted that prison reform is urgently required. Due to the high security setting in prisons characterised by depersonalisation and total control of prisoners (Hill et al., 2015), participatory research practice is very difficult to achieve in practical terms. Nevertheless, the refocus of some prison environments from punishment and incarceration to empowerment and education has facilitated some interesting participatory research projects with prisoners and their families. So far, most of these have been with female prisoners in low or medium security prison settings.

One of the first and, so far, largest participatory projects undertaken in prisons was that of Martin et al. (2009) – see also Ramsden et al. (2015). The purpose of this research was to engage and empower female prisoners to enhance their health and wellbeing. Using the setting of a women's prison in Canada, the research team, which included prison staff, academic researchers and female prisoners as co-researchers, initially explored the feasibility of undertaking a CBPR project with incarcerated women with a focus on primary health care provision in prisons. Once the authors concluded that this was feasible the research commenced. Around 200 women participated. Themes were identified and monthly health forums in prisons were subsequently organised around these themes by the female prisoners working on the project.

An earlier study using participatory methods in the prison context was conducted by Fine and Torre (2006). Their PAR design explored the impact of college in prison which exposed some of the structural issues within the prison system. Fine and Torre also explored issues around the ethics of undertaking participatory research projects with prisoners.

The mental health of prisoners has also been the focus of a number of studies. Ward, Bailey and Boyd (2012) undertook a three-year PAR project with the aim of developing an awareness of self-harm among prison staff. Six female prisoners with personal experiences of self-injury helped to deliver training sessions to prison staff. Elwood Martin et al. (2009) report the findings of another health-related participatory research project with female prisoners in Canada. In this case, female prisoners in a minimum/medium security women's prison undertook a participatory multi-method ethnographic study, from which nine common themes on health goals emerged. The authors concluded that incarceration provided a good opportunity for academic researchers and primary care workers to engage with prisoners to improve their health.

Vandermause, Severtsen and Roll (2013) undertook a CBPR project with the aim of helping mothers with young children who were recovering from drug abuse in the CJS to reclaim a vision of parenting whilst Sherwood and Kendall's CBPR study (2013) focused on aboriginal mothers in prisons in Australia. Aboriginal prisoners are significantly over-represented in the Australian prison system. Sherwood and Kendall reiterate the need to apply an indigenous informed conceptual framework and a decolonising research methodology in studies of this nature.

Not all participatory research in prisons focuses primarily on health. Hill et al. (2015) used a PAR approach in a maximum security prison to study the effects of restrictions on choice in an institutional setting, whilst Crabtree, Wall and Ohm (2016) used an informal occupational therapy education programme in a prison to explore the utility of a PAR approach in this context.

Children and young people

Arguably, children and young people do not per se fall into the category of 'marginalised' or 'disadvantaged' population, but in practice, as we have seen above in the section on rights-based approaches to research, often children and young people remain excluded from making decisions about issues that affect their lives simply because of their age, despite the fact that the UNCRC provides a legal framework for their involvement in these matters. Not unlike the disability rights movement, there is now a well-established children's rights lobby. Some countries have the statutory infrastructure in place to implement and promote children's and young people's rights, such as children's commissioners. The emergence of the children's rights movement and the impact that it has had on the participation of children and young people in policy making has resulted in a large body of literature on co-production methods with children and young people. Many studies describe the process and the value of involving children and young people actively in research – Brady's (2007) participatory IT project undertaken by Barnardo's in Galway in Ireland and the Scottish Human Services Trust PAR study (2002) on young school leavers which involved young people with disabilities as co-researchers would be examples for this.

However, the literature on children's participation has also received criticism. Tisdall and Davis (2004) critically reviewed what they call the 'largely self-referential' participation literature in relation to children and young people and contested the actual effect it has had on policy making. Whilst the authors found evidence for increasingly supportive environments for children's participation, they were critical of the limited impact and tangible outcomes that these measures actually had at a policy level. Their review suggests that in fact children's and young people's voices are still often ignored. Based on a participatory study of teenage parenthood, which included young mothers as co-researchers, Petrie, Fiorelli and O'Donnell (2006) also discusses the issue of how young people can be involved in non-tokenistic ways in the research process so that both the researchers and research participants benefit from their involvement.

One of the issues frequently discussed in children's research literature is the minimum age at which very young children can be meaningfully consulted. A significant contribution to this debate was the development of the so-called 'Mosaic approach' by Alison Clark. In a publication in 2011, Clark and Moss describe how participatory methods can be used to capture the perspectives of very young pre-school children on their lives, using methods such as child conferencing and role play. Aldiss et al.'s (2009) participatory research project explored children's experiences and views of cancer care services and is such an example of including very young children (3–5-year-olds) in research. The authors used play and puppets to elicit children's views. Maconochie and McNeill (2010) worked with even younger children in a parent–baby group in Sheffield in England. Whilst this PAR project also included parents, the authors argued that the project led to changes in professional attitudes towards children and a redistribution of resources, structures and spaces within children's services. Most of all, the project led to a recognition of the importance of the children's voice and the fact that even very young children are not just passive recipients of services.

Play is naturally a very important issue for children and young people of all ages. Sutton (2008) explored the relationship of children's play and children's socio-economic background and the freedom given to play, the safety of their play and the use of public spaces. Sutton's participatory study with 72 children from various socio-economic backgrounds highlighted the importance of street play in the lives of disadvantaged children who may not have access to other play venues due to lack of resources or transport. The study found contradictions in government policy on children's play and wellbeing, and concluded that safeguards should make open public spaces suitable for street play. Fox and Fine's (2013) study is equally critical towards neo-liberal urban public policy and planning and its negative impact on young people. Fox and Fine's article is based on a PAR project which was initiated by young people and adults in New York.

Young people in care and care leavers

Whilst children and young people are not principally disadvantaged or disempowered just because they are young, young people in care and care leavers are one group with persistently poorer outcomes in education, but also health. One of the issues related to young people in care is the instability of the settings which sometimes lead young people to 'go missing'. High-profile cases show that these young people are particularly vulnerable to abuse, including sexual abuse (Beckett and Warrington, 2015). In 2012 the NSPCC (National Society for the Prevention of Cruelty to Children) published a report on a participatory project involving care-experienced young people as co-researchers which explored this issue, including the trigger factors that contributed to young people running away from care settings (Taylor et al., 2012). VOYPIC (Voices of Young People in Care, 2014), an advocacy group for care-experienced young people in Northern Ireland, has on a regular basis undertaken surveys with young people in care settings and care leavers to capture their experiences. These surveys were co-designed by an advocacy group that VOYPIC runs, and some of the young people were involved in the data collection as well as the dissemination of results. Torronen and Vormanen's (2014) participatory research project in Finland, which also employed care-leaving young people as peer researchers, aimed to improve the ease of transition from care to independent living arrangements. The authors argue that participatory research methods provide opportunities for better understanding of health and social care services from a user's perspective.

Summary

This chapter demonstrates the striking diversity of participatory and collaborative research practice. It also shows that certain approaches such as CBPR have focused on particular settings, such as health and social care, whilst others, such as rights-based approaches, are concerned with population groups, for example children and young people, but also prisoners and older people in care settings who are often left out when decisions are being made about their lives. What this extensive but still incomplete range of examples presented in this chapter show is that there are very few limitations to the subject areas and populations which can be included in participatory research practice. It is, however, noticeable that many of the projects address issues of powerlessness and inequality. Many of the population groups included in these collaborative studies have been at the receiving end of persistent disadvantage and marginality. This reiterates the points made in the previous two chapters that participatory research practice emerged because of the failure of conventional research to capture these voices appropriately and to address the existing disadvantage.

The final chapter in this first part of this book will now consider some of the ethical implications in using participatory research methods.

FURTHER READING

Groundwater-Smith, S., Dockett, S. and Bottrell, D. (2014). *Participatory Research with Children and Young People*. London: Sage.
Minkler, M. and Wallerstein, N. (eds) (2011). *Community-based Participatory Research for Health: From Process to Outcomes*. San Francisco: Jossey-Bass.

EXERCISE 3.1

IN OR OUT? DEFINING YOUR STUDY POPULATION AND THE LEVEL OF INVOLVEMENT

One of the main challenges in collaborative research is to decide what individuals or groups need to be included in your research. Even when a study is initiated by a community or community organisation itself, the issue of what inclusion criteria need to be applied will arise. Diversity always exists not just between but also within communities. Whether your study is a collaboration with people who have never worked together before, or with an established group, power relations will have to be managed, so who is in and who is out and

(Continued)

who should be making this decision are important factors to consider in the planning of a project. The question trail below is a good tool to start this decision-making process.

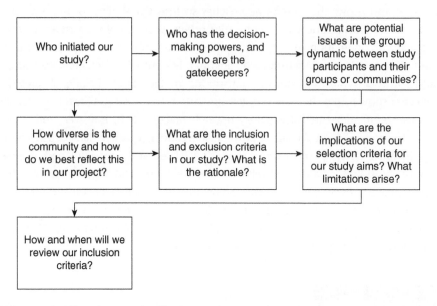

Figure 3.2   Question trail for defining your study population

4

RESEARCH ETHICS IN PARTICIPATORY RESEARCH PRACTICE

What you will learn

This chapter will address the main ethical implications of participatory research approaches and knowledge co-production. It first reviews the development of ethical thinking in research and how what we would now consider as malpractice in the past has informed this. We will then look at the challenges that institutional research ethics processes pose to participatory projects. The second part of this chapter considers the particulars and specifics of ethical research in participatory approaches, such as the management of power relations and expectations, but also risks associated with participatory approaches.

Introduction

In this chapter I will discuss ethical issues related to participatory and collaborative research approaches. In many countries, academic researchers and students are now duty-bound to submit any research project they intend to undertake which involves human participants or their data for institutional ethical review. Even when research takes place in a context where ethical scrutiny is not an institutional requirement or is not as such formalised, it is simply good practice to consider how we should undertake research so that it is safe for both research participants and researchers, and how ethical issues that may arise can be addressed. Although there are of course disagreements in relation to what *exactly* ethical research entails and how this should look in practice, as well as who has the power to decide what is ethical and what is not, we have come to expect that we apply an ethical approach and attitude to research involving people and their data.

In participatory research practice, where the boundaries between participant and researcher are sometimes blurred, very specific ethical issues may arise in terms of the participant–researcher relationship, but also with regard to the management of promises and expectations. This chapter now starts with a brief discussion of the principles of ethical research and institutional ethics review processes more generally before it considers the particulars and specifics of ethical research in participatory approaches.

The development of common research ethics standards and review processes

Very few legal and ethical regulations governed social research practice before the 1960s. As a result, some highly questionable (Berg and Lune, 2014) and exploitative practices in research occurred, which arguably disregarded the wellbeing of participants and were oblivious or indifferent in relation to issues such as confidentiality and data security. Some of the most notorious examples of what we would today consider breaches of ethical codes of practice in the social sciences occurred in the 1970s, and marginalised and disadvantaged groups of people or communities have historically been more likely to be at the receiving end of such unacceptable, exploitative or unethical research practice. Three frequently quoted, infamous and notorious examples of this exploitative practice are the Stanford prison experiments (Haney, Banks and Zimbardo, 1972), which put prisoners at risk; Humphreys' (1970) 'tearoom trade' study, which deceived gay men; and Rosenhan's 1974 'On being sane in insane places' study, which set out surreptitiously to test the reliability of psychiatric diagnoses using both pseudopatients and people suffering from mental health problems. Whilst there is little clear evidence that the researchers undertaking these studies *deliberately* set out to harm their participants, what is perhaps common to these examples is that the wellbeing and dignity of study participants was compromised in the name of science. Since then, what we now regard as acceptable minimum standards in ethical research practice has changed to an extent that none of these three projects would be reasonably likely to gain approval, due of the lack of informed consent, the level of deception used in these projects and the risk to study participants respectively. Nevertheless, various views on research ethics and how these should be applied continue to co-exist.

Bryman (2016) identifies the main stances in relation to the position that authors have taken in relation to research ethics. According to Bryman (2016: 123) a *universalist stance* 'takes the view that ethical precepts should never be broken' and that a breach of ethical principles would ultimately be 'damaging to research'. A *situation ethics stance*, on the other hand, considers deception as a means to get access to participants on a 'case-by-case basis' (2016: 124). The argument here is that under certain circumstances the end justifies the means, or that there is sometimes no choice but to use deception as a means to access participants. Undercover participatory observation into football hooliganism (Giulianotti, 1995) or research on corruption (Girodo, 1991) come to mind as examples where this may be seen as appropriate or necessary. According to Bryman (2016: 124), some authors take the view that 'ethical transgression is pervasive' and that complete honesty with participants about the research intentions potentially changes participant behaviour and the kind of information revealed. Others go further and argue that 'anything goes' (2016: 124). Bryman refers here to Norman K. Denzin's view that social scientists should have the right to study anything if it aids science, as long as it does not harm participants. Finally, Bryman (2016) refers to the discourse between 'deontological' and 'consequentialist' positions in relation to ethics, whereby 'deontological ethics considers certain acts as wrong (or good) in and of themselves' whereas a consequentialist ethical stance takes the view that certain ambivalent ethical practices such as deception whilst justifiable in certain circumstances may be harmful for the academic discipline and community as a whole in the long run, and must therefore be avoided. It would be fair to say that current ethical research practice leans towards the universalist stance, although there is an ongoing discourse around the need to facilitate a necessary level of deception, for example in criminological research in order to investigate and uncover harmful and illegal behaviours. As already discussed above, the prevalent approach is that there has to be a good rationale for eschewing a universalist approach, which would assume that participants are fully informed about the project aims and objectives and have been given an opportunity to consent actively, i.e. opt in, to take part in the research.

In order to impose minimum standards of ethical research, over the last two or three decades, many professional organisations involved in research have formalised and institutionalised ethical approval processes and have produced new guidelines and codes of ethical research practice. Whilst these codes may vary in their detail, in an attempt to agree the smallest common denominator and minimum standards, in March 2015 the Academy of Social Sciences in the UK adopted five core ethical principles for social science research, which aptly capture the current understanding of what ethical research entails (Figure 4.1).

Whilst these principles essentially represent a *universalist* stance to research ethics, the first of the five ethical principles addresses the main criticism pointed at research ethics review processes, namely the view that the formalisation of ethical approval processes potentially inhibits and limits academic freedom, or as Berg and Lune (2014) put it, that Institutional Review Boards (IRBs) or Research Ethics Committees (RECs) are basically functioning as 'handcuffs' for researchers and impede research. There is a perception, in particular – but not exclusively – among some qualitative researchers, that IRBs/RECs are exceeding their authority beyond their actual function, namely the assessment of potential harm to research participants (Berg and Lune, 2014). Truman

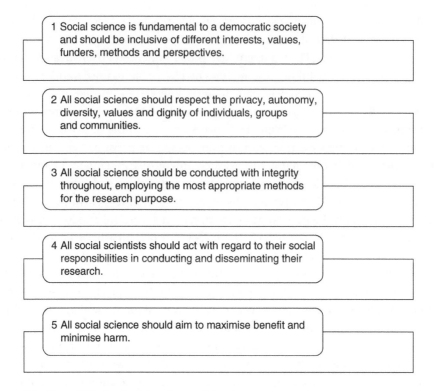

1 Social science is fundamental to a democratic society and should be inclusive of different interests, values, funders, methods and perspectives.

2 All social science should respect the privacy, autonomy, diversity, values and dignity of individuals, groups and communities.

3 All social science should be conducted with integrity throughout, employing the most appropriate methods for the research purpose.

4 All social scientists should act with regard to their social responsibilities in conducting and disseminating their research.

5 All social science should aim to maximise benefit and minimise harm.

Figure 4.1 Five ethical principles for social science research

Source: UK Academy of Social Sciences: www.acss.org.uk/developing-generic-ethics-principles-social-science/academy-adopts-five-ethical-principles-for-social-science-research/ (accessed March 2019)

(2003) also asserts that ethics review processes often reinforce experts' control of knowledge, which for researchers that follow a participatory and emancipatory approach can be particularly problematic.

It is undoubtedly the case that some qualitative research approaches such as ethnographic and participatory studies do present greater challenges to IRBs/RECs because of their more flexible approach to data collection and their greater emphasis on the relationship between researchers and participants, which make it harder to foresee and therefore address all ethical challenges before any data collection begins. I will discuss this in detail later in the second part of this chapter. However, by putting a clear and unambiguous statement of support for diversity in research at the start of the list of their ethical research principles, the UK Academy of Social Sciences arguably takes some wind out of the sails of the critics who are sceptical towards institutionalised ethical scrutiny. Indeed, research is central to democratic societies, but at the same time it is no longer acceptable that the freedom to undertake research should be offset by the unethical treatment of research participants without whom research could not be undertaken in the first place.

The Academy's Principles 2–5 therefore deal with the way research should be undertaken: respectfully towards the participants and their communities and with integrity. Ultimately the aim of research must be to maximise the benefits of the research and to avoid or minimise harmful effects, as Principle 5 states. Again, this confirms the essentially *universalist* undertone of these principles. In order to uphold the integrity of their research studies and their compliance with general ethical standards of research, the questions that researchers should ask when planning their projects are these:

1   How do I achieve informed consent from my research participants and/or their legal guardians or representatives for my study, including the right to withdraw from the study without negative consequences? If it is impractical or impossible to gain informed consent, what is the rationale for undertaking the study anyway, and what are the implications for direct and indirect participants?
2   How will I make sure that I protect the privacy of my participants?
3   How do ensure that I treat my participants and their experiences respectfully?
4   How do I ensure that I minimise the risk for participants and researchers to be harmed?
5   What measures do I put in place to treat my data with confidentiality and store it securely?

The working rule in research projects is now that fully informed and voluntary consent should be sought. There will be few cases where it is impractical, impossible or even unsafe for a researcher to seek informed consent from participants. The most obvious example is covert research, for example for criminological and investigative observations, such as the already mentioned studies on corruption or hooliganism/violence. The exploration of very controversial or sensitive issues may under certain circumstances also merit the decision that informed consent is not sought prior to the study, as this may actually increase the risk to researchers and participants. In these cases, normally the expectation is that researchers evidence the measures they put in place to minimise risk to participants, including the risk of exposure. This may include safety protocols for both researchers and participants, including exit strategies.

The principle of active informed consent, however, has also been contested. Aldridge (2015) raises the question whether stringent research ethics frameworks that insist on active informed and voluntary consent actually prevent people regarded as 'vulnerable' (e.g. young children, people with dementia or severe learning disabilities, prisoners, patients in the health system) from being included in research – for example, if they are deemed unfit to give informed consent and the right to opt in or opt out of taking part in research is transferred to guardians or gatekeepers who *in loco parentis* police the access that researchers can have to vulnerable participants. Making their case for passive consent (opting out) versus active consent (opting in), Berg and Lune (2014: 80) also argue that if all studies only included those who voluntarily participated in research, in many cases the consequence would be that we really do not gain a meaningful understanding of the issue under investigation. Perhaps this is more of a substantial issue for quantitative survey-based research where the ambition is to yield generalisable data, but the issue of voluntary active consent may also affect qualitative studies which may aim to uncover institutional malpractice or abuse.

In the European Union, the General Data Protection Regulation (GDPR), which came into force in 2018 and which regulates the handing of personal data, provides a legal gateway for research institutions to collect and process data, if this is deemed to be in the interest of the public, even if informed consent is not in place. This is a mechanism which can be applied, on a case-by-case basis, if and when there is a clear rationale for this. Generally, waiving the need to seek consent in the name of ambitious or self-satisfying pursuit of knowledge or 'truth' is not an acceptable strategy as such. As we have seen earlier in this volume, qualitative researchers tend to struggle with this notion of a 'discoverable objective truth' anyway, so a more appropriate approach is to consider the issue of consent as an integral part of research and as an ethical and moral endeavour.

Specific ethical issues in participatory research practice

The five ethical principles discussed above apply to all research projects in the social sciences. However, participatory research practice raises some unique ethical questions, mainly due to the close relationship and sometimes blurred boundaries between researchers and participants, as well as the emancipatory ambition and the desire to initiate positive change for the participants, their communities and institutions. When discussing these specific ethical issues here, I do this with an empowerment rather than efficiency rationale in mind. According to Brownlie (2009: 701), the 'efficiency rationale' is based on the belief that participation produces better outcomes, whereas the 'empowerment rationale' of participation is centred around the desire to improve people's lives via participatory research means. Whilst these two rationales are by no means mutually exclusive and can be complementary, for the purpose of this chapter it makes more sense to assume that the main rationale for the adoption of a collaborative, participatory approach is the improvement of the lives of the people involved in the research and/or their communities.

Figure 4.2 shows the seven main principles that according to the Centre for Social Justice and Community Action & the National Co-ordinating Centre for Public Engagement (2012) form the ethical framework of participatory research. Whilst integrity and respect are also important aspects of ethical research practice in conventional research, the other aspects, such as inclusion, active learning, the aim to make a difference and democratic participation are aspects of ethical research practice that are not necessarily central in conventional research, but highlight here the focus on action and change in collaborative and participatory research practice.

As Banks and Brydon-Miller (2019) stress, these elements also highlight the collective nature of participatory research. Some of the steps involved in ethical participatory research practice include active conversations around the issue of mutual respect; proactive involvement in research of disadvantaged and under- and

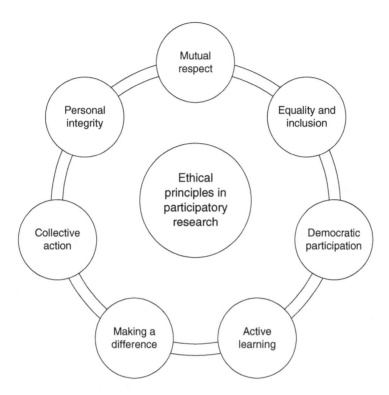

Figure 4.2 Ethical principles in participatory research

misrepresented individuals and communities; an acknowledgement and addressing of power imbalances; a focus on learning and skills development; working
towards an agreed vision of positive social change; and the honesty and willingness to accept and work with conflict and diversity of opinions.

The researcher and participant role conflation in participatory research

Blake (2007), Boser (2006), and Brydon-Miller and Greenwood (2006) all point out
that the way participatory action research projects are run poses significant challenges with regard to the increasingly formalised and institutionalised ethical review
structures via IRBs/RECs. Boser (2006) claims that the current ethics framework is
essentially based on post-positivist epistemological assumptions characterised by a
distant researcher–participant relationship, and this is at odds with participatory and
collaborative research approaches, where boundaries are more fluid and may shift
during a research project. Brydon-Miller and Greenwood (2006) agree with this sentiment and argue that the process character of participatory projects does not follow the
assumed predictability logic as conventional positivist research where:

the researcher can predict (or believes she can predict) with reasonable certainty how the research will be carried out and what the possible outcomes might be. In action research, because the articulation of the issues to be addressed, the development of possible interventions, and the processes of group reflection and ensuing actions are all under the control of the participants themselves, rather than the researcher, there is no such control. (2006: 121)

This normally strict differentiation between researcher and participant does not usually occur in the same way in participatory and collaborative approaches. This poses challenges around issues such as informed consent, agreeing roles and responsibilities, assuring confidentiality – even in relation to the establishment of a clear research question and methodology – all of which are fluid and subject to ongoing negotiations and renegotiations. Further tensions may arise between the roles a researcher has to adopt in participatory research. According to Stoecker (1999) there are four main roles: animator, community organiser, popular educator and participatory researcher. The two main functions are being a researcher, but also an activist. Not all people are good organisers, animators, educators and researchers at the same time, as Stoecker notes.

Unlike in conventional research where social change is not necessarily an explicit research target, in participatory research practice, personal and social transformation are commonly both an aim and a desired outcome of the research. This blurs the boundaries between researchers and researched as well as between researcher and activist (Durham Community Research Team, 2011). The assumption of new roles, such as co-researcher or peer researcher and the new competencies and insider status that ultimately go hand in hand with this means that community researchers are no longer 'full peers' in their communities. Equally, the longer professional researchers are involved in a collaborative research project the more they lose their outsider status, as MacFarlane and Roche (2019) note. These processes need to be managed, including the potential disappointments if desired social changes do not or only partially materialise.

In participatory projects, research relationships normally extend over longer periods and this demands that ethics are considered as an integral part of the entire research process. Boser (2006: 14) argues that ethical implications of participatory research practice do not narrowly arise from, and therefore should not be solely judged on, 'the impact of the research process on the individual participant' but also 'the social location of the research itself, … the context and the potential intended/unintended consequences in a politicized environment'. Again, this points to a practice where ethical issues are understood to be part of an ongoing process and are revisited and renegotiated routinely for the duration of the study. This is a good illustration of the constant reflexive process characteristic of participatory research. Bengtsson and Mølholt (2016) have termed this approach 'situated ethics', by which they mean that, in order to handle ethical challenges, proactive and reactive strategies should be applied that are guided by local and specific circumstances and not just by universal principles. Note here the similarity to the term 'situation ethics' used by Bryman (2016).

Individual versus group consent

Williamson and Prosser (2002) go as far as to claim that conventional notions of informed consent are inadequate for participatory practice. In their view, consent cannot be meaningfully given at the start of a project, which is designed to evolve and develop collaboratively in open dialogue among all research participants, and which does not have fixed aims and objectives or agreed methods at the project initiation stage.

Further, as Flicker et al. (2007) point out, informed consent is usually understood in relation to individual-level consent, but this disregards the potentially difficult issues that community representation (for example via advocacy groups, project board membership or co-research) may raise for communities at the centre of the research. This can, for example, be the case if co-researchers do not express the views of the majority of people of a community that they are appointed to represent, or if the research findings sit uneasily with the respective community. As Flicker et al. point out, unflattering research data may further stigmatise disadvantaged communities and may have negative rather than empowering effects, so it is important to strike a good balance between academic rigour on the one hand and sensitivity towards the needs of the community on the other.

However, attempts to extend informed consent to group or community level will ultimately pose other challenges as well, as the Durham Community Research Team (2011) points out. These start with the difficulty to define what exactly the respective 'community' is. Who is in and who is out?! What if the community is divided? What if the groups' or communities' own ethical standards are different from our common standards? All these questions point to the need to find common denominators with those involved in collaborative research projects. What I would argue strongly is that communities must not be regarded as homogeneous groups, even if they appear to have strong representation of specific community interests. Because all groups and communities tend to be diverse, community consent should therefore not offset individual consent, but should be regarded as an additional challenge. In indigenous communities, where community consent is often of particular importance due to what may be perceived as exploitative research practice in the past, a key question is whether the planned research is sensitive and responsive to community needs, likely to assist in building local capacity and is potentially able to solve problems that the respective community itself identifies as priorities (Glass and Kaufert, 2007).

Research training

One of the mechanisms by which ethical research practice can be implemented in participatory and collaborative projects is researcher training. Writing about the involvement of children as co-researchers, Brownlie (2009) argues that critics of participatory approaches raise concerns about the lack of competence of non-professional researchers and the impact that this has for the rigour of the research. The question posed is basically what the purpose of involving co-researchers is if they need to be trained. Also writing about children as researchers, Kellet (2005: 10) argues 'that a barrier to empowering children as researchers is not their lack of adult status but their lack of research skills'. And she asks: 'So why not teach them?'

The research methods capacity building among non-academic researchers generally, and not just as far as children are concerned, is indeed one of the challenges of participatory research approaches. Together with colleagues I have argued elsewhere (McCartan, Burns and Schubotz, 2012) that the research training has three main functions:

1   Introducing basic research methods skills and principles of research ethics (such as consent and confidentiality, dealing with disclosures).
2   Sensitising for the subject area researched.
3   Team building.

Researcher training ultimately helps to identify roles and responsibilities based on interest, ability, skills, availability and commitment. Research training and capacity building are here not simply a one-way process in which professional researchers educate community researchers. Fox (2013: 987) therefore warns that research training should not be about 'teaching conventional research practices which participation should be aiming to avoid'. One of the greatest benefits of participatory and collaborative research practice is indeed that it also helps professional researchers to understand the culture and socio-economic context of the people and communities that they research. Having said that, and as I alluded to in Chapter 1, research projects afford participants different levels of participation, and not all achieve the 'gold standard' of full participation, and there could be very practical reasons for this. So, in response to Fox (2013), and in preparation of Part II of this book, I would hold that conventional methods (such as surveys or group discussions) do not have to be avoided at all cost, and as in all other research it is the research questions alongside the context in which the research takes place that determine what methods should or should not be used. Conventional methods used in a participatory way can be suitable approaches, and in these cases, training co-researchers in how to conduct group discussions, how to ask good survey questions, and how to analyse data arising from these methods can be necessary and empowering experiences.

From a research ethical point of view, co-researchers need to be sensitised in relation to the principles of consent and confidentiality during a research project, and awareness also needs to be raised about the limitations of confidentiality in relation to their own role as co-researchers in a participatory research project. The issue of confidentiality is particularly difficult to negotiate in participatory research practice where multiple actors are involved in the running of the research process and where the roles of participant and researcher are blurred (Williamson and Prosser, 2002; MacFarlane and Roche, 2019), as just discussed. The level of confidentiality that can be offered is therefore at best conditional. There is an inherent risk to disclosures in group projects, so the need to secure internal confidentiality between group members needs to be addressed. It is for that reason that transparency about these limits to confidentiality is required at the training stage, and informed consent must be routinely renegotiated and renewed throughout all stages of a participatory project. The option to opt in or out of participating in the whole study or certain aspects of it should exist throughout the research process.

Brydon-Miller and Greenwood (2006) remind us that this issue of confidentiality continues into the dissemination phase of a project where authorship and ownership issues need to be negotiated. Confidentiality could, for example, be compromised through research outputs, i.e. by naming members of the research team who were also informants in the project. So, paradoxically, the ethically commendable praxis of acknowledging the contribution of co-researchers may compromise one core ethical principle, namely confidentiality.

Whilst co-researchers may have an inside knowledge of the issue under investigation, the collection of data requires not only research skills and commitment, but also the adoption of a critical distance towards the subject area itself and reflexivity about one's own positionality. In order for the project to be completed with ethical integrity and with rigour, awareness needs to be raised for the ability to respect the attitudes and values of other research participants and informants, even if they do not correspond with one's own views. An understanding of the dynamic in group projects is essential for the success of collaborative projects, and ethically it is important to communicate this. This connects directly with the next point discussed here, i.e. the nature of power and trust relationships in participatory and collaborative research practice.

Power and trust relations in participatory research practice

Central to the philosophy of participatory research is the ambition to work in the best interest of the research participants. It is for that reason that some academics engaged in participatory or collaborative research practice have argued that this in itself represents a more ethical way to undertake research. Kershaw, Castleden and Laroque (2014), for example, conclude that a CBPR approach is an 'effective practice and an ethical way to respond' to calls for respect of indigenous communities, whilst Ward, Barnes and Gahagan (2012) utilised a participatory approach with the aim to develop ethical practice to enhance wellbeing among older people. In my view, however, there is no automatic link between ethical and participatory research practice; rather, the negotiation of trusting and equal relationships between participants and researchers does take a lot of effort and planning, as participation is an interactive and complex process. As Aldridge (2015) emphasises, in particular if participatory research practice involves vulnerable or marginalised individuals or communities, it is often the intention of the researchers to tackle inequality and powerlessness and to give voice to those who are marginalised and excluded, not least by affording them full participation in research.

This is often not the case in conventional research practice because these individuals and communities are deemed 'hard to reach' and too difficult to be included.

In fact, in participatory research practice, often the people or communities involved are not simply members of disadvantaged or disempowered communities, but they are architects of their research studies themselves and/or become co-researchers in these projects. These studies consequently generate a different group dynamic from projects initiated by professional researchers. This means that the ethical principle to maximise benefit and minimise harm also gains a different dimension from conventional research practice, as it is not the researcher's sole responsibility to ensure that risk is minimised, but it becomes an integral part of the group dynamic to negotiate how participants and their organisations and communities are protected.

Jupp Kina (2012) draws on the writing of Paulo Freire, one of the pioneers of and core contributors to our understanding of participatory research practice, when she highlights the main challenge that researchers involved in participatory practice face in relation to their position in research projects. Jupp Kina argues that the decision to 'be participatory' still too often remains an intellectual decision that fails to recognise the commitment to personal change that is connected to this decision. Jupp Kina (2012: 205) quotes from Freire (1971): 'Political action on the side of the oppressed must be pedagogical action in the authentic sense of the word, and, therefore, action with the oppressed.' She argues with Freire that as a participatory researcher – or 'pedagogue' in Freire's terminology – one has to be willing to place oneself 'as a subject of the process alongside those with whom you are working' (Jupp Kina, 2012: 205). This may be challenging and uncomfortable at times, but – again quoting from Freire – 'it is only through accepting this aspect of the process that it is possible to avoid making people "the objects of ... humanitarianism" which "itself maintains and embodies oppression"' (Jupp Kina, 2012: 205). It is this willingness to become the subject of the participatory process itself that is required for the equality power relations. In short, there is no alternative for researchers to place themselves in the centre of continually informed and negotiated participation.

One of the first steps required in order to achieve this is to recognise and acknowledge the role of power, how it operates, and its positive and negative aspects in participatory and collaborative research endeavours. This includes some reflection on who determines the rules of the engagement (Carr, 2012). Clear strategies are required for maintaining these relationships with co-researchers and participants for the duration of a project. Following Foucauldian thinking, Hilsen (2006) proposes that it is the responsibility of those involved in participatory research to address power relations that arise from this practice and to reconceptualise power as 'a network of social boundaries that constrain and enable action for all actors' (2006: 31). The power relations that need to be explored are those between and within the groups of professional researchers and those with the co-researchers and the participants. Factors that influence these relationships are context factors – for example the community in which the research takes place and its status, but also issues such as age, gender, race, socio-economic status, educational background and so forth (see Figure 4.3). Not all of these factors are always of equal importance and further context factors not captured in the model in Figure 4.3 could also play a part.

As colleagues of mine and I have pointed out in the publication from which this model is reproduced (McCartan, Schubotz and Murphy, 2012: para. 47), the negotiation of power relations within participatory projects 'demands flexibility and the potential to exchange power either temporarily or permanently. This needs to be both constructed and carried out in an artificial and self-conscious way, a post-modern approach, which acknowledges the fluctuating levels of power among the research partners.'

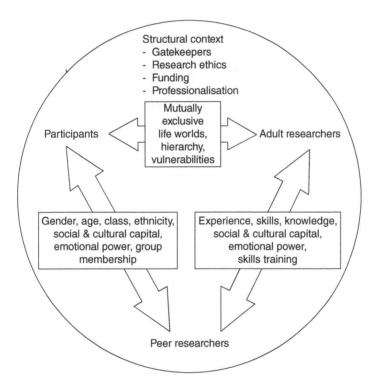

Figure 4.3 Model of power relations in participatory research

Source: McCartan, Schubotz and Murphy (2012). Licensed under a Creative Commons Attribution 4.0 International License.

The ethics of compensating and valuing contributions

Whether or not compensations or reimbursements are offered to co-researchers or volunteers in collaborative research projects, and what form these take is an important ethical issue as this may impact the relationships between researchers, co-researchers and other participants. Interestingly, beyond the agreement that covering incurred expenses (such as travelling costs) is a minimum standard, the guidance on the compensation of co-researchers in collaborative research practice is quite vague and diverse. This is probably a reflection of the financial constraints under which some projects are undertaken. The question really is: should we pay co-researchers if we can afford to and, if so, how and how much should we pay them?

In the projects that I was involved in with any decision-making capacity, our approach was always that if we expect co-researchers to make a significant contribution to the research, then we ought to pay them for this, if we can. In my view, reasonably formal contracts for co-researchers which specify their tasks and time commitments and the respective compensation they will receive can be useful tools that can support mutual trust and can help to reinforce the message about how much we value the contribution that co-researchers make. This may lead to a more professional relationship between co-researchers and professional researchers, especially, but not exclusively, in projects in which children and young people are involved as co-researchers. This is where most of my own expertise lies. Pay can be given in the form of cash, but also vouchers, if this is more feasible. When we paid in cash, we always paid an hourly wage which reflected the fact that research is a very skilled activity.

However, for some participants, short-term cash payments may have undesirable effects, for example the loss of benefit payments, so as with all other aspects of a research project, openness and transparency are very important when it comes to the compensation of co-researchers, and that includes information about what kind of income needs to be declared for tax purposes. It is also possible that individual payments contribute to coercive relationships which may impact on the ability to freely express discontent, in particular if co-researchers are in need of monetary compensation.

Alternative non-cash forms of formal recognition should therefore not be ruled out. These include certificates of achievement or thank-you letters, accreditations, references, offers of free training courses, payment of fees for such training, or payments being made to a community organisation or charity instead of individual payments.

More informal recognition may include vouchers for days out, such as cinema or meal vouchers, a party, opportunities to present research to high-profile audiences, or generous catering during research meetings.

Whilst recognition and compensation are generally positive aspects of a project, there is also the potential that jealousy may arise among participants who may not get compensated. So if a difference is being made in terms of the level of compensation received – say between a co-researcher and an 'ordinary' participant in a project, then it is important to communicate the reasons for this very clearly to the whole group. In some cases it may be more appropriate to formally or informally acknowledge the contributions of the whole community group and to not give any individual monetary compensation to co-researchers.

Reciprocity, trust and the ethics of care

Riecken et al. (2005) remind us that the desire alone to work with participants as 'co-equals' cannot change the power imbalance itself, and Carr (2012) found that power issues were at the heart of cases where participation had *not* achieved the change that was desired.

In order to deal with the power differentials and to develop mutual ownership of the research process, Maiter et al. (2008: 307) state that it is necessary to develop 'reciprocal dialogue' between researchers and participants 'in which an individual researcher and study participant communicate as equals'. Maiter et al. argue that reciprocal practices are a common and fundamental form of exchange in different spheres in our life. Whilst reinforcing egalitarian relationships, reciprocity also carries a certain moral weight and inherent psychological power until an obligation to reciprocate is met. In participatory research practice this reciprocal dialogue offers the opportunity to create a level playing field between different researchers and participants, but it also highlights potential risks when it comes to the distribution of tasks and the related issue of consent. Academic researchers involved in participatory projects have to master the balance between building and maintaining positive reciprocal non-hierarchical relationships with co-researchers and study participants whilst at the same time upholding academic obligations in relation to rigour in the research.

Franks (2011) acknowledges that full participation in all aspects of a project is not always possible or feasible, for example due to the nature of the research, funding or methodological constraints, practicalities, interests of the participants and so on. He suggests that in these cases meaningful 'pockets of participation' can be created, and that the limits of participation and decision making should then be clearly communicated

In Hilsen's (2006) view, the only response possible to address power differentials is to develop ethical research practice, and by that she means that the researchers have to take responsibility overall for their research participants and for how the research affects their life worlds. Ward and Gahagen (2010) propose a similar 'ethic of care framework', which they see as materialising via interconnected principles of attentiveness, responsibility, competence, responsiveness and trust. In practice this often means that researchers involved in collaborative research practice with community organisations have to find the right balance between closeness and distance which allows them to gain the trust from participants and co-researchers whilst at the same time honouring confidentiality and privacy. In qualitative research the expectation to maintain a professional relationship with participants, including appropriate exit strategies, on the one hand can be in conflict with participants' desire to form 'friendships' with the researcher on the other. One of the consequences of too friendly relationships with participants may be that the principle of ethical consent is compromised as participants may find it hard to say 'no' to participation in a study. On the other hand, too great a distance from participants may mean that the reciprocal practices that Maiter et al. (2008) demands will not materialise and the necessary trust between researchers and co-researchers as well as participants cannot develop.

For Hilsen (2006), trust is the most important ingredient in this, and she draws on some theoretical ontological insights when she makes her argument. From a constructivist perspective, 'not trusting other people at all would make life ontologically impossible', Hilsen (2006: 28) argues. She continues: 'Without trust, there could be no communication, as the fundamentals of communication, the speech acts, are acts of trust toward other people' (2006: 28). Hilsen makes this point because she argues that in action research trust should be used *as a method*: She writes: 'AR enables the participants to trust their own powers of action and decision' (2006: 28). In Hilsen's view, the radical ethical demand arises from fairer power relations which include the willingness to trust the participants and their judgement in the decision making in the projects, even – or especially! – if these decisions do not agree with the professional researcher's views or judgement. This can be very difficult to do, but determining to what extend participants are afforded decision-making capacity is central for each participatory project. The level of decision-making power in each project must be negotiated from the start and regularly revisited, otherwise the researchers are likely to fall into the tokenism trap. In these cases, ethically a participatory design should perhaps rather be avoided.

Referring to participatory research involving children, Gallagher and Gallagher (2008) reiterate that participatory methods do not per se 'empower' children. In fact, they can also be used to regulate children, especially if the assumption is that adults need to 'empower' children. For example, participatory projects only involve a small number of co-researchers. If these are 'hand-picked' by gatekeepers – children as researchers, picked by teachers is a good and common example – then there is a real possibility that those with mainstream opinions and experiences (e.g. 'professionalised children' – Tisdall, 2008) are privileged. Thus, if not used appropriately, participatory methods can also have potentially counter-productive effects. Gallagher and Gallagher (2008: 499) hold that 'participatory approaches, in their insistence that children should take part in research, may in fact involve children in processes that aim to regulate them'. This is an issue that transcends research with children and young people and equally applies to projects with adults. Beresford and Carr (2012) express similar concerns about the potential abuse of user-led research approaches. They argue that user involvement in research can sometimes be abused to rubber-stamp decisions that have already been made. This could lead to people being even more vulnerable.

Undertaking research in one's own organisation or community

One of the common issues that occurs in participatory research practice is that people with authority and those who they have authority over are involved in the same research project. Examples of this are: teachers and students, youth workers and young people, social workers and clients, prisoners and prison staff, or social work managers and their staff. In conventional research projects this would be seen as potentially problematic, and for good reason, as it raises substantial questions around the ability to give or withhold informed consent and to maintain a basic level of confidentiality. However, in collaborative projects, which may include whole communities, networks or organisations, the participation of those with authority alongside those they have authority over is often unavoidable and may even be desirable.

Again, essentially, the only way to deal with this is to openly explore and address the power differentials and power relations that arise in these contexts. Together in a team, attempts should be made to raise awareness for potential conflicts of interest and to agree suitable strategies to deal with these, 'distinguishing between coercion on the one hand and a shared interest in promoting the generation of knowledge and positive social change on the other' (Brydon-Miller and Greenwood, 2006: 125). Brydon-Miller and Greenwood suggest that consent issues could be dealt with by third parties, if this is feasible, so that participants do not have to fear negative consequences from their participation or non-participation, if they decide to opt out, although this may not always be very practical.

Unfortunately, within established community groups, in addition to the formal hierarchical structure there are also informal power differentials and hierarchies that are much harder to deal with because they are not as easy to identify. The only way to do so is through openness and transparency about decision-making processes throughout a study. As Williamson and Prosser (2002: 590) state, if participatory approaches are truly collaborative, 'then the only way to resolve these [ethical] issues is through mutual discussion and reflection'.

Alongside openness and transparency, some structural mechanisms can be employed to counteract hierarchical relationships. For example, a quorate of co-researchers and 'professional' researchers could be introduced. In many cases in collaborative research practice, co-researchers outnumber professional researchers in the project, and this in itself can help shift the power relations towards the community researchers in team meetings or generally when strategic decisions are being made. Similar quotas can be introduced among co-researchers to make sure a variety of views and experiences is reflected. For example, in one of the studies that I was involved in (NCB NI and ARK YLT, 2010) which focused on newcomer children and young people's experiences in Northern Ireland and the attitudes of young people from established communities towards them, we made sure that the team of co-researchers was diverse in terms of ethnic background, but also gender and school background. The purpose of a quorate is to ensure that no group is over-represented thus attempting to maintain a power balance, although this of course may not always and automatically translate into practice. The aim is to create an appropriate discursive space which is accessible to all participants and acknowledges that co-production is a mutually beneficial exercise which cannot be completed successfully without a collaborative and inclusive approach.

Managing expectations, emotions and the promise of change

The participatory turn in research provides new opportunities as the academic community is much more open now towards innovative collaborative approaches than in the past. At the same time, the increasing endorsement of participatory and collaborative approaches may drive researchers to adopt participatory designs when it is neither appropriate nor genuine, and this is when participation may turn into tokenism and the promise of change may remain elusive. Whilst Lundy (2018) has spoken out about the unintended positive effects that tokenistic participation may yield, ethically, the ambition in collaborative research practice should certainly be that it is genuine and real. Thus, whilst it is important to develop and improve participation opportunities, it is equally important to have realistic expectations of what participatory approaches can achieve. Of course, participation may never be perfect, and there is always more that can be done, but that goes without saying.

Two of the core ethical issues that will have to be managed carefully are therefore participant expectations and this promise of change. Petrie, Fiorelli and O'Donnell's (2006) article 'If we help you what will change?' captures this sense of promise and expectation of change. Their study of teenage pregnancy and early parenthood, in which young people were involved as co-researchers, epitomises this need to manage participant expectations. This is something that all collaborative research projects have to address. Potential study participants may have previously been at the receiving end of broken promises – either from taking part in previous research projects that did not yield the expected outcomes, or from feeling let down by service providers. The result could be a disillusionment with any kind of consultation or research project that promises positive change to the lives of the people and communities involved. Some participants may therefore give conditional offers to participate, and some may request promises that the desired impact is going to materialise – a promise that cannot and should not be given. In participatory projects it is therefore important to explore and manage expectations from the onset of a project and to revisit this on a regular basis. Giving participants and co-researchers as much information and control as possible about the research design and process is ethically a good strategy; however, it is equally important to help participants understand that research, lobbying and advocacy are only three pieces in the large puzzle of policy and decision making, so one of the ethical responsibilities that professional researchers involved in collaborative research practice have is to protect participants and their communities from unrealistic expectations about the outcomes and impact of a research study. Even in well-established group contexts disappointment or anger may arise alongside passion for a project and social engagement in its name.

Jupp Kina (2012) explores the role of emotions in participatory work alluding to the connection between what we think and what we feel. She found that feelings such as tiredness, nervousness, excitement, stress, disappointment or anger can easily affect people's capacity and willingness to contribute to the research. However, emotions do not just affect participants but also researchers themselves, as Brownlie (2009: 712) reminds us, when she writes that 'we need to unpack our emotional investment in such participation and acknowledge the differentiated, sometimes unintended, consequences which can arise from it'. This relates to some of the potential risks that I have just discussed, but also disappointment when things are not going as planned, or if the intended impact of the research fails to materialise.

One of the main tasks at the start of each project is therefore the development of an understanding of realistic expectations on what policy and practice interventions can and cannot be achieved (Brodie et al., 2011). Williamson and Prosser (2002: 588) warn that participatory projects can potentially result in 'much self-reflection with little change'. Service user-led research, which was developed to inform the way social services are being run, is particularly affected by this issue. Carr (2012) found that even if research is specifically set up to inform change and to accommodate user voice in service delivery, as is the case in user-led research, there is no guarantee that participation strategies result in change. Carr also found particular deficits in relation to the feedback that the service users received about the outcomes and impact of their studies. At the core of this deficit is the lack of responsiveness and commitment to change at an organisational and institutional level.

One of the causes of this can be an essentially tokenistic approach to user participation which lacks the fundamental commitment to deliver and implement change. This is often fostered by an institutional culture, characterised by bureaucracy, inefficiency, inflexibility and micro-management of work processes, all of which cultivate organisational and professional resistance when it comes to implementing change generated from user participation. The additional issue is that disadvantaged and marginalised service users who need change the most are often under-represented when it comes to participatory involvement, so their voices are either disregarded or treated as 'off limit' (Hodge, 2005).

At the same time, the process of engaging with service delivery and the development of policy does take time, as research evidence is not the only evidence taken into consideration when policies and interventions are developed. The evidence available may also be contradictory and stakeholders may be resistant to change, or the financial remit for desired change may be limited. The discussion of policy-making processes should therefore form part of the programme initiation process when expectations are being explored.

When research is undertaken in highly controlled environments, such as prisons, very practical organisational and ethical issues may also arise, for example, where and how to store sensitive or confidential information, such as interview transcripts (Fine and Torre, 2006). Generally, effective participation requires access and support for people to get together and work together collectively and collegiately.

Undertaking research with particularly vulnerable groups such as people with learning difficulties will pose additional challenges in relation to the management of expectations and emotions. Conder, Milner and Mirfin-Veitch (2011) developed a quality of life tool with a group of people with an intellectual disability who they engaged as co-researchers. They reported on the ethical dilemma of 'providing the vehicle for greater insight into how an individual's life might improve whilst not being in a position to effect change' (2011: 46).

Risk management – protecting and safeguarding research participants

As Petrie, Fiorelli and O'Donnell (2006) conclude, there is an inherent contradiction in participatory research, namely: allowing people and communities real and meaningful influence on the research process has tangible benefits for them, but the same process also exposes them to risks. It is therefore important to enable participants to make informed choices about their participation in the research, whilst at the same time trying to manage the risks that they are exposed to. These risks can sometimes be unpredictable and far-reaching, and this is more likely the more political and sensitive the research areas are.

Gubrium, Hill and Flicker (2014) discuss the individual and community risks involved in participatory digital story-telling projects. They argue that the storytellers' wellbeing should be the main concern here. Participants in story-telling projects need to understand the implications and potential consequences of the publication of personal stories. Whilst they should ideally retain ownership of their stories and should be credited with their work, the rights and interests of indirect participants, i.e. those who appear in the story or who might be identified as a result of a story, must also be respected. For example, ethical and legal issues arise when a participant identifies people, experiences or events which are related to harmful or abusive behaviour.

Brydon-Miller and Greenwood (2006) point out that in projects which are led by members of the community, professional researchers have little control of what actions the group decides to take and what consequences these actions can have. This has implications for the management of risk in participatory research practice. The authors argue that 'efforts to minimize the likelihood of harm to human subjects by severely limiting the kinds of research that can be done' can result in social research becoming 'largely impotent in terms of addressing issues of real importance' (2006: 122), which would be a paradoxical and indeed unwanted effect.

Williamson and Prosser (2002) question how one can 'guarantee' risk-free and harm-free research for participants in light of the political character of many action research projects and the intention to initiate change. Political action, such as highlighting social inadequacies or inequalities, per se involves a certain element of personal risk, and sometimes this is not an undesirable by-product of a research product but an intentional outcome. Action research *is* a political enterprise which has potential consequences for the participants' careers and their lives more generally. On the other hand, the responsibility of being a co-researcher can also weigh heavily, so various potential risks should be discussed and addressed throughout a project. Bengtsson and Mølholt's (2016) term 'ethical red flags' is quite useful in that respect as it can be used to identify boundaries in relation to risk management. One of these 'red flags' should be, for example, that if there is a sense that participation in the research would create problems for a participant, especially if they are considered vulnerable, then it would not be in the best interest of this participant to pursue the research participation. Bernard's (2013) study on black teenage mothers with harmful childhood histories, for example, explores questions of the limitations of consent and confidentiality, the management of risk and the duty of care for her vulnerable study participants. She concludes that acting in the best interest of a participant who is under the legal age of consent could mean that compromises may have to be made when legal, ethical and duty of care issues are in conflict with each other, for example in relation to confidentiality or consent.

The concept of the 'Gillick competency', which originated in a 1985 court ruling in the UK and which gave children and young people under the age of 16 years the right to access contraception if they are deemed competent to do so, and which was applied to various research settings where seeking parental consent was deemed impossible, impractical or counter-productive, can be an appropriate vehicle to apply. However, the question in research contexts is whether a researcher is always competent to decide whether or not the 'Gillick competency' should be applied, and this process of decision making about competency is certainly susceptible to ambiguities and errors. The United Nations' Convention on the Rights of the Child (UNCRC) provides an alternative and perhaps more convincing framework. The UNCRC stipulates that children who are capable of forming their own views should be given the opportunity to express those views freely. It also states that these views should be given due weight in accordance with their age and maturity, and all of this has to be done with the children's best interest in mind. However, as Archard and Skivenes (2009) have eloquently shown, a child's best interest is not always and automatically served by hearing a child's view, in fact a child's view may be contradictory to his or her own interests. Archard and Skivenes propose a checklist that can be modified and, by doing so, become a useful tool for researchers in participatory research projects with children and young people, but also other participants who are deemed unable to give consent themselves (such as people with severe learning disabilities), to assess the relationship between 'best interest' and the 'right to be heard'. Applied to the research context, this list includes questions such as:

- Who makes the judgement of 'best interest' and how is this made?
- What opportunities are there to contest this judgement and its assumptions?
- How are the views of participants sought and what steps are taken to ensure that these are genuinely their views?
- Who decides when a participant is 'mature' enough to give consent, and on what basis is this decided?
- Who decides how this maturity is manifested and demonstrated? What is the standard of maturity and competency against which this is judged?

Generally, it has to be said that the legal threshold for the age of maturity and competency (e.g. voting, having sex, drinking alcohol, smoking, driving a car, working for a wage, getting married) varies in different contexts and jurisdictions. This naturally raises questions about the basis of these thresholds. Ethically, research must take place within the legal context that the respective environment provides.

Whilst potential risks have to be addressed as part of the research process, sometimes unintended consequences occur which are external to the actual project. Petrie, Fiorelly and O'Donnell (2006) undertook a large-scale study on teenage pregnancy and young parenthood in which they employed young mothers as peer researchers. In their case, the study received some harmful press coverage which affected some of the young people negatively and personally. From their experience in this study the authors conclude that meaningful participation which gives participants real influence on the process of the research 'brings potential risks as well as benefits and these risks are largely carried by the research participants rather than the researcher' (Petrie, Fiorelly and O'Donnell, 2006: 43–44). Having learned from their experience they suggest that it would be sensible in participatory research practice to undertake a risk audit in order to be prepared and have strategies in place should potentially damaging consequences arise.

One of these potentially damaging consequences is directly related to the nature of participatory research itself. A common perception, and one of the main reasons why participatory research takes place, is that compared to conventional research projects, participatory approaches have the advantage that co-researchers have easier and better access to the life worlds of their peers. However, not all people may want to be researched by members of their peer groups, nor is this automatically and always an advantage. In fact, too much familiarity between researcher and participant and too much insider knowledge can actually have a detrimental effect on any study. For example, there is the risk of 'going native'. This concept originated in ethnography and describes the process where researchers get so immersed in the context that they study that they lose sight of their role and position as researcher. Co-researchers helping to carry out research among their own communities will be particularly prone to this. The role and positionality of a researcher is therefore a crucial aspect that needs to be addressed in the initial researcher training in any participatory project. However, risks to co-researchers may also arise if they come across research participants in their communities who share neither their views nor their experiences. Being a peer researcher may open doors and provide access to participants, but it may also come with additional risks, notably in areas where communities experience significant conflict or segregation.

Summary

In conclusion, the best advice that can be given about ethical research is not simply to adhere blindly to standardised common ethical principles, but to exercise common sense when applying these standards and principles as they play out differently in different social and cultural contexts. Researchers need to be mindful about the dilemmas and contradictions that may arise in collaborative research practice.

Looking back to the initial question of why common ethical standards have developed, there can be no doubt that the dominant *universalist* attitude with its formalised research review processes is at least partially a result of unethical research practice, in particular in research among vulnerable and disadvantaged communities who had no voice to protect themselves. However, there can equally be no doubt that these universal principles such as informed consent, confidentiality, privacy, avoidance of risk and so forth are not always straightforward, unambiguous concepts which are easy to apply.

In practice, for participatory and collaborative research projects this means that research ethics should be treated not as a one-off tick-box exercise at the start of a project. Instead, researchers and participants need to be mindful of all their actions and their potential consequences as a research project progresses. It is important to maintain a sense of rigour and integrity towards both the research participants and their communities, but also towards the principles of participatory research practice, which, at the end of the day, is supposed to improve the lives of those who are involved in the research, even though this may not be immediately and decisively. This may mean that, paradoxically, by being sensitive towards the social and cultural context in which the research takes place, and by prioritising agency and choice of participants, compromises have to be made in relation to universalist ethics standards in order to protect the participants and their communities. Thus, there is equally a strong case for a *situated* approach to research ethics.

As I have shown in this chapter, there are good examples from existing research projects, where such compromises needed to be made and were made successfully. In participatory research, these decisions should not be made solely by a professional researcher or principal investigator, but in conjunction with the participants and co-researchers in the project. In collaborative research, being ethically responsible means first and foremost to be transparent with research participants, not just about the aims and objectives of the research, but also about ethical standards and ethical responsibility, about risk, choice and agency, and about boundaries in what is and is not acceptable research practice. The overarching ethical principles that can arguably guide these processes and negotiations are that research should always act in the best interest of participants and their communities and that the risk of being harmed should be minimised during the research and as a result of it. A risk audit produced jointly by researchers, co-researchers and participants can be a useful tool to support this process. Ultimately, research studies, even longitudinal ones, are time-limited undertakings; however, the lives of participants and their communities continue after research projects are completed, and whilst research project always carry a degree of risk, they should not make the lives of those who participate more difficult than they were before.

FURTHER READING

Banks, S. and Brydon-Miller, M. (eds) (2019) *Ethics in Participatory Research for Health and Social Wellbeing: Cases and Commentaries*. Abingdon: Routledge.

Shaw, C., Brady, L. M. and Davey, C. (2011). *Guidelines for Research with Children and Young People*. London: NCB.

EXERCISE 4.1

DESIGNING A CONSENT FORM AND INFORMATION SHEET

Thinking about your research project, design an appropriate consent form and participant information sheet that takes account of the dynamic and required flexibility of collaborative research. What are the aspects that should be considered? Think about the power relations in the project. In a participatory project, what do participants give their consent for? How will you address the possibility that participants themselves may determine the direction the research project is going to take? How much detail is required for informed consent? How will you detail your own limitations as a researcher? To what extent does an information sheet look like a 'research contract' and what areas should this cover?

ANALYSING A CONSENT FORM

Take an existing consent form and participant information sheet of a study to analyse the underlying and subtle power relations that the forms assume. Can you make changes to the wording in the consent form and participant information sheet that shift the power relations towards participants in order to reflect the more equal power relations desirable in participatory projects.

EXERCISE 4.2

THE MEANING AND BOUNDARIES OF CONFIDENTIALITY

Understanding the meaning and boundaries of confidentiality is one of the necessities in participatory research practice. The orientation of collaborative research towards advocacy and change inevitably raises issues around the limitations of confidentiality, as participants and co-researchers may become co-authors and activists, and at this point confidentiality normally ends. This can be associated with a range of risks to individuals, groups and communities. However, on a more basic level, confidentiality is also about understanding the implications of sharing personal information in a group context.

I have used this exercise below successfully as part of research training days for co-researchers in a variety of group settings, and it can be adapted to different contexts:

1   Hand out a small piece of paper to all participants.
2   Ask them to write a piece of personal information about themselves on this piece of paper and fold the paper over several times, so that this cannot be seen.

3   Ask participants how they would feel handing this paper over to the person next to them. Depending on the group dynamic and the level of trust at this information stage it may be possible to ask participants to actually hand this over, but not before advising everyone strongly that this piece of paper must not be opened.

4   Discuss how it feels to trust someone with personal information or to be trusted with someone's personal information. Discuss limits of confidentiality. What are the situations where we cannot guarantee confidentiality (e.g. disclosures of abusive situations, but also implications of sharing information in a group context). Often some participants decide not to write anything on their papers or to write only trivial information. If this has happened, point out that some people are happy to share personal information, but others aren't, and that both are okay.

5   Finally, ask participants to take back and destroy their pieces of paper.

PART II

APPLICATIONS OF PARTICIPATORY METHODS

5

PARTICIPATORY ACTION RESEARCH

What you will learn

This chapter will introduce the reader to action research and then more specifically participatory action research. It will pay particular attention to the way engaged participatory research is designed and organised. The chapter discusses PAR's epistemological origins and how PAR designs and practice have diversified over time. As with any other research method, PAR has weaknesses which critics have pointed out, and these will be discussed too.

Introduction

Action research was one of the original collaborative approaches that contributed to the participatory turn in research methods, and participatory action research was often regarded as synonymous with participatory research methods. AR and PAR approaches use a range of research methods, which include any number of established conventional methods (e.g. surveys, group discussions, observation) as well as emergent or novel methods, including visual and online tools. This chapter will concentrate on the planning and organisation of AR and PAR projects including the participatory and engaging elements of such research, without paying too much attention to these individual methods, which will be discussed in subsequent chapters. In a sense, this chapter deals with the macro-issues of participatory designs and processes rather than the nitty-gritty of the actual mechanics of data collection and data analysis in AR and PAR.

Defining action research and its origins

The social psychologist Kurt Lewin is often credited with developing and pioneering AR methodology at his Tavistock Institute in the late 1940s. As a social psychologist Lewin's principal interest was in organisational behaviour, development and system change, and he used his research to develop thinking around issues such as group productivity and communication, social perception, inter-group relations and group membership. He was also interested in how awareness and sensitivity training could contribute to better group functioning and democratic leadership and management, and how this could enhance organisational performance. The nature of his research was action-oriented; this means that the aim was not just to find out about these issues, but to transform the practice itself. The fundamental principle of Lewin's enquiry was to practise dialogue and engagement with his research participants in order to inform his work. Training, feedback and role play were some of the activities which formed part of the research process in order to explore and initiate change in attitudes and behaviours and to build capacity. So, the views and voices of participants were central to the whole process. In his original article on inter-group relations Lewin defines the rationale of 'action research' as follows:

> The research needed for social practice can best be characterized as research for social management or social engineering. It is a type of action-research, a comparative research on the conditions and effects of various forms of social action, and research leading to social action. Research that produces nothing but books will not suffice. (1946: 35)

Lewin contends that social research should be guided by two aims: finding out things; and making positive changes. His notion of research going hand in hand with positive action has prevailed over the years and is evident in the work of those using and describing AR methodologies. In fact, over time AR has become a label for a multitude of research methods and activities which at their heart combine a focus on social action with collaborative research practice. As a result, Susman and Evered (1978: 601) identified AR as producing 'a different kind of knowledge'. In their view, AR as a methodology is future-oriented and collaborative: orientated towards system development, theory-generating, grounded in action and situational. They argue that this distinguishes AR significantly from positivist approaches.

Using Lewin's rationale for AR, Coghlan and Brannick (2014: 46) propose that the key idea of AR is that it 'uses a scientific approach to study the resolution of important social or organisational issues together with those who experience these issues directly'.

According to Ladkin (2007: 478) 'action research is grounded in the belief that research with human beings should be participative and democratic' and has the primary purpose to 'produce knowledge that is useful to people in the everyday conduct of their lives'. Like Lewin pointed out 70 years ago, it can be argued that the practice orientation of AR and its focus on change sets it apart from 'ordinary' social science research (Ladkin, 2007). This difference between applied research, led by experts, and action research, led jointly by participants and professional researchers, is core. Coghlan and Brannick (2014) therefore propose that there is an epistemological difference in how action researchers approach their work. The authors claim that 'action researchers work on the epistemological assumption that the purpose of academic research and discourse is not just to describe, understand and explain the world, but also to change it' (2014: 50).

This quote has remarkable similarities to Karl Marx's 11th thesis on Feuerbach, first written in 1845, in which he states: 'Philosophers have hitherto only interpreted the world in various ways; the point is to change it' (Marx and Engels, 2001: 170). It is therefore no coincidence that, alongside Lewin's original contribution, Marxist theory has been seen as one of the founding blocks of AR methodology; the others being Paulo Freire's (1971) work on consciousness raising within his *Pedagogy of the Oppressed*; feminist theory; and pragmatic philosophy (Coghlan and Brannick, 2014). The key characteristic of these approaches is that they seek to develop emancipatory practices by engaging local and community knowledge systems through participatory practices (Lykes and Coquillon, 2007).

AR is therefore fundamentally built on emancipatory, democratic and social justice values which are core to these theoretical and conceptual founding blocks of AR. Methodologically this has implications for how researchers approach their projects. As Silver (2008: 104) states, 'it is generally considered that Action Research is achieved through collaboration between researchers and participants and by following a cyclical process of planning, acting, observing and reflecting'. According to Coghlan and Brannick (2014: 52), 'reflection is the activity which integrates action and research'.

However, social change can also be the aim of many conventional projects and Coghlan and Brannick (2014) caution that recently the label of AR has been devalued due to the tendency to call anything 'action research' which involves clients or co-researchers in the research process. Coghlan and Brannick highlight that AR really ought to be seen and utilised as:

> a powerful conceptual tool for uncovering truth of practical knowing [...] [that is] genuinely scientific in the emphasis on careful observation and study of the effects of behaviours on human systems as their members manage change. (2014: 61)

Hart and Bond (1995: 40–44) produced an AR typology in which they attempted to classify different approaches to AR, incorporating aspects of Lewin's original model. Hart and Bond identified seven criteria and characteristics that AR projects share. According to these, AR is a cyclical process that has an educative basis with collaborative relationships between researchers and participants; a fluid membership of individuals; and a problem focus with the aim to initiate positive change and improvement (Figure 5.1).

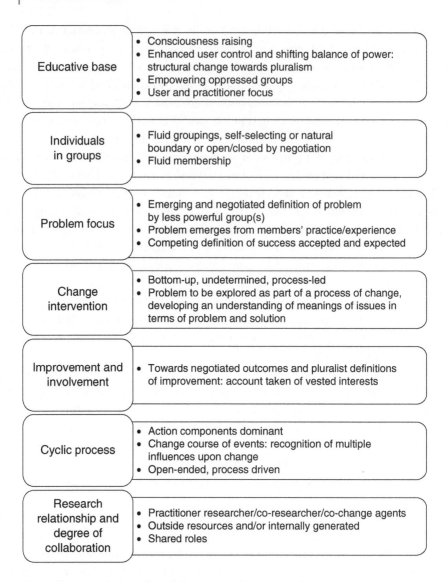

Figure 5.1 Characteristics of participatory action research

Source: adapted from Hart and Bond (1995)

The participatory nature of action research

An important difference between AR projects and conventional research, including projects that include some participatory elements, is that the research agenda is not set by a professional researcher alone, but rather jointly with the research participants, for example members of a community or organisation involved in the research. Community-based participatory research partnerships are an example of this (see Chapter 3). The members of the AR team share the power of knowledge production and *actively work towards* social change rather than *hoping* that the study results are convincing enough to trigger such change. Reason and Torbert (2001: 6, cited in Coghlan and Brannick, 2014: 50) argue that ultimately AR aims to contribute 'directly to the flourishing of human persons, their communities and the ecosystems of which they are part', and the involvement in the research process aids that process.

This transformational focus of AR means that it is usually conducted in real time and often with the aim of developing interventions. Whilst a retrospective focus of AR is also possible, for example with the aim of fostering retrospective learning, sometimes referred to as 'learning history' (Bradbury and Mainemelis, 2001) or 'action learning' (Revans, 2011), this learning is still used to address a current issue or to trigger learning for future practices. A good example of this is Lundy and McGovern's (2006) work on community-based truth telling in the peace process in Northern Ireland. Whilst truth telling played an important part in the transformation from apartheid in South Africa, it never achieved the same role or status in the Northern Ireland peace process. After the completion of their project, the authors concluded that truth telling as a reconciliatory measure raised major issues and had limitations in the context of a society where the very nature of (historic) 'truth' is contested.

Reason and Bradbury (2016) argue that the inclusion of different ways of learning and knowing – namely experiential, practical and presentational knowing – is imperative to AR approaches. Generally what sets AR apart from conventional research practice is: firstly, what Ladkin (2007: 480) describes as 'intentionality for the outcome of the

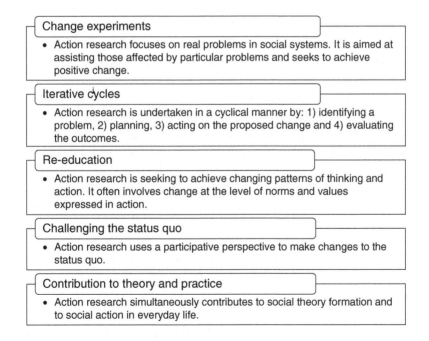

Figure 5.2 Model of Kurt Lewin's five-tier concept of action research

project', namely 'that it should have practical consequences in the bettering of, or deeper understanding of, a situation'; and, secondly, the assumption that those affected by the issue or situation which is at the core of a research project are also best placed to inform the research process. So, in AR the participatory process of undertaking a study has at least the same weight as the study outcome itself. In other words: the journey is the destination! Lewin's model of the concept of AR incorporates all these aspects aptly (Figure 5.2).

Participatory action research

I will now turn my attention to participatory action research. PAR and AR share many theoretical and conceptual roots, but PAR emphasises even more its participatory nature. Study participants are regarded and treated as the experts in the field and play a vital role in the entire research process, often becoming 'co-researchers' or 'peer researchers' alongside academic or professional researchers. In fact, it is not unusual in PAR that communities or organisations initiate a research project themselves. Similar to the term 'participatory methods', the term 'participatory action research' originated in the 1970s. Fals-Borda (2001) was one of the first scholars to use the approach and terminology of PAR, namely when he undertook his research on locally controlled development projects in Colombia.

Like in AR, the main aim of PAR is to use the research process to change and improve the situation of those being researched. In short: 'PAR seeks to understand and improve the world by changing it' (Baum, MacDougall and Smith, 2006: 854), or as Brydon-Miller (2001: 76) puts it: 'The goal of PAR is transformation.' Traditionally, professional researchers involved in PAR work with members of disadvantaged or marginalised communities in order to bring about positive change for that community. Over time the scope and subject range of PAR has been widened to include areas such as environmental planning and climate change, which do not just affect disadvantaged communities. PAR projects are characterised by not only addressing the specific concerns of the respective community or organisation involved in a study but also the fundamental causes of the problem with the goal of achieving positive social change.

According to Sample (1996: 318), the first studies using PAR approaches were undertaken in the fields of agriculture (Rhoades and Booth, 1982), social services (Sarri and Sarri, 1992), social sciences (Whyte, Greenwood and Lazes, 1989; Chisholm and Elden, 1993) and rehabilitation (Turnbull and Turnbull, 1991; Zarb, 1992). The first book on PAR appeared in the early 1990s (Whyte, 1991). Two years earlier Whyte had described PAR in an article published with two colleagues in the following way:

In participatory action research (PAR), some of the people in the organization or community under study participate actively with the professional researcher throughout the research process from the initial design to the final presentation of results and discussion of their action implications ... some of the members of the organization ... are actively engaged in the quest for information and ideas to guide their future actions. (Whyte, Greenwood and Lazes, 1989: 514)

As stated in this definition, PAR is not a distinct methodology as such, but rather a research approach, or a 'process' with some guiding principles. For Chevalier and Buckles (2013: 4), PAR 'is an expression of science that assumes reflectivity and self-experimentation in history'. They define five key areas that PAR is related to and has had an impact on:

1 Work life approached experimentally (after Lewin).
2 Psycho-sociology (using the insights of psychoanalysis).
3 Freirian education.
4 Community development in the international arena.
5 The emerging technologies of public engagement.

These contributions represent significant efforts to integrate the three fundamental components of participation, action and research.

Theoretical background and conceptualisation of PAR

Paulo Freire's *Pedagogy of the Oppressed* (1971) has been a particularly influential theoretical guide for many PAR practitioners, highlighting the importance of radical education reform as one of the elements in the three-part process of PAR, alongside social investigation and social action. For Freire, research itself *is* education, but it is a reciprocal process of educating and being educated at the same time for both the researcher and the participants. In his concept of pedagogy, understanding the individuals and communities that take part in the research process is a critical condition required to facilitate social transformation and to confront inequalities – something that Freire calls 'conscientisation'. In the Freirean tradition, research has therefore the function of critical enquiry which goes hand in hand with the task of promoting radical democracy, and this starts with education. In that sense, PAR is a form of critical knowledge generation which is a result of a dialectical process of action and reflection. As Brydon-Miller (2001: 79) puts it:

Critically informed inquiry generates a form of knowledge that results in and grows out of the liberation of those generating the knowledge; it is simultaneously knowledge based in action and action based in knowledge.

In that sense, PAR methods provide a framework which allows the integration of critical social science with the interest of human liberation. The role of the researcher is to engage in a process of critical research praxis which facilitates the pursuit of social justice and social action, thus rejecting the notion that knowledge generation can be or should be value-free. Rather, participatory action researchers should be aware of the political and social nature of their research project.

Feminist researchers expressed concern that early participatory and action researchers addressed power inequalities, but failed to include women appropriately in their projects, failing to problematise hetero-sexism and gender oppression (Lykes and Coquillon, 2007). Sandra Harding's (1986, 1987) work belongs to a group of early feminist contributions to the field of research methodologies. Feminism itself is obviously a field of great disciplinary variety, but what is important here is that the smallest common denominator for feminist researchers is that they use gender as an analytical category whilst addressing issues of disadvantage and that have been left out by conventional research. The way that feminism has critically addressed the power relations between the researcher and the participants (for example Finch, 1984) and explored subject positionality and status of participants in research projects has influenced the design and direction of PAR and AR methods just as much as Freire's and Lewin's contributions have. However, according to Reinharz (1992) feminism has provided a new perspective to research in general.

As Lykes and Coquillon (2007) point out, some feminist researchers have raised concern about the spread and diversification of PAR and AR methods, which at first glance appears paradoxical. However, as pointed out earlier, participatory research methods have become increasingly utilised for public engagement and decision making by governments, and some action researchers have argued that the mainstreaming of collaborative research practice potentially leads to a de-politicisation of participatory approaches.

As stated above, PAR emerged as a means to undertake applied research with the aim to achieve change, and as a consequence of what Turnbull and Turnbull (1991, cited in Sample 1996) called the 'credibility gap' in traditional research practice between researchers and those researched. Interestingly, in one of the earliest publications that attended to the need of a participatory turn in research practice, Brown and Tandon (1983) still differentiated between *action research* isolated mostly to developed countries, and *participatory research* evolving in developing countries. In both developments, they felt that the impetus for this came from some researchers who had started to set themselves apart from the existing researcher-led positivist practice.

In today's research landscape, participatory approaches are more commonly an integral part of AR, with action *and* change often the aim of co-production. Both 'action research' and 'participatory research' have therefore become part of one tradition and under one label – PAR – rather than continuing to co-exist as two distinct movements. In fact, the ultimate symbiosis of the two formerly distinct approaches materialised during the 1980s when Brown and Tandon (1983) laid out a theoretical rationale for this interdependence.

Today, PAR approaches are seen to evolve around the following three main epistemological principles.

1   *Ordinary people become co-researchers.* Those affected by the issues that are being researched are considered subject experts and are given a role and some responsibility in deciding the direction and the process of the research project. Often these study participants and co-researchers come from disadvantaged populations and communities, although this is not always the case. The goals of the research are action-focused and determined by these study participants and co-researchers. The aim is to bring about positive change in the lives of the study participants, their families and communities.

2   By involving people from the respective study populations or communities as active participants and co-researchers in the studies and giving them responsibility to determine the direction of the research process, *PAR projects fundamentally differ from the hierarchical power relations in conventional research projects.* This change in the power relations is not just a fundamental methodological principle in how PAR projects are conducted, it is also one of the core aims of the research itself. The 'empowerment' of marginalised groups of people is central to PAR approaches, with the challenges of the paradoxical concept 'empowerment' at the forefront of researchers' thinking.[1]

3   *PAR projects are transformative and praxis orientated.* Whilst theoretical academic knowledge is a possible outcome of PAR projects, they are firmly embedded in the praxis context. PAR projects are often explicitly informed by political and civic values, such as equality and justice, and not only aim to address these, but also transform the lives of people and the communities they live in.

Process and design of participatory and action research

In principle, PAR projects are characterised by a research design which integrates the three main elements of PAR, namely action, research and training – or 'ART'. Chevalier and Buckles' simplified ART Venn diagram (Figure 5.3) is meant to illustrate that only a small proportion of the activities in a PAR project actually deals with all three elements – action, research and training – at the same time. However, all three elements must be present in a PAR methodology. The proportion and order of these activities will depend on the

---

1   The paradox of empowerment has been discussed by Eylon (1998) and others, referring to the work of the American social worker, management consultant and philosopher Mary Parker Follett who undertook pioneering work in the fields of organisational theory and behaviour. Follett (1919: 576) saw 'community' as a 'creative process [...] a process of integrating' and also recognised the paradox in empowerment in that respect. She wrote that genuine power cannot be given, but needs to be grown. As Eylon (1998: 16) states: 'The paradox of empowerment is that the very existence of circumstances that place one group in a position to "provide" another group with power implies that power is a finite commodity controlled by a sub-set within the organization. In other words, the very fact that one group is in the position to judge if others are dis-empowered and then to decide what to "give" so that they will become "empowered" indicates that true empowerment is not occurring.'

needs of the community and the specific PAR project. Hall (2001) refers to these three core elements of PAR as an integrated three-pronged process of (1) social investigation, (2) education and (3) action.

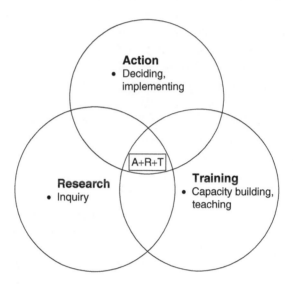

Figure 5.3 ART Venn diagram

Source: adapted from Chevalier and Buckles (2013: 61)

PAR projects usually start with a reflective process within an organisation which leads to the formulation of the research questions. In some cases, this process is initiated by the affected community groups themselves, but it is equally likely that a professional researcher, for example from an academic or NGO background, approaches a community group or organisation to instigate a research project. At a time where there is an increasing expectation of academic researchers to play a more proactive role and engage with their local communities, the researcher-initiated model is perhaps the more common one.

McIntyre produced a useful categorisation of typical PAR questions, which are reproduced in Figure 5.4. These are very general questions which can easily be adapted to specific PAR projects. How exactly the project is to be conducted, how the process and design is going to unfold and what the outcomes ought to be is a matter of negotiation between all partners in a PAR project, it is subject to change, and often does not become very clear until later in a project.

This required openness in relation to outcome, process and design can be a potential stumbling block in research ethics applications, as these often require very specific information about the project design, as we have seen in Chapter 4. However, with the increase in participatory projects, ethics committees and IRBs will also adapt and accommodate the required flexibility.

Identifying the issue

- What do we perceive as a problem or an issue in our community?
- How does it relate to our and our community's life?
- Why do these problems exist?

Thinking about a solution

- What can we do about these problems?
- What do we already know?
- What do we also need to know?

Planning the study

- What resources do we need to undertake the study?
- How will this project benefit the participants and the whole community?
- Who will control the research project? Who will make decisions?
- How will we address confidentiality and privacy throughout the study and dissemination?
- Should our research only represent the reality of the people involved or of the whole community?

Planning the impact

- What are the common themes that have emerged in the research?
- How can these themes be summarised to benefit the participants and the community?
- How will we disseminate the results of the study to others?
- What are the criteria we use to assess the adequacy and efficacy of the project?

Figure 5.4 Typical PAR research questions

Source: adapted from McIntyre (2008: 50)

The identification and assignment of roles and responsibilities as well as establishing clear expectations, aims and objectives should be one of the first steps in any PAR project. Mutual trust is one of the key ingredients in any participatory research project. Ladkin (2007) warns that all participants in a PAR project need to be aware of, and manage, their emotional response to the study. As in any situation which involves a diversity of actors, there will be situations where decisions are taken that not everybody necessarily agrees with. This is okay as long as there is an agreed balance of power between all participants in the project and the decision-making processes and the manner in which differences and conflict are dealt with are settled within the group.

What follows is an ongoing process of exploration, reflection and action, characterised by a fluid, cyclical course of action where explorative research practice, knowledge construction and social action coincide throughout the project (McIntyre, 2008: 6). Ladkin (2007: 482) refers to these as 'cycles of action and reflection' and reminds us that the PAR process is usually not linear. Furthermore, significant periods of time may lapse between research and reflection, which may pose challenges for researchers who are under time pressure from funders or employers. Again, negotiating and agreeing progress and timelines is a matter for all participants. Referencing McTaggart (1997), McIntyre (2008: 1) describes PAR as a 'living dialectical process, changing the researcher, the participants, and the situations in which they act'. However, consistent with Ladkin's experience, she also warns that 'the process of linking the meaning of participation to the actualisation of participation [can be] slow and time-consuming' (McIntyre, 2008: 17). She describes how she sometimes spent entire sessions with participants exploring the meaning of participation, but these also tended to be valuable sessions where the project participants realised that they were the ones who had to 'make things happen' (2008: 17). Normally, the outcome or product of a PAR project should not just be a simple research report, but actual change/action (or at least the prospect or the initiation of it).

McIntyre (2008) explains how participants in PAR critically reflect on their work during the research process and have to simultaneously address internal as well as external aspects of the research process. Internal aspects relate to the way data is collected and to internal power relations within the project team whereas external aspects deal with decision making on how to best disseminate research findings in order to effect change.

Diversity of PAR projects and common principles

As with AR more generally, PAR projects vary in context, method, subject area and even underlying political ideology. Coghlan and Brannick (2014) point out that apart from its emancipatory and egalitarian approach, the unique feature of PAR approaches compared to AR more generally is that PAR typically focuses on an issue outside the organisation and/or community which is involved in the project. According to McIntyre (2008: 1), the majority of PAR projects share therefore four common characteristics:

1   A *collective commitment* to investigate an issue or problem.
2   A *desire to engage in self- and collective reflection* to gain clarity about the issue under investigation.
3   A joint decision to *engage in individual and/or collective action* that leads to a useful solution that benefits the people involved.
4   The building of *alliance between researchers and participants* in the planning, implementation and dissemination of the research process.

As McIntyre highlights, the needs and desires of research participants are central to PAR projects; in fact, these needs tailor the design and direction of PAR projects in the first place. PAR is fundamentally embedded in communities and community organisations and seeks to address their needs. McIntyre (2008: 15) stresses the importance of the quality of the participation and engagement in PAR and makes the critical point that the strategy of involvement and participation should not simply follow some proportionality rationale, but that rather a common-sense approach should be applied which involves a negotiation between the researcher and the respective group involved about the nature of the participatory design used.

Generally, all PAR projects will have to develop their own appropriate and meaningful way of organising participation, within an appropriate ethical framework – see Chapter 4. Thus, each PAR project is likely to be unique and there is no recipe for guaranteed success. The type of (social) actions that derive from PAR projects will also depend on the needs of the research participants and the context and topic being researched.

Research methods and activities in PAR

PAR projects draw on a wide range of research methods, some of which are also used in conventional research projects, such as surveys, interviews, observations and group discussions, as well as a wide range of explorative, experimental and creative methods, including visual and performative arts-based methods, participatory mapping, story telling and oral history methods. They may include political campaigning and actions, and educational and training activities. McIntyre (2008) highlights the importance of employing research methods that are in tune with communities' histories, traditions and practices.

Data analysis is also typically undertaken with participants using a range of data analysis methods. Participants can be included in a variety of ways including small group work or data analysis workshops with the aim to identify themes that have emerged in the project. Joint discussions about drafts and re-drafts of data or transcripts are common. Participants should be enabled to come up with their own ideas of how to make sense of the data and how to present this to different audiences. Whether or not it is meaningful to utilise data analysis software packages will depend on the nature of the data collected, the capacity of the community organisation and qualifications of participants. Participants can be trained in data input and data analysis if the time frame permits this and if there are the financial resources to acquire suitable software packages. If a survey is used, simple descriptive survey analysis software is now often built into online survey tools. Equally, participants and co-researchers can manually analyse data.

The planning of the fieldwork and the development of data collection and analysis tools is intrinsically embedded into the PAR process, enabling the members of the respective project or community organisation to be involved in the decision making on what questions to ask and what methods to use. This does not mean that all project partners have to be actively involved in all research activities, but they should be given an opportunity to be involved as much or as little as they wish. It is important that the decision-making process is transparent, and that there are options to be involved in all aspects of a project.

Research areas covered by AR and PAR

AR and PAR studies have been undertaken in various fields, including social policy, law, government and public services, education, health and employment. The actions arising from AR and PAR projects may, for example, focus on national or local policy changes, changes to local service delivery (e.g. in education or health care provision), health promotion, equality or awareness raising of a particular issue.

As mentioned in the introductory sections in this chapter, Lewin, who is regarded by many as a founder of AR methodology, was interested in organisational change. Participatory organisational research (POR) and organisational development (OD) have remained important branches of AR and PAR (see Chapter 3). The ultimate aim of POR and OD is generally to improve the social and organisational conditions within organisations by drawing on the perspectives of participants that are part of the respective organisation. Burns et al. (2014), for example, undertook a participatory research project on the mistreatment of care home residents, using the POR method, whilst Craig's 1997 study on elder abuse is also a notable contribution to this field. From the onset of their study, Burns and colleagues incorporated the views of older people living in care homes who were then also recruited as members of an advisory panel which jointly made decisions with the researchers about the methodology and direction of the research project. The authors reflect on the apparent paradox already alluded to, namely, that the participation of marginalised members of organisations, who are often also deemed 'vulnerable', may unintentionally further their vulnerability, e.g. if they do not comply with norms or expectations at public events.

BOX 5.1

CASE STUDY ON PARTICIPATORY ORGANISATIONAL RESEARCH

The diversity in the field of POR and OD is highlighted by a study undertaken by Puente-Rodríguez et al. (2016) on the knowledge co-production of the management of environmental management systems in Dutch ports. The impetus for this study was the need to implement new environmental standards in coastal zone management and the authors describe how they used participatory methods to gain the understanding and insights of both internal and external stakeholders to inform the new policy. Whilst predominantly traditional methods such as interviews and group discussions were used, the authors conclude that participatory knowledge arrangement and co-production practices could become mandatory practice when it comes to making policy decisions of that scale and nature. This highlights the potential for participatory methods in relation to large-scale policy decisions, whilst at the same time reminding us about the inherent dangers around the potential devaluing of participatory processes if they become mainstreamed.

Another study on environmental issues using a PAR approach was undertaken by Cloutier et al. (2015). The study aimed for a policy change within local government in relation to the implementation of climate change measures in urban areas. The main aim of Cloutier et al.'s three-year PAR study undertaken in Quebec in Canada was to identify factors that can increase local engagement with environmental and climate change planning. According to the authors, one of the outcomes of this study was that local actors were more valued as experts of territorial management, while there was also increased engagement of different actors in the planning. The authors conclude that this project will lead to better practices in planning and better understanding of local concerns as well as improved collaboration between local stakeholders.

Cultural and community-based work

A significant number of PAR and AR studies have been undertaken with minority eth-nic or migrant communities as well as socially deprived and disadvantaged indigenous communities. The principal aims of these studies are to help these marginalised commu-nities and to give voice to their needs and experiences. Story telling, awareness raising and health and education interventions have also been part of PAR designs.

Two of the original and pioneering PAR projects were those undertaken by Sarri and Sarri (1992) with the aim of fostering community development among disadvantaged communities in Bolivia and the USA. The authors argue that one of the main outcomes of these studies was the evidence that AR can help enable people, who previously per-ceived themselves as powerless, to take part in decision making on issues that affect their lives. Sarri and Sarri contend that this provides balance to the tendencies of spe-cialisation, professionalisation and privatisation.

Another of the earlier PAR examples is Osteria and Ramos-Jimenez's (1988) study of the health care needs in the Mangyan community in the Philippines. The purpose was to investigate the feasibility and effectiveness of a village-based health care system. This was done by training and involving community members in health care and health care planning, taking account of indigenous resources. The study had an ideal-typical PAR design with a specific action in mind but also with elements of training and assessment.

Not all PAR studies follow such a strict model, but many more have been undertaken in this field. Cornwall and Jewkes' (1995) study also addressed indigenous knowledge and resources to investigate health-related issues. The authors used body mapping as a participatory method with women in Zimbabwe to differentiate between local (non-Western) and 'white' (Western) medicine.

MacKinnon (2011), for example, undertook a PAR study with Winnipeg's disadvan-taged inner-city Aboriginal communities with the aim of helping voice the experiences of the people living in some of Canada's poorest communities. Balcazar, Garcia-Iriarte and Suarez-Balcazar (2009) conducted a participatory project with Colombian immigrants in Chicago. They used the Concerns Report Method (CRM) which is geared towards community change and incorporates Freire's praxis framework; namely, an ongoing interaction between reflection and action through a process development of critical awareness. CRM therefore combines needs assessment with a brainstorming of solutions and a promotion of action and problem solving that involve the respective communities and take action from the perspective of community members. Community volunteers were actively involved in the data collection and the authors found this methodology to have a mobilising effect on the individuals involved.

Temple et al.'s (2005) study on refugee communities in Britain undertaken on behalf of the Joseph Rowntree Foundation is a good example of a team of researchers address-ing a contemporary global issue with the aim of making policy changes. The researchers worked with a charity, Refugee and Asylum Seeker Participatory Action Research (RAPAR), and three diverse community organisations in the north of England in order to explore the ways people from dispersed asylum seeker communities interact with each other. The report directly explores barriers to community cohesion and proposes policy interventions to improve legislation and government policy on asylum seeking. Temple et al.'s study shows how critical participatory policy research at a larger scale is possible with the help of a well-placed and respected funder.

Francisco (2014) explored the situation of migrant Filipino workers, particularly domestic workers in New York, with regard to their health and involvement in society. The researcher employed story telling and arts-based approaches using theatre in the native Tagalog language as part of a PAR design to explore the domestic workers' experiences and life stories.

O'Neill, Woods and Webster's (2005) study on 'new arrivals' in the UK had a similar topic and PAR approach. A range of methods were used including interviews, a survey, group discussions and visual methods. Some participants were trained in PAR methods, becoming co-researchers on the project. The results of the study were presented as part of an engagement event with the local community including local government representatives of the city where the research took place.

Another example for timely and policy-relevant critical PAR is the same author's research with sex workers in the UK (O'Neill, 2010). At the time of writing, a number of countries have implemented, or are considering the implementation of new legislation that regulates sex work. Some have followed the so called 'Swedish model' which criminalises the purchase of sex. Other countries (e.g. Netherlands and Germany) have strengthened the legal position of sex workers in the hope that this reduces the risk of exploitation. O'Neill's work with female sex workers is guided by the work of Nancy Fraser and uses a PAR approach involving sex workers, agencies and policy makers to explore the diverse perspectives and experiences of sex workers and their views on the preferred legislative framework for sex work.

One country which used a decriminalisation strategy for sex workers is New Zealand and Abel and Fitzgerald (2008) studied the impact that this has had on the health and safety of young street-based sex workers in three cities in New Zealand. They used a CBPR design and conducted their research in partnership with the New Zealand Prostitutes' Collective (NZPC). The NZPC was involved throughout the research project, including the design of the data collection tools, data collection itself, write-up and dissemination.

Gender identity, sexual identity and sexual health are also topics which have been explored using PAR approaches. Conventional research practice has often failed to address sexual and gender issues outside the hetero-normative mainstream. Fenge's (2010) study of older gay men and lesbian women, a particularly 'invisible' population group, not only explored sexuality outside the hetero-normative mainstream but also sexuality at an older age. Fenge's 'Gay and Grey' project in Dorset, England, involved a number of older lesbian women and gay men in research about their experiences of social exclusion and marginalisation with the aim of identifying their needs and communicating these to local agencies. The author addresses some of the ethical issues and paradoxes of participatory research, which have been discussed before, including the need to publicise information whilst guaranteeing the right of privacy and confidentiality.

A (culturally) very sensitive topic is female genital cutting (FGC), and we know very little about the attitudes of male members from communities where FGC is practised. This was the topic of a participatory investigation undertaken by Johnson-Agbakwu et al. (2014) with male members of the Somali immigrant population in the UK. CBPR partnerships were formed with stakeholders within the Somali refugee community in the UK. The study found that the support for FGC practices was primarily based on traditional matriarchal support and that men were generally not supportive of FGC.

Some of the key areas in which PAR methods have been utilised are *health, social care* and *social work*. Fieldhouse (2012) for example reports on a project which addressed the exclusion of mental health service users, undertaken in Bristol in England. The small-scale participatory project was initiated from within the local community's mental health sector and aimed to explore the experiences of mental health service users who had been involved in an advocacy and assertive outreach (AO) service. According to the author, the AO service is geared towards people who are normally unwilling to engage with existing services and this is significant in that research projects normally rely on volunteers and on self-selection. This does not suggest that people should be coerced into participating, but the authors clearly evidence the benefits of trying to involve marginalised and disengaged people for whom very positive outcomes were recorded. The author claims that participants had managed to overcome barriers to community engagement. One aspect of this work related to the improvement of educational opportunities for mental health service users. Other project outcomes included improved inter-agency working and better joint planning between mental health services and the learning community with the aim of promoting social inclusion and community development.

A study by Kreitzer et al. (2009) investigated culturally appropriate social work training in Ghana. Using a PAR approach, the authors explored the relationship between historically dominant Western knowledge and social work thinking in relation to traditional approaches to practice. The data collection techniques included native oral tradition, guest speakers, story telling, drama and proverbs as well as exchanges about the personal experiences group members had in their own educational social work experience. One outcome was an action plan for future challenges for social work in Africa.

Ringstad et al. (2012) addressed the issue of critical service learning in social work through a CBPR project. The project arose essentially out of a public consultation exercise on the need for a homeless shelter in a local area. The researchers located at two UK universities engaged their students in this project. They concluded that this led to both critical service learning and community transformation.

Using a PAR approach, Reese (1999) investigated cultural and institutional barriers to hospice access and use by Americans with African community backgrounds compared to Americans with European heritage. Cultural barriers included values regarding medical care and spiritual beliefs, whilst lack of knowledge and trust in health care services and economic factors served as institutional barriers prohibiting African Americans from accessing hospice services. The project resulted in recommendations on how social work practice should be organised to better meet the needs of African Americans.

Another area that has seen a range of participatory and AR projects is that of *disability research*. Again, people with disabilities have often been under-represented in or excluded from conventional research projects, so engaged participatory approaches have been utilised by some researchers to give voice to the experiences and issues of disabled people. One such example is the project undertaken by Lorenzo (2003) with disabled women in disadvantaged suburbs of Cape Town, South Africa. This project used story-telling workshops alongside other methods to explore the struggles that these women experienced daily at an individual, family and community level as well as their physical, emotional and spiritual needs, and their resourcefulness and resilience. The study included some of the stakeholders as partners, namely the Division of Occupational Therapy, University of Cape Town, an advocacy organisation for people with disabilities (Disabled People South Africa, DPSA) and a local health trust and primary health care project.

An area which has seen a notable number of AR and PAR projects is that of the experiences of *women affected by war and conflict*. An example of this is McIntyre's (2002) study exploring the biographies and identities of a group of working-class women living in Belfast, a society that has emerged from a long-term violent conflict. According to the author, this long-term feminist PAR project is trying to help the women involved to better understand the historical and political contexts in which they live.

Critique of action research

As with all other research methods, AR and PAR have their critics. Interestingly, it is the very nature of most AR and PAR projects that has been the focus of most criticism; namely, that they tend to focus on powerlessness and disadvantage as a means to help affected communities tackle disadvantage, influence decision making, or give a voice to those who are overlooked or disadvantaged by society. Advocates of the appreciative inquiry (AI) tradition (Cooperrider and Whitney, 2005) have taken issue with this problem orientation of AR and with what they see as the inherent negativity that is connected to that focus. They argue that AR can equally focus on the *improvement* of what has already been achieved rather than just on deficiencies or problems, thus giving AR a more positive spin.

So, rather than dwelling on deficiencies, gaps and problems, AI targets effective organisational change using a positive problem-solving approach, focusing on core strengths, past stories of success, positive experiences, existing trust and other assets that a community or organisation might have. The aim is to use and take inspiration from these stories of past and present success (Srivastva and Cooperrider, 1999). The authors hold that a more optimistic outlook can lead to positive changes in organisations that are not actually doing badly. To some extent this work is aligned to the theory tradition of positive psychology (Seligman, 2002; 2006). Cooperrider and his advocates have developed two cyclical processes, firstly the *Four Ds* (discovery, dream, design and delivery) and *Four Is* (initiate, inquire, imagine, innovate) which action researchers and practitioners are supposed to organise their AR project around to make positive changes to their organisation.

Chevalier and Buckles (2013: 5) point to three key challenges within PAR, namely:

1 The need to strengthen the theoretical foundations of PAR.
2 Finding a solution for the fundamental question of 'how to create a careful action-learning process based on abilities to think with rigour, combined with genuine caring for expressions of difference social and natural history'.
3 The challenge to make sure that PAR addresses the burning issues and questions at hand, something that the authors call 'up-scaling' of PAR research.

Due to its context-specificity and applied nature, which involves small group work with non-academic and often socially deprived or disadvantages communities, the contribution of AR and PAR to theoretical developments in science has been at best modest. To change that, engaged academics need to work towards a better integration of academic theoretical and methodological advancements and community development and action. The authors appropriately remind us of Lewin's view that 'there is nothing so practical as a good theory' (cited in Chevalier and Buckles, 2013: 11), emphasising the fact that theory development and practice relevance are by no means mutually exclusive.

On a more practical level, Chevalier and Buckles (2013) note the actual limitations that AR strategies have in relation to their use in public engagement and decision-making processes. Whilst aiming to change things and to take action to improve the lives of those involved in the research, their often small-scale approach significantly weakens the ability to address necessary changes on a societal level – something which is also pointed out by Mead (2016). According to Chevalier and Buckles (2013: 29), the tendency of action researchers to take a micro-perspective on social action, i.e. 'to keep things small and close to natural communities and environments [...], either ignores or remains naively optimistic in its opposition to the exclusionary and authoritarian character of positive science and an academic life largely deaf to pressing individual and community needs'. As a consequence, the promise of change and action remains potentially unfulfilled.

One positive example of such an up-scaled approach is the study by Carney, Dundon and Léime (2012). Rather than working with one community, the project aimed to explore how PAR approaches could be used on a national level among the Irish Civil Society Organisation (CSO) sector in order to strengthen their collective voice when negotiating welfare support during a severe economic crisis. The authors argue that use of AR has contributed to better relationships between the Irish government and CSOs that are involved in the process of consensus policy making in negotiating levels of welfare support. The point the authors are making is that, despite limitations, participatory approaches can be used to achieve collective action beyond individual organisations and communities.

In their European-level action research project, Moschitz and Home (2014) used a reflective learning methodology to address the challenge of up-scaling from local to regional and international learning. This related specifically to innovation in sustainable agriculture in Europe and had the ultimate aim of influencing the European agricultural policy framework. However, Cornwall (1996) also warns about risks of involvement in larger-scale projects, particularly if they are set by external interests, e.g. government. Cornwall reminds us that the parameters which define the nature of participation, or underlying norms and values, need to be interrogated. The type or form of democratic participation that participatory action researchers promote and practise is not necessarily the same as the one encouraged by public engagement and consultation exercises, which can at times be tokenistic, even though this may not be intentionally the case. So, this challenge to go beyond the small scale whilst at the same time to remain truthful to the values of participatory and action research is perhaps the greatest test of all.

The flip-side of attempts to scale up AR and PAR projects means, however, that participatory action researchers have to make conscious decisions about inclusion and exclusion criteria. The larger a project, the less inclusive the sample of co-researchers and participants can be. Whilst small community-based projects can be very inclusive, at a larger scale there are often neither the resources nor the time to ask everyone to participate. This is a very fine balance that has to be struck (see Exercise 3.1). Again, auditability and transparency are very important criteria of rigour in any project, but in particular when it comes to making recommendations for action at a macro-level. Resource implications will also affect the relationship between the emancipatory goals of a project – participatory projects can be time- and resource-intensive – and the need to bring a project to a close.

Finally, Chevalier and Buckles urge action researchers to address the profound and wide-ranging changes we have experienced as a result of the technological development in information and communication technology (ICT). They argue:

> More than ever, engaged researchers must adapt to new ways of understanding and constructing social life, beyond small groups and organic communities. They must show greater flexibility and creativity in their use of *techné* to support the kind of collaborative enquiry and social engagement that can be brought to bear on the pressing issues of our day. (Chevalier and Buckles, 2013: 32–33)

As the authors rightly point out, the digital revolution has fundamentally changed the way we communicate with each other and PAR researchers need to show a greater interest in this. As Romero, Kwan and Chavkin's (2013) review of a number of PAR and CBPR case studies shows, the conditions for this to be successful are methodological rigour, incorporation of post-research evaluation, and an acceptance that advocacy is part of the job profile for academic researchers involved in participatory research. The authors claim that they found evidence for a growing acceptance of PAR approaches, so, from that point of view, the conditions for an up-scaled participatory agenda are just about right.

Summary

In this chapter I discussed the origins and approaches of AR and PAR. I looked at the theoretical framework and practical implications of combining participation, research and action in research studies, and I gave some examples of the applications of AR and

PAR. The possibility to use a range of different conventional, but also novel methods in PAR contexts means that PAR really provides researchers and participants with multiple and creative opportunities to co-construct knowledge. PAR approaches give participants the opportunity to engage in research whilst maintaining their individual and collective identities. However, I also showed that there are concerns about PAR approaches in relation to their scale and generalisability – i.e. the practical and theoretical relevance at a macro-level.

In the following three chapters I will now focus on the application of the very commonly used research methods in participatory projects.

FURTHER READING

Bradbury, H. (ed.) (2015). *The Sage Handbook of Action Research: Participatory Inquiry and Practice.* London: Sage.

Chevalier, J. M. and Buckles, D. J. (2013). *Participatory Action Research: Theory and Methods for Engaged Inquiry.* London: Routledge.

Walmsley, J. and Johnson, K. (2003). *Inclusive Research with People with Learning Difficulties: Past, Present and Future.* London: Jessica Kingsley.

EXERCISE 5.1

AGREEING A GROUP CONTRACT

A really crucial part of a participatory project is to agree the timeline and schedule of the project. In many projects, participants are likely to have a range of diverse commitments, so it is important to be aware of this and to fit the project work around participants' needs. A timeline and tasks should be agreed early on in the project to give participants an opportunity to plan their input. This can take the form of a group contract which people may want to sign. It is important to have a discussion about, and include in the contract, how everyone will participate in the project. Also, what action would they like to see? (Aims!) So, what activities will be undertaken to generate this action? Discuss the consequences of not attending team meetings regularly and non-participation. What input can everyone realistically have? The group contract can be displayed on the wall if the same meeting space is being used for regular meetings or it could be copied and handed out to all participants. The contract should have the agreed overall aims of the research and perhaps ground rules at the top and then specific tasks and timelines below. Training and qualifications could also be part of this, if applicable. A Gantt chart or colour-coded table can be a visually useful tool to display

(Continued)

what objectives and actions were agreed. Instead of putting names against tasks, it could be photographs or symbols that people choose to represent themselves.

A contract can also take an audio-visual form if participants are comfortable with this. Every participant could make a statement about what he or she wants to get out of this project and what they intend to contribute. This could be part of a video diary of the project.

It is really important to find suitable tasks for everyone, even if these are very small, so that no one feels left out.

_____

6

PARTICIPATORY APPROACHES TO PARTICIPANT OBSERVATION

What you will learn

This chapter focuses on participant observation and its links to ethnography. A short discussion of the historic roots of participant observation and ethnography as a field method is followed by an introduction to participatory approaches to ethnography. The reader will then be introduced to practical steps involved in undertaking participant observations, such as initial rapport building, note taking and recording of information as well as ethical strategies of exiting the field. The chapter also discusses how various methods are being used in participant observation, and in what contexts observation has been used.

Introduction

In 1982 Burgess described participant observation as the 'principal method that has been used by anthropologists and sociologists to conduct field research' (1982: 45).

For a long time, these 'field methods' were chiefly thought to be what many would today call 'ethnography'. According to Delamont (2007), the term 'participant observation' is being used interchangeably with 'ethnography' and 'fieldwork' to describe a range of research methods aimed at studying and understanding people's lives. Delamont feels that ethnography is perhaps the most inclusive term. Bryman (2016) agrees that ethnography and participant observation have often been thought to be more or less the same thing but argues that the terminology simply changed from 'participant observation' to 'ethnography' during the 1970s. Conversely, Boellstorff et al. (2012) refer to Han Vermeulen's 2008 PhD thesis that identified that the term 'ethnography' was actually coined much earlier (namely in the middle of the eighteenth century as part of Romanticism in German-speaking Europe) and that the practice of ethnography also happened much earlier than Bryman suggests. However, we have to agree with Bryman who points out that many recent textbooks have dealt with ethnography and participant observation in one chapter and under one heading. There is therefore no question that there is a very close connection between participant observation as a social science method and ethnography as the study of cultures.

Ethnography is fundamentally a holistic activity which typically involves more than just one data collection method, and, just to reiterate Bryman's statement, research methods textbooks (e.g. Burgess' (1982) volume on field methods) assume that participant observation comprises a range of predominantly but not exclusively qualitative data collection techniques including document analyses, interviews and group discussions, but also surveys. The ethnographer's chief aim is to engage in the lives of the people and communities at the centre of the study over an extended period of time. Carried out within the participants' setting, it observes how the context informs participants' views, beliefs and actions. According to Evans (2012), ethnography or participant observation can be conceived of as a research strategy rather than a unitary research method.

Recent work has attempted to position observation as a method in its own right once again. Perhaps this is a reflection of an increasing acknowledgment that traditional immersive ethnographic research practice is often resource-intensive and always time-consuming; something that in the current outcome and impact-driven research landscape, few academics can afford. It is therefore perhaps no coincidence that the term 'mixed methods research' has become the term of choice when describing a research approach that encompasses more than just one data collection method. In a changing culture of ethnography short-term projects characterised by a lesser degree of actual immersion in the culture and everyday life of the communities or the phenomena studied have become the *modus operandi*. As a result, we have increasingly seen a move from ethnographic studies to studies that apply ethnographic techniques, including observation.

In this chapter I will briefly discuss the origins of ethnography and participant observation. I will then focus on key aspects of participant observation as a field method before turning to participatory approaches to observation – i.e. *participatory* observation. I understand participatory observation as a critical approach to ethnography, or collaborative action ethnography (Cole, 2005), which involves participants actively as co-researchers throughout the research process.

Theoretical background/conceptualisation

Burgess (1982) reminds us that field observations and descriptive reporting about other cultures goes back many centuries and is, among other motives, connected to the activities of religious missionaries, merchants and travellers. Early 'ethnographic accounts' were therefore produced by people without academic background and ambitions. A good example of such an 'ethnographic' study on the back of expansive endeavours of monotheistic churches to bring heretics in line with their religious conventions and norms is Emmanuel Le Roy Ladurie's *Montaillou: Cathars and Catholics in a French Village 1294–1324*. The book first appeared in French in 1975 and analyses the inquisition register that Catholic bishop Jacques Fournier produced in the Pyrenean village of Montaillou as part of a missionary trip to deal with what the Catholic church regarded as heresy. Fournier was later to become Pope Benedict XII.

According to Hammersley and Atkinson (2007: 1), the origins of the term 'ethnography' as we would use today go back to nineteenth-century anthropological studies undertaken by Western scholars in Asia, South America and Africa 'where an ethnography was a descriptive account of a community or culture, usually one located outside the West'. These studies are connected to names such as Bronisław Malinowski, Margaret Mead and Edward Evans-Pritchard. The fieldwork of ethnographers often demanded that they would spend significant periods of time, usually over several months, immersing themselves socially and culturally in these communities, participating in, and subsequently documenting and interpreting, their ways of life. The primary methodology to do this was therefore described as 'participant observation'. Boellstorff et al. (2012) remind us that participant observation has a similarly long tradition in sociology with works such as Simmel's famous essay 'The stranger' (1950 [1908]) but also Webb's studies of London society (1926) using participant observations. Arguably, especially considering his own deprived circumstances, one can also make the argument to add to the list of early ethnographic sociological works Marx's studies of the milieu of the working classes during the time of industrial revolution in England, which informed his theory.

One unique form of ethnography is institutional ethnography (IE) which was developed by Dorothy Smith as an 'alternative' sociology *for* the people, not *of* the people from the late 1970s onwards (e.g. Smith, 2005). IE has strong connections with Marxist feminism and is interested in the social organisation of knowledge, particularly in how institutions and institutional processes structure and control our everyday lives. IE as a theory is very strongly related to a particular methodology which focuses on the exploration of work processes, especially how they are structured through discourses and texts. The starting point in all of that are participants' standpoints and a 'research problematic' which is supposed to assure that the research is undertaken from the point of view of people's everyday tasks and experiences. IE takes an anti-positivist approach to scientific enquiry and follows critical and constructivist perspectives. The fieldwork itself is not dissimilar to the fieldwork in other ethnographic studies, and this is discussed in the following section.

Participant observation as a method of data collection

As the term suggests, participant observation involves the participation in, and observation of, the everyday life of the people and communities under investigation. Participant observation therefore requires simultaneous engagement and observation with the aim to develop a holistic understanding of everyday life from the point of view of the people and communities that are being studied. Mears (2013: 22) suggests that 'observant participation allows researchers to engage in the same rhythms, rates of movement, and same emotional and physical sensations of the people about whom we are most curious'. However, for Heinonen (2013) the term 'participant' is a bit of a misnomer in projects where researchers do not *really* participate in study participants' lives. According to Kawulich (2005), a successful accomplishment of studies utilising participant observation require the researcher to have an open and non-judgmental attitude. They need to be careful observers and good listeners, whilst being curious about the lives of other people and open to the unexpected.

Whilst observations are perhaps the main method used in ethnography, researchers also routinely engage in conversations and exchanges. These exchanges are an integral part of participant observation and take the form of unstructured and flexible informal interviews. What differentiates them from formal interviews, which also form part of the ethnographer's toolkit, is that they occur in natural settings and not in isolation. These interviews are useful tools to collect information that is not really observable, such as attitudes and perceptions or not visible aspects of cultures, for example hidden meanings. They also provide an opportunity to help the researcher in informing the future direction of the research. These interviews can be quite short or more substantial, and they should really be conducted in a sensitive, non-judgemental, non-threatening manner.

Kawulich (2005), but also Clark et al. (2009), list a number of reasons why participant observation might be used as a research methodology. This can be summarised as follows. Firstly, participant observation may help the researcher understand and document cultural parameters of the community or phenomenon under investigation and how they are organised. This first-hand experience of behaviours and events in context facilitates an inductive approach to the enquiry and reduces the researcher's reliance on prior conceptualisations of the study field. The observer may start to understand cultural norms, practices and taboos and he or she may develop an insight into how people communicate and interact socially. Participant observation provides opportunities for the researcher to gain access to members in the respective community or setting who in turn may facilitate the research process further, for example by consciously or unconsciously helping to distil core research questions which are culturally appropriate and relevant.

Therefore, in the first instance, observation provides an opportunity for the researchers to familiarise themselves with the community and context of their study. Observation has the potential to 'reveal the mundane, routine activities that collectively make up those practices of everyday life that may escape the discursive attention of participants' (Clark et al., 2009: 348). Thus, over time, involvement in more sensitive and private activities may be facilitated which would normally not be open to those who undertake one-off field visits to conduct interviews or group discussions in often artificial settings. An ongoing presence and engagement in the field also increases the likelihood that study participants 'forget' that they are being observed, and therefore act more like they would when they are not part of a study.

Whilst providing opportunities to engage, observation methods also allow the researcher to document aspects of the life world of those who are unable to express themselves verbally, or who are unwilling to engage in research methods that rely on verbal communication and engagement, such as interviews, group discussions or surveys. As an observer, one can step back, disengage and document the things one sees and hears without taking part actively in these encounters. This flexibility of observation types was captured by Gold (1958) who developed an ideal-typical four-tier model of researcher roles in participant observation ranging from complete participation to complete observation (Figure 6.1).

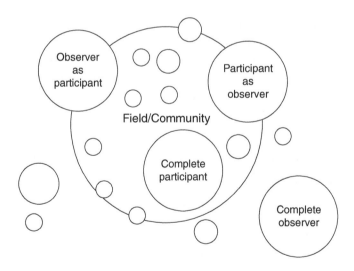

Figure 6.1 Ideal-typical researcher roles

Source: after Gold (1958)

Delamont (2007) states that complete participation and immersion in the field is neither very easy to achieve nor particularly desirable as it could potentially prevent the researcher from doing the things he or she really needs to do (taking notes, studying documents, conducting interviews, etc.). The notion of a researcher coming to a field and becoming a 'complete participant' also ignores what we've learned from the classic writings of Schütz (1944) and Simmel (1950 [1908]) in relation to being a 'stranger'. Whilst it is possible for a stranger – here ethnographer – to gradually become familiar with and part of a social setting, slowly acquiring an inside knowledge of the people and processes, the ethnographer cannot escape the contradictive participant–observer relationship. He or she can never be fully outside or inside the research setting (i.e. community or organisation) and will always remain partly an observer, and as such can never become a full participant. As an ethnographer of one's own community setting, the successful researcher will have to ultimately abdicate their role of full participant.

The more realistic scenario then is one where a researcher partially engages in everyday activities, e.g. helping out with tasks in order to learn about the nature of the activities and routines that are being studied. Observation with no participation is equally difficult to achieve, except in lab settings. Representing the views of many other authors, I refer to Hammersley and Atkinson (2007) who state that in participant observation a researcher can never really be fully outside the community they are researching. I would add here that 'full participation' is perhaps also just an academic notion which in reality is very difficult to achieve. The 'observer as participant' and 'participant as observer' roles perhaps encompass the most common and realistic description of ethnography and observation practice. Even in anthropological studies where the researcher spends prolonged time periods in the community setting, this is often just an activity limited to a certain number of hours each day. The night is usually spent at home or in accommodation which is separate from this setting. According to Kawulich (2005: para. 22) this partial immersion of 'observer as participant' is also the ethically most appropriate way of conducting participant observation, 'as the researcher's observation activities are known to the group being studied, yet the emphasis for the researcher is on collecting data, rather than participating in the activity being observed'.

The emergence of participatory and collaborative forms of ethnography

Over the years, ethnography has diversified both theoretically and methodologically. Theoretically, significant stimuli have come from Marxism and critical theory, feminism, the Chicago School, but also from post-modernism and post-structuralism. Central to these contributions about ethnography are discourses of power, interpretation and meaning, whilst the core questions posed interrogate whether or not ethnographers can reliably capture the meaning of people's behaviours, cultural values and 'realities'. As a result of this discourse we have come to an understanding that meanings are not secure and stable but can change over time. Much of this is mediated via language which is also subject to change. So a key question is whether 'reality' or 'realities' can even be captured meaningfully. As Evans (2012) puts it, in traditional participant observation approaches, the final decisions on what informants' accounts are being selected, and how they are represented and interpreted, lie with the researcher which can limit the 'participatoriness' in participant observation.

Comparing participant observation and participatory research, Heinonen (2013: 37) reminds us of the similarities between the two – namely that they are both bottom-up approaches 'with a focus on locally defined priorities, perspectives and knowledge'. What divides the two approaches is that the focus of participatory approaches is 'on knowledge for action', whereas anthropologists and ethnographers 'generally tend to (at least initially) go for "knowledge for knowledge's sake"' – see Figure 6.2.

Participant observation

- Researcher-led: researcher has control and power over the research process
- Researcher as main research 'instrument'
- Participants are not engaged in data collection or data processing
- Observation for knowledge: knowledge may or may not result in change

Participatory observation

- Collaborative research approach: researcher shares control and power with participants and co-researchers
- Participants and co-researchers engage in all aspects of a project
- Capacity building: training and supervision for co-observers. Co-researchers' expertise informs project design and enhances capacity among professional researchers
- Observation for action: intention to effect change

Figure 6.2 Distinguishing key features of participant and participatory observation

---

One element of this discourse is also the question about the relational distance between study participants and communities and the researcher. The notion of the researcher being a participant whilst at the same time maintaining a distance from the field has been contested.

All of this has fed into the development of more participatory and collaborative approaches to participant observation which aim to generate a theoretically more dynamic and generally more proactive social science. Participatory approaches to participant observation give greater agency to study participants, whilst the focus of the study is on change and advocacy. This takes account of two insights, namely the realisation that participants are knowledgeable about the social world in which they live and operate and, secondly, that social scientists should not just study issues and communities but have a moral responsibility to help bring about positive change, even though, of course, this cannot be guaranteed. As a result, however, we have seen the emergence of collaborative participatory projects with a much more active involvement of participants in the fieldwork. According to Evans (2012), a more participatory approach to participant observation engages participants in determining research questions whilst also attempting to increase their understanding of their situation, and their ability to use this information to create change for themselves. This can lead to the development of research questions that are more relevant to participants' lives. Thus, it is the extent to which participants are involved in all aspects of an ethnographic study that determines whether or not the terms 'participatory' or 'collaborative' ethnography are justified. In practice, collaborative approaches to ethnography should enable participants to develop and bring to the table their own understandings of the research questions and process. They should be afforded the position where they can act upon their newly gained knowledge to challenge the status quo. This is perhaps more easily achieved in research within institutional settings, provided that there is support at all levels. The example of Rekalde, Vizcarra and Macazaga's (2014) study based on an all-school approach to participant observation aimed at improving school sport is a good example of this, as is Tetley's (2013) study of choices made by older people in institutional care settings about using, or refusing, a range of health and social care services.

Collaborative and action ethnography

One type of collaborative approach to participant observation is *action ethnography*. For Cole (2005), action ethnography is characterised by a commitment to insider perspectives and citizen advocacy. It sets out not only to learn something about the communities where the observations take place, but also to help them harness the social power derived from new knowledge in order to achieve positive change. According to Cole, central to action ethnography are group decision-making processes. Whilst in traditional ethnographic studies the researcher holds all the interpretive and decision-making power, in collaborative approaches to participant observation the researcher must relinquish some of this power to the study participants. Evans (2012) states that the engagement of people as collaborators has the potential to make the research more meaningful. Action ethnography is therefore about providing study participants with opportunities to represent their own community, identify problems and make suggestions concerning how positive change might be implemented, rather than just being reliant on the interpretations and conclusions of the ethnographer. The participants' power should also extend to some control over study resources and should identify and publicise solutions to the recognised problem or need.

Collaborative ethnography (Lassiter, 2005) is very closely related to action ethnography and is also characterised by shared authority, goals and visions for the research between the researcher and participants. In collaborative ethnography, like in other participatory approaches, the collaboration is not accidental but deliberate and explicit and typically includes all parts of a research project from the planning stage to writing up. A collaborative approach to ethnographic fieldwork can help address and resolve the disparities between the community research site, its members and the academic researchers themselves. A more reciprocal ethnography has the capacity to facilitate the construction of deeper levels of co-interpretation. Lassiter emphasises that this shared authority extends to the texts and all other outputs that are being produced from participant observation. Commonly, participants and researchers therefore assume co-authorship when research findings are being produced and disseminated.

Lassiter (2005) sees ethnography more broadly as a 'kind of dialogue'. He therefore uses the term 'interlocutor' (i.e. a participant in a dialogue or conversation) instead of 'participant' or 'informant' because he feels that this emphasises the greater equality in the exchanges between members of the culture or community that is being studied and the researcher. However, Boellstorff et al. (2012) argues that the term 'interlocutor' perhaps overemphasises the importance of verbal exchanges in participant observation, which is characterised by a multitude of research methods including non-verbal ones, such as desk-based document analysis and observation. Boellstorff et al. also feel that power relations between study participants and researchers are perhaps not as equal as they are made out to be. Lassiter himself argues that a collaborative approach to ethnography is not always appropriate, for example when structured and standardised data collection methods (such as standardised surveys) are being used which leave little or no room for collaboration or participant input.

For this book, I will not dismiss the term 'interlocutor' completely, as of course the ambition of many collaborative and participatory projects is to arrive at a point where the research is undertaken in dialogical rather than in hierarchical format with communities and their members. Lassiter notes that one of the effects of collaborative and reciprocal ethnography can be that the research deepens the commitment of friendship between researchers and participants as well as the mutual moral responsibility experienced. Again, as we will see later on, this may not only have positive implications.

Feminist ethnography

Similar to action ethnography and collaborative ethnography, *feminist ethnography* has also contributed to the promotion, development and application of non-exploitative relationships in ethnographic fieldwork – not just in research by women on women, but more generally in participatory research practice. Again, feminist ethnography aims to make power relations in the field visible and to redress these, by giving a voice to the 'voiceless' and to help improve the lives of disempowered and disadvantaged communities. Skeggs (2001: 426) argues that feminism and ethnography suit each other because 'they both have experience, participants, definitions, meanings and sometimes subjectivity as a focus and they do not lose sight of the context'.

As Skeggs (2001) correctly points out, feminist ethnography should really be thought of in the plural – i.e. 'feminist ethnographies' – as there is not just one type or one approach. However, for this volume, we are particularly interested in the feminist ethnographies that are committed to enabling participants to collaborate in the establishment of the research agenda and to have some say in how the research is undertaken. From that point of view, the notion of 'giving voice' is of interest. Skeggs (2001: 431) argues that the 'idea of giving voice deflects away all the attention from existing power relations' as researchers allocate those whose experiences they are recording into existing categories of class, gender and race, and by doing so reproduce these categories without unique contexts. Feminist standpoint theories, for example by Dorothy Smith (2005) who also developed the institutional ethnography methodology, attempt to address this by introducing the notion of 'tacit knowledge', which focuses on everyday knowledge that people have about doing things without thinking about what and how they do these. This introduces a bottom-up approach to participant observation that prioritises people's experiences and standpoints and puts (academic) social constructs and theories second. Of course, risks and questions remain in terms of the ownership of interpretative power, as is discussed further below and in Chapter 4 on research ethics. However, one of the strengths of feminist approaches to ethnography is that they are generally very mindful of ethical discourses of positionality, power and objectification, thus asking the question in whose interest the research is being undertaken. This is a central question to collaborative research practice generally, as discussed elsewhere in this book, and as a guiding principle this question helps participatory researchers to interrogate their approach to research and to retain a sense of responsibility for participants when undertaking the research and reporting the results.

Methodological and practical impetuses

Methodologically, developments in narrative methods, interview and group discussion techniques have had an influence on how we undertake and understand ethnographic studies today, but also increased ethical awareness for what is and is not acceptable behaviour for researchers in the field. This ethical awareness has changed the nature of ethnography, as have technological developments which have led to the emergence of visual and virtual ethnography and will be discussed later in this chapter. Notably, ethnography has been impacted by epistemological, ontological and philosophical discourses about how research should be undertaken and interpreted (see Chapters 1 and 2). In comparison to other approaches, data collection in ethnographic research occurs normally in 'natural' settings that have not been specifically arranged for research purposes. According to Hammersley and Atkinson (2007: x), 'a particular virtue of ethnographic research [is] that it remains flexible and responsive to local circumstances'.

Whilst the conceptual frameworks for participatory approaches have already been discussed, practical concerns may also play a part in the decision to involve local people as co-researchers. One example of this is where the area being studied could be physically or substantially too large for one researcher and the task may just be too complex. Local community members may also be able to help with the access to informers. This can help the researcher to blend in more in the field and can improve rapport. Community members can provide insider perspectives that may enrich the research and help in an understanding of their culture. This will not necessarily make the research better, but it may trigger a more analytical and critical approach to the observation. Hammersley and Atkinson (2007) remind us that the researcher as 'stranger' brings a certain objectivity to the field whereas those who live inside the culture that is being studied tend to see it as simply a reflection of 'how the world is'. A participatory approach to participant observation, which involves community members as co-researchers, therefore creates a kind of 'insider ethnography' (O'Reilly, 2009).

Data collection in participant observation

Data collection in participant observation is not normally theory-driven and takes a fundamentally inductive approach using multiple kinds of data and various data collection strategies. This can appear quite unsystematic at the start and may only be refined and become more structured later in the fieldwork. The focus is really on the everyday simple tasks, routines and common patterns starting with a panoramic view and finishing with a focus on the details.

One of the key characteristics of data collection in participant observation is its flexibility in the use of various research methods and the required open-mindedness of the researcher and their ability to adapt to the unexpected. Data collection methods include observation, physical and virtual document and object analysis (e.g. letters, diaries, emails, artefacts, social media profiles), individual and group interviews, creative and arts-based methods, all of which increasingly incorporate visual and online elements. The essential openness and flexibility to this approach has perhaps led to the perception by some that one cannot meaningfully prepare for participant observation. At this point it is appropriate to refer to the writings of Malinowski (2013 [1922]), one of the pioneers of ethnography. He stated that researchers arrive in the field with what he called 'foreshadowed problems'. These are not preconceived ideas of how things are or work, but foreshadowed problems that arise from researchers acquainting themselves with the latest results in their field of study and with good knowledge of, and training in, research methods. So, Malinowski's notion of foreshadowed problems really takes account and raises awareness of the fact that researchers bring tools and knowledge to the field which inform the way they view and research it. This does not question the point of open-mindedness and flexibility but contextualises it, addressing the myth that research can be undertaken without any prior knowledge or perceptions.

What probably best describes the aim of the fieldwork in participatory observation is Clifford Geertz's (1973) classic term 'thick description'. The purpose of fieldwork in participant observation is really to collect as much and as diverse information as possible about the lives and culture of the people in the communities and settings under investigation whilst being flexible and adaptable about how to go about this. This process is broadly driven by the problem or issue that is being studied. So ethnographic fieldwork is not a completely open process but is, to quote Hammersley and Atkinson (2007: 16):

an active process, in which accounts of the world are produced through selective observation and theoretical interpretation of what is seen, through asking particular questions and interpreting what is said in reply, through writing fieldnotes and transcribing audio- and video-recordings, as well as through writing research reports.

Data collection in participant observation is therefore characterised by an open approach during which the research questions develop gradually and may change, the focus of which then narrows gradually and, as Burgess (1993) states, the research roles are regularly renegotiated in the field during this data collection period.

Using observations in participatory research

In this section I will now turn my attention to how participatory approaches to observation methods can be implemented in practice. I acknowledge at this point that there are a number of studies that fall into the participatory mass observation category in the natural sciences or astronomy which can be broadly captured under the header of citizen science (Hemment, Ellis and Wynne, 2011), which I have briefly discussed in Chapter 3. Many of these use observations as their chief method, for example in order to explore space or to count wildlife, but I will not focus on this here.

As stated in the background section of this chapter, the earliest versions of what we now consider ethnographic accounts were almost exclusively produced by people with academic backgrounds and aspirations. The published accounts of the fieldwork in these traditional ethnographic studies are often inaccessible to those being studied and, as Evans (2012) notes, conventional ethnographic research has been criticised for the lack of control it affords to participants over research questions and resulting outcomes and publications. Kawulich (2005: para. 5) for example recalls that during her own ethnographic studies she was made aware that other 'researchers were perceived to have taken information they had obtained through interviews or observations and had published their findings without permission of the Creek people or done so without giving proper credit to the participants who had shared their lives with the researchers'.

In Robins' (2010) ethnographic post-conflict study of human rights violations in Nepal, families of the disappeared helped to set the research agenda which was informed by their desire for dissemination and publicity of their needs. The researcher accepted from the start that the victims knew best how these needs should be articulated. The agency of the victims involved in the study was not in doubt having been included in designing the research.

As we can see, in collaborative approaches to participant observation participants have some ownership of the research design and conceptualisation, and their local knowledge is being utilised to inform the research questions and process. Participatory approaches to observation may therefore be described as collegiate activities involving researchers and local people – a kind of 'team ethnography' (O'Reilly, 2009). O'Reilly states that such a collaborative approach can lead to unique insights that can only emerge when the participants play a key role in directing the research process.

The rationale why this might be sensible has been described in earlier chapters in this book, therefore I will focus on the practical steps here. If successful, participatory ethnography can be transformative and empowering for both the researcher and the community. The idea of participatory observation is to use local resources in order to build capacity and develop advocacy tools. As in all participatory projects, the underlying assumption is that ordinary people are capable of providing and collecting valid data about their own and their peers' experiences, as Evans (2012) puts it. The knowledge generated from these participatory approaches is not just knowledge for better understanding, but knowledge for action and change.

Apart from actual observations, participatory activities, such as participatory diagramming and mapping, visual and online methods, and arts-based methods can be used as part of a participatory observation project, and some of these will be discussed in this section. Alongside observations and other qualitative methods, surveys and structured observations may also be used. A good example of how this can work is Siri and Chantraprayoon's (2017) community participatory learning project which aimed to involve the local community in the development of tourism to ensure their needs were met.

Preparation and training

Typically, research training and sensitisation towards the research topic are the first steps taken to enable community members to conduct their own research. Before fieldwork starts, co-researchers need to be given guidance on how to undertake observations and what to observe in order to answer the research questions. During the initial researcher training, the research topic and its rationale should be explored which will help co-researchers in their focus. This will also include issues around research ethics, including confidentiality, privacy and researcher and participant safety. It must be made clear that participant observations are usually a time-consuming activity, which may involve different emotions, such as discomfort and embarrassment, and may also involve certain risks and lead to negative effects. The pathway to withdraw from the research project must be clearly mapped out, as should the support mechanisms for the co-researchers.

Practically, researcher training for observations should also include hands-on observation exercises which help to establish and develop co-researchers' ability to collect and return robust data (Clark et al., 2009). Co-researchers need to learn how to differentiate between their reflections and interpretations and their actual observations. Structured and unstructured observation protocols and examples of fieldnotes could be provided and discussed. Figure 6.3 shows that many elements of observation protocols and records are identical in structured and unstructured observations. The main difference really is that for structured observation, very specific observations tasks are set which often include the counting of events or activities happening whereas unstructured observations may also be aligned to research questions, but are much more open in terms of what is being recorded.

Unstructured observations

- Date, time, duration and location of observation (later to be anonymised)
- Name or initials of observer
- Some context information, e.g. additional information about the location or event, where the observation takes place
- Details about people being observed
- **Unstructured fieldnotes** taken during the observation
- Some initial reflections/memos – kept separate from observations
- Reference or copies of documents related to observation activity

---
Structured observations

- Date, time, duration and location of observation (later to be anonymised)
- Name or initials of observer
- Some context information, e.g. additional information about the location or event, where the observation takes place
- Details about people being observed
- **List of specific observation tasks, such as particular events or actions occurring, and space for recording the frequency of and/or details about this happening**
- Some initial reflections/memos – kept separate from observations
- Reference or copies of documents related to observation activity

Figure 6.3 Elements that should be contained in structured and unstructured observation schedules and records

The initial training needs to be followed up by ongoing supervision, guidance and continued support in the field. This should include joint de-briefing sessions, data analysis and writing workshops but also reflections on the experiences of the observations. Not all co-researchers may want to be involved in all aspects of the research, so this needs to be taken into consideration when the research role distributions are being agreed. The most important thing to remember in participatory studies is that participants and co-researchers have agency and will act in their best interest. In her study of street children (see Box 6.1), Heinonen (2013) experienced these children not as passive actors, but as participants who decided when and how to engage with her as a researcher, sometimes without her initially noticing. Researcher–participant relationships and the direction of the interaction are determined by the nature of the fieldwork undertaken.

— BOX 6.1 —

CASE STUDY: HEINONEN

Talking about her experience of undertaking participatory observation among street children, Heinonen (2013: 38) describes an episode which led her to the conclusion that children are the experts of their lives:

When I finished, the boy told me: 'You forgot to ask me about my father'. I answered: 'I am new at this and I am not working for them (meaning the NGO). I am learning how to do it'. He replied: 'It is easy, I will teach you. Ask me if I have a father'. I put down my pen and questionnaire and asked him: 'Do you have a father?' He answered: 'No'. I said: 'But everyone has a father'. He answered: 'Yes, but sometimes if you say that you have a father, they do not include you in their program'. I insisted: 'Is that so, but do you have a father?' The boy answered: 'I have already given you the answer you need for your job'. I asked the others to teach me and we had fun.

This was the first indication to me that the children had become the experts themselves and that they knew more about what they were doing than I did and that some were as much in control of the situation as the adults in charge.

Access to the field and rapport building

The first step in an empirical research project before the fieldwork can commence is to gain access or negotiate a way into the field. How this happens can vary and will depend on the context of the research project. Whether or not formal access (for example by written request) is necessary will depend on whether or not the research project takes place in an open (public) or closed setting and whether or not the researcher intends to assume an overt or covert position (Figure 6.4). For participatory and collaborative approaches in observation, the latter is not normally appropriate.

Ethically, usually active, written opt-in by study participants is regarded as good practice and in all ethnographic studies taking place in closed settings requiring institutional permissions, ethnographers may need to request access from formal gatekeepers. Paradoxically, gaining access to formal, covert settings, such as companies, schools or large public institutions, such as health trusts, may be easier, simply because clear processes may be in place that determine not only who has to be asked for permission, but also under what circumstances access may be granted. When assuming a covert role as a researcher, formal informed opt-in may not be feasible or could be counter-productive, as discussed in Chapter 4.

For observations in public settings, hanging around in the field and having informal conversations in order to have your 'path smoothed by individuals who act as both sponsor and gatekeeper' (Bryman, 2016: 428) may be the first required activity. According to Hammersley and Atkinson (2007: 4) this not only requires implicit or

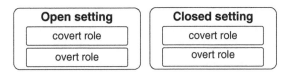

Figure 6.4 Types of fieldwork settings and researcher roles in participant observation

explicit negotiation with these gatekeepers, but access 'will also have to be negotiated and renegotiated with the people being studied; and this is true even where ethnographers are studying settings in which they are already participants'.

Informal gatekeepers can be people in powerful positions in the field or people with connections and access to important informers. Often these are community members that are highly respected, well connected or influential. A good example of a study where a highly influential gatekeeper was instrumental for its success is 'Doc', the gang leader in Whyte's 1955 bestseller *Street Corner Society*, a study undertaken in the 1930s in a deprived community of mainly Italian migrants in Boston. In participatory projects, key informers may indeed become co-researchers. However, availing of the support and assistance from gatekeepers and key informants is not always without risk. In Cornish and Ghosh's (2007) ethnographic study undertaken in an Indian red light district, access to sex workers (whose health and interests were central to the study) was only possible because the researchers were willing and prepared to accommodate the interests of local men's clubs and brothel managers. The authors argue that without this engagement with other interest groups the project could not have succeeded. In Chopel's (2014) study of maternal risks associated with unaccompanied birth practices in an indigenous Chihuahua community it is clear that the intimacy of the study subject required whole community support as well as the consent of the actual study participants.

Researchers need to understand and respect the dynamic in a community. Not all gatekeepers may be equally regarded in all sections of a community or in an organisation, especially if the community is divided or segregated. To avoid conflict with other participants, multiple gatekeepers for multiple factions of communities may be required in these cases. Too close connections with gatekeepers and key informants may also increase the likelihood that researchers start seeing the field through the eyes of their key informants, rather than their own eyes, which is an issue I come back to later in this chapter, when discussing the notion of 'going native'.

Delamont (2007) reminds us that information about gaining access or the failure to gain access are part of the 'data' that is being recorded. She claims that there is a positive link between hard access to the field and rewarding fieldwork. What she probably means by that is that the harder access is the more likely it is associated with very powerful gatekeepers who, once 'bought over', can really help with the facilitation of the research. Equally, having to work hard for access to the field may be seen as commitment to the study, which again may lead to the co-operation of target communities.

It is important at this point to remind ourselves that qualitative research practice generally relies heavily on developing a good rapport with participants and the researcher is therefore the main research instrument. In participant observation, where contact with research participants is more intensive and more enduring than in one-off data collection encounters, a comprehensive communicative skills set is required, including the ability to build and maintain close relationships but also the sense and vision to be at the right place at the right time. Of course this is something that can be learned and practised, but a general interest in people and an appreciation and empathy for their life world is a good starting point. It may not be immediately obvious what value there is in attending particular events or venues (in fact there may be no immediate use or benefit at all) but in the long run it contributes to engaging with the community and their members and it means being visible, showing respect and commitment and sharing an interest. There are of course cases where researchers may find it difficult to build close relationships and rapport because they may disagree with participants' world views, may find them disturbing, or because there is simply a personality clash. Blee's (1991) study of women involved in the Ku Klux Klan is such an example. This does not mean that researchers cannot complete their study, although the failure to build rapport may ultimately lead to failure overall, but the advice would be to seek possible points of connection with participants in areas which are less contentious and where some agreement can be found.

Rapport is built over time, and as the classic Hawthorne experiments that took place from the mid-1920s to the early 1930s (Roethlisberger and Dickson, 1939) have taught us, the effect of the presence of ethnographers on participants wears off over time (for a systematic review of the Hawthorne effect see: McCambridge, Witton and Elbourne, 2013). Thus, building rapport involves establishing a trusting relationship with the community that is being studied so that study participants can feel happy to share information and trust the researcher that the information they give will be presented accurately and not to their disadvantage. 'Hanging around' in the community that is being studied is itself a strategy that potentially contributes to trust building. It gives potential participants an opportunity to 'check out' the researcher and his or her intentions, and it may contribute to a reduction in suspicion.

I agree with Kawulich (2005: para. 39) that rapport is related to reciprocity – 'the giving back of something in return for their sharing their lives with the researcher'. As researchers we expect participants to share information honestly with us, to invite us into their lives to an extent. Giving something back, in return, even if it is just a sense of appreciation, interest and respect is, in my view, an integral part of good research practice. Boundaries between researcher and participants can break down if the researcher is willing to get involved in communities, for example by taking on volunteering tasks at events or in organisations. A strategy of observant participation helps to soften the boundaries between researchers and participants and can result in a community's informal permission given to the researchers to undertake their study.

Generally, the key advice in relation to access and rapport is to be flexible and adaptable, taking account and advantage of the circumstances that present themselves.

Undertaking observations

Observations can be undertaken either in a structured or an unstructured way. Structured observation involves direct observation and systematic recording, using specific observation schedules and coding schemes, with explicit rules on what to observe, for example specific behaviours or activities. One could, for example, undertake a simple study on how people use roads, which could involve the counting of the number of passengers travelling in each car. Another example could be that one takes part in a community meeting and records systematically the contributions made by community members by gender, or how often certain terms or phrases are being used. Structured observations are often used with a cross-sectional design, facilitating between-group comparisons, for example between men and women, and the results of such an observation are more often than not processed and reported quantitatively. Structured observations and the collection of quantitative data form very much part of the ethnographer's toolkit and are definitely not *taboo* in ethnographic research approaches, but the approach overall is predominantly unstructured. Therefore, unstructured open-ended observations are much more common.

Like in structured observations, the researcher still needs to take prior decisions about the focus of the observations and their timing, duration and location but there is much more flexibility around unstructured observations. Kawulich (2005) differentiates between descriptive, focused and selective observations.

Descriptive observations are completely open and are not guided by a prior focus. I recall an exercise from my own undergraduate studies when we were sent to a train station with the task to observe and record anything and everything we noticed for 30 minutes. Descriptive observations are typically undertaken at the start of the fieldwork. Whilst they are useful in order to get to know the study context, it is likely that some of the material observed and recorded may prove irrelevant to the study in the end.

Focused observations typically take place once the researcher has gained some insight in the field and has a better idea about the research questions that need to be answered, although they are still open-ended activities. Coming back to the example of the observation task in a train station, a focused observation could concentrate on the purchase of train tickets and ignore everything else that is going on.

Selective observations are more specific again and, depending on the nature of the observation task, feasibly can be structured rather than unstructured observations. To exploit the example of the train station one last time, a student observation task could have been to observe the difference between men and women and younger and older people using ticket desks and ticket machines respectively. This would likely involve quite a specific observation schedule which requires the counting of different kinds of customers at the ticket desk and at ticket machines.

For unobtrusive observations undertaken in a public space, regardless of its kind and focus, it is a good idea for the researcher to attempt to blend in with the environment. This is not too difficult in large train stations or shopping malls which are typically used by a great variety of diverse people who engage in different activities, but it may not be just as easy in less diverse environments. In non-public closed settings, such as organisations or institutions or specific closed communities, the need to blend in is less important. In fact, attempts to blend in may be counter-productive and could be interpreted as an attempt to disguise and hide. Nevertheless, researchers should respect cultural habits and codes, including dress codes in closed settings. In closed observation settings, researchers should also be up-front about what they are doing and should be open in explaining to participants the focus of their observation.

Regardless of the nature of the observation task and the setting in which the fieldwork takes place, researchers need to familiarise themselves with the environment and identify suitable locations from which to undertake their fieldwork.

The length of the observation sessions will be determined by the needs of the project and again the ability to be flexible in relation to the opportunities that present themselves needs to be emphasised strongly. However, overly long observation sessions are potentially not very productive as it is likely that one loses concentration and focus. The longer the observation goes on the harder it is to take systematic notes. For structured and focused observations this may still be feasible, as these are very specific. For unstructured, descriptive observations, it is nearly impossible to maintain attention for a very long time. Kawulich (2005) suggests that a good strategy to maintain concentration is to change the focus of the observation task from time to time, initially taking a descriptive approach but occasionally being more selective or focused on specific aspects or interactions. It is really important to take short breaks from observations in order to facilitate the recording of fieldnotes. This can be done by paper and pen, but also electronically on tablet computers or voice recorders for verbal note taking and even mobile phones, which may be the most unobtrusive data recording method, considering the increasing proliferation and everyday use of mobile technology.

When observing interactions, non-verbal aspects should be recorded in addition to the actual verbal exchanges. Where and how people sit, their body language, how decisions are being made and identifying which people's opinions are acknowledged and whose opinions are ignored gives insight into the power dynamics at work during group interactions.

Delamont (2007) argues that observations in an unfamiliar culture are at the same time harder *and* easier than those in familiar societies. Whilst the strangeness of unfamiliar environments is likely to spark greater awareness, hidden aspects of unfamiliar cultures and communities are much harder to uncover and more likely to be misinterpreted. On the other hand, whilst observations in one's own culture or community are likely to be more detailed, insightful and coherent, there is the risk that proximity and familiarity may lead to less care and rigour, with certain aspects taken for granted that really should be interrogated more closely.

This claim links to the discourse about the distinction between emic (insider) and etic (outsider) perspectives in ethnography and the difficulties researchers undertaking participant observation may face when they try to clearly differentiate between the emic insights of the study participants and the etic interpretations of researchers. In truth, the notion that these can be completely separate is increasingly regarded as a moot point as the two typically overlap and/or influence each other. As we will see, it is important that the researcher's standpoint towards their fieldwork is transparent.

Participant observation in cyberspace – virtual and online ethnography

Currently, one of the aspects of modern life for many people is the increasing amount of time spent online and in the virtual world. Expanding portions of people's communications and exchanges now take place via social networks (such as Facebook, Twitter, WhatsApp, Snapchat or Instagram) and via text messaging services using mobile phone networks, Skype and Facetime. Many everyday tasks and activities in our lives such as shopping, banking and paying bills, arranging meetings and dates, making appointments, entertainment and reading, playing games, but also advice, guidance and counselling are accessed through digital computer and online technology. There are various online communities and fan clubs built around multitudes of interests. Some of these occur alongside the physical world, whilst others exist exclusively online or virtually. Opting out of and consciously avoiding computer technology, social media and the virtual world is getting increasingly difficult. For many people, social media and the virtual world are now all-encompassing and have become an integral part of their reality. The main difference between the virtual and the real physical world is that it is possible to exit and log off from virtual worlds. Thus people are never really fully submerged in the virtual world, but they are also always still in the real world at the same time, and it is the person in the real world that decides how to act in the virtual world.

For participant observation, this provides both opportunities and challenges. Unlike traditional observation, 'netnography' – i.e. the immersion of the researcher in online worlds – is in a way 'placeless'. According to Hine (2000), internet ethnography is not bound to a physical place where researchers come and spend time. In fact, the observations and engagements usually take place from the relative safety of the office or home computer devices – including tablets or smartphones. Pink (2012), on the other hand, looks at the concept of space in the virtual world slightly differently. She argues that the internet itself becomes one of the 'ethnographic places' that needs to be explored. For her, place is more a theoretical concept, which can be simultaneously open and a visible virtual landscape with defined boundaries. Pink suggests that this requires a firm distinction in the meaning of the term 'place' for theoretical and conceptual analysis on the one hand and place as a multi-sensory environment where ethnographers can go and undertake their virtual ethnography on the other.

In any case, the resource and time challenges of undertaking physical observations have all but disappeared for virtual ethnography although it is possible to meet up in a physical space, for example with gamers, and then enter the virtual world together. When undertaking virtual ethnography it is also much clearer from the outset that there is no such thing as an objective truth that needs to be discovered, rather the focus of a netnographer is on the understanding of subjective representations and constructions of reality. The online world affords people the ability to be who they want to be, to create new identities of themselves, and to adopt various identities at the same time. Then again, this is not that different from the physical world where people also adopt different identities, tied to particular times, spaces and different roles. Someone can be a parent, a child to a parent, a partner or spouse, an employer or employee, a hobbyist and sports person all at the same time. Thus, constructed virtual reality in the online world is really still a multi-sensory part of people's real lives that needs to be explored.

One of the remarkable and thought-provoking revelations in Boellstorff's ethnographic study of the virtual world of Second Life (2008) can be found in his final chapter where he quotes one of the Second Life residents: 'That's the dirty secret of virtual worlds; all people end up doing is replicating their real lives' (2008: 239). Boellstorff himself admits that he was stuck by the banality of Second Life. Despite the quite literal castles in the sky built in Second Life, he experienced this virtual reality world very much as a place where 'mundane' everyday things like shopping, entertainment and conversations took place – all activities that indeed replicated engagement and experiences from the physical world. To reiterate this point, Boellstorff (2008: 240) quotes another Second Life resident who felt that 'Second Life is part of real life'. Boellstorff therefore suggests that virtual worlds such as Second Life, which generate and are based on cybersociality, should be treated as a kind of culture.

Boellstorff et al. (2012) propose some strategies for effective participation in virtual worlds that participant observers need to use. Researchers need to prepare their real and virtual self for participation in the virtual world. They need to prepare and get used to the required technology to be able to immerse themselves in the virtual world. Certain virtual worlds, such as Second Life, or games require a particular language or linguistic conventions that the researcher has to acquire before starting the observations. This technical preparation may also include the planning of one's own identity or avatar in the respective social worlds. Boellstorff et al. argue that, in fact, the preparation for online ethnography needs to be better than in the physical world. Physically, research-ers need to be prepared for the strains that long-term computer use will ultimately entail (such as strains on eyes, the back and neck). Lastly, the authors warn not to give in to the temptation to spend less time in the virtual world due to the convenience of the fieldwork. Just like in the physical world, virtual ethnography demands full or partial participation in online communities for prolonged periods of time.

Appropriating Malinowski's famous first lines from his 1922 publication *Argonauts of the Western Pacific*, in his study of the virtual world of Second Life, Boellstorff (2008) argues that the challenges that a novice ethnographer faces upon arrival in a virtual world can be very similar to those faced by ethnographers arriving in a 'real place' and a 'real culture'. He suggests that the internet can actually provide field sites which are very similar to those in the 'real' physical world, with houses, particular environments, specific inhibi-tors and with definite boundaries. Like in participant observation in the physical world, access to influential members and gatekeepers who may become key informants is equally crucial in the virtual world and the first steps in the fieldwork should be geared towards this. Ethical principles of informed consent of course also apply here.

Extensive fieldnotes need to be recorded just the same as in the real world but tech-nical solutions, such as chatlogs, video and sound recordings, screenshots, etc. perhaps provide a more comprehensive toolkit for the recording of events and observations.

Platforms such as Second Life, or gaming platforms, but also Facebook groups, require full participation whereas other internet forums such as chatrooms perhaps facilitate observation with minimal or no participation. Boellstorff et al. (2012) note that multi-tasking, such as observing, participating and recording fieldnotes, can be difficult in the online world because playing games and other tasks and activities require full attention.

One of the issues in online ethnography is, as Tom Boellstorff in his 2008 book *Coming of Age in Second Life* highlights, that the subject matter can not be too big or too small. He argues that the number of existing virtual platforms and networks have become so enormous and diverse that it is basically impossible to capture people's online lives comprehensively. At the same time, many of the virtual networks are too vast and have too many members to be able to produce a comprehensive picture.

Visual ethnography

Whilst participant observation always contained a visual dimension to support textual information (e.g. via drawings, analysis of visual documents, videos and photography) and to challenge its hegemony (Madden, 2017), the new technological context with ever increasing availability, flexibility and affordability of digital technology means that the possibilities of visual ethnography have significantly expanded and actually shaped the context of the current research landscape. Pink (2012) argues that the emergence of visual and internet ethnography is connected to the emergence of visual technologies and the internet in the 1990s. Rose (2014) feels that this relationship between the growth in visual research methods and the increasing importance of visual images in contemporary social and cultural practice still requires further investigation.

Ardévol (2012) also sees a clear intersection between visual and virtual ethnography. On the one hand, with its visual textual and non-textual content, the internet has increasingly become an object of study, on the other hand, with its diversification and increasing storage of data and information, the internet has also become a powerful tool to undertake and aid research facilitating the access and sharing of textual, visual and audio-visual information. As already alluded to above, the ethnographer's interest in this is primarily what this content and platforms represent rather than whether the content is truthful, reliable and valid. It is of interest *how* online group activities create a sense of belonging. In many ways, the internet itself has fostered and facilitated a participatory culture where people regardless of their position and status can make contributions. There are some examples where online activities have counteracted and subverted privileged cultures, although arguably the grand promise of greater equality has not been fulfilled.

Participatory visual ethnography

O'Neill (2010, 2012) used a combination of participatory research practice and visual artistic representations of research to explore the lives of street-based sex workers and the safety concerns in the communities where they live and work. O'Neill calls this approach 'ethno-mimesis'. For her, visual and artistic representations can also make a contribution to the change of reality and are therefore creating something new. Alongside story telling and walking interviews, visual methods can help to connect research with the public.

In her study of sex work, O'Neill worked with local people who she trained and employed as co-researchers. One of the outputs was a website that displayed some of the artwork and visual images alongside textual representations produced as part of the research project. In another project, O'Neill worked with Bosnian refugees and showcased their work and art produced in participatory art workshops. For O'Neill, these visual and online methods offer opportunities for participants to represent themselves and, by doing so, transcend power relations. She argues that 'participants involved in PAR research are both objects and subjects (authors) of their own narratives and cultures' (O'Neill, 2012: 165).

Ross et al. (2009) used the mobile methods of car journey interactions and guided walks to explore the sense of locality of residential care-experienced young people in Wales. As in O'Neill's work, mobile methods were used to connect the spoken word to physical locations, introducing a visual element to the study to capture young people's memories and connections to specific places.

O'Hara and Higgins (2017) used participant photography to research drug use and antisocial behaviour among young people living in areas of deprivation and high levels of sectarian violence in Northern Ireland. Young people were asked to take photos of the places where they socialised and spent time. Images were then sorted and thematically analysed, then discussed in interactive group discussions.

Gotschi, Delve and Freyer (2009) used a similar approach with participatory photography to inform and stimulate interviews and group discussions about farming culture and social capital in Mozambique. The authors argue that the use of participatory photography enabled them to identify and explore issues of social capital at the level of members that otherwise could not have been explored.

Lowe et al. (2014) used visual ethnographic methods, such as visual probes and mapping tools, in their study of adults with autism who had limited verbal speech and learning disabilities. Using visual ethnographic methods, the researchers were able to involve participants actively in the study design. Panek (2015) describes how a participatory mapping project, which gives control to communities in relation to what is and is not included on maps, can empower these communities.

Taking fieldnotes and writing up

Data collected during participant observation will usually be recorded in unstructured format, consisting predominantly of descriptive fieldnotes, quick memos and jottings, aided by audio or visual (video or photo) recordings, if this is feasible and appropriate. The recording equipment used in participant observation may include a voice recorder, mobile phone and pen and paper, but also worksheets and survey questionnaires for more structured observations and recordings. Mobile phone use is very common now in most societies, so the recording of fieldnotes, but also voice and video recordings and photography, can be undertaken unobtrusively, and therefore has much less impact now on conversations and activities than even one or two decades ago.

Fieldnotes should be as extensive as possible and can therefore initially be quite rough, for example notes taken during or after informal conversations or unstructured interviews, but also observation notes taken at informal activities or official ceremonies. The fieldnotes may contain drawings or interaction maps as well as notes on any relevant background information. Date, time, place and name of researcher should be routinely included on each set of notes. The descriptive fieldnotes can be accompanied by initial reflections and thoughts, although analytical reflective notes are not usually added until later at home or in the office when writing up fieldnotes. In any case, these thoughts and interpretations should be kept separate from the recorded observations. Relevant documents (such as programmes of events, background about locations, maps, etc.) can also be included and may later aid the analysis. When it is not possible or appropriate to take fieldnotes during observations, for example in Corman's (2018) study of paramedics, these should be taken as soon as possible after the observation activity.

As noted at the start of this chapter, ethnography is not just a method but also a product, so whilst fieldnotes are in the first instance records of data collected, they are equally the start of the analysis. When writing up the fieldnotes, anonymisation and pseudonomisation should take place in order to protect the participants' confidentiality. The end product should represent what Geertz (1973) called 'thick description'. For participatory ethnography, the accounts of the fieldwork have an advocacy and social change focus whilst their format should be accessible to a large and diverse audience.

Participatory data analysis can involve interactive group discussions, workshops and joint thematic analysis with co-researchers, as described in more detail in Chapters 5 and 7 in this book. What characterises participatory observation is that co-researchers arrive at the data analysis session with their own fieldnotes and interpretations and quite possibly already have themes in their head that emerged in their observations. Further, members of the community or setting that is being observed will have a strong sense of competency and ownership of the data. For collaborative approaches, it is therefore important that the ethnographic tales that are being produced as the output of the participatory observations are a 'team story' (O'Reilly, 2009) and represent a combination of the ideas of the researcher and the co-researchers/participants. The decisions about which elements of the research should be included should be a joint decision and co-authors' voices and opinions and their interpretations must be given due weight.

Collaborative approaches to ethnography, such as action ethnography or feminist ethnography, do not finish with the writing-up but involve active and engaged steps of dissemination that are geared towards initiating and facilitating change. This may involve workshops with, and presentations to, statutory or voluntary agencies and journalists as well as the public events for the community where the research was located.

Study results are typically presented in various formats to suit different purposes and audiences, and this may include visual material (videos, posters, photos, drawings) and arts-based activities, such as dramatisations of the study results or public exhibitions. This also allows for flexibility in terms of co-authorship, making sure that co-researchers are not potentially at risk of status change in their own community, for example by being publicly associated with the study.

Exiting the field

Even though ethnographic fieldwork traditionally lasts for prolonged time periods, none can last forever and exit strategies must be planned as much as access to the field and rapport building. Of course, there is always more data that can be collected but a study also has to be concluded. The question is when is it the right time to leave the field and how is this done?

In most cases the end of a research project is determined by the financial limitations or the time pressures to complete a project. In an ideal world of limitless resources and no time constraints, the guiding principle for the completion of a study would probably be the notion of 'saturation'. This occurs when all the research questions are answered, only familiar situations occur and no new insights emerge from new data collected. However, field exit strategies in participatory and collaborative research projects also have to be considerate of a number of other factors.

Firstly, in most participatory projects, co-researchers are volunteers. Even though a community or community organisation may have initiated a research project, they generally have other work or family commitments and pressures which means that their involvement in a research project is time-limited. Their involvement in a project may also serve a particular purpose, for example a particular consultation or input in a decision-making process, so the purpose of their involvement may have simply ceased to exist. These are still common reasons to end a research project which are not unlike the reasons in conventional projects.

However, in collaborative research projects which rely on close relationships between researchers, co-researchers and participants, the planning of the ending of these relationships is just as important. As was discussed in Chapter 4 of this volume, it is the responsibility of a researcher to anticipate the ending of the fieldwork and they should prepare co-researchers and participants for this from the outset of a project. This includes that a good rationale must be given for the departure from the field. Nonetheless, unrealistic expectations may have manifested themselves during a research project. These may include naïve hopes about the outcomes of a project, such as the speed or extent of promised changes, but very close trust relationships may have developed between researcher and co-researchers or participants, and the latter may have a sense of betrayal when the research project is ended. Sometimes the nature of the relationship between participants and researcher also slowly changes and this can be an indication that it is time to leave the field, as Cole (2005) reports when she reflects about her experience of ending a ten-year long ethnographic action research project about the effects of tourism on two communities in Indonesia. She found that 'balancing the giving and taking of knowledge' became 'increasingly difficult', evidenced by the fact that her 'interviews would be turned into their interviews', and she would become 'the giver rather than the taker of knowledge' (Cole, 2005: 70).

Participatory projects are also not always without risks to co-researchers. They may lead to stressful situations for participants and co-researchers and to ethical dilemmas, for example when the research itself puts researchers and participants at risk. Researchers may, for example, become vulnerable if they become involved in political action or other active engagement which may compromise their status and security.

Overrapport or 'going native'

The term 'going native' essentially refers to the failure of ethnographers to maintain the 'delicate balance of empathy and distance' (O'Reilly, 2009: 89) with research participants. For some, the term 'going native' itself is now considered to be a derogatory expression as it originally referred to predominantly Western anthropologists getting 'too close' to, and too involved with, 'native' or indigenous communities during their fieldwork. The rejection of the term 'going native' can perhaps also be seen as a stance against ethnographic studies that were funded and supported to justify and inform colonial and imperial endeavours.

The result of this 'overrapport' with participants (Hammersley and Atkinson, 2007: 87) – which is suggested to be a more appropriate way of describing the issue at hand – is that researchers increasingly see the world through their participants' eyes and as a result may lose track of their role. Getting 'too involved' with the community being researched may result in a loss of objectivity and the inability to answer research questions with the necessary rigour. For Madden (2017), giving participants some space to be 'off' from the fieldwork is a good strategy to counteract overrapport and to avoid total immersion in the field and being too close to the subject.

For participatory researchers, how much involvement they should have with their participants is a critical question. Wacquant's (2009: 119) much quoted phrase 'Go native, but go native armed' – suggests that immersion in the field is a possibility without necessarily losing one's position as a researcher. The phrase suggests that researchers should have an awareness of their reflexivity, but also their vulnerability, before they enter the field in an ethnographic study and in my view this is the right approach that should be adapted in participatory observation projects.

Critique of participant observation

Critics point out that data derived from participant observation is not representative because observation can only ever be selective. This selection is ultimately made, and the observation undertaken, by a biased human on whom much of what is found and being reported depends. Researchers involved in collaborative ethnographic studies themselves sometimes highlight the difficulties around generalisability. Robins (2010: 193), for example, writes about his study involving families of the disappeared in Nepal:

> The greatest limitation to the generalization of this [collaborative] methodology is the need for mutuality between the research agenda and the goals of the community being researched. Equivalently, a participatory research design demands that the researcher yields some control of the research agenda, and indeed the research question, to the researched. Whilst this can be considered a violation of the positivist view of social research aims, it is a prerequisite of participatory research design and indeed of any emancipatory approach. Such an approach can only work where the research agenda seeks articulation or addressing of issues that the community prioritizes.

Feminist academics would of course respond to this critique that bias is inevitable regardless of which research method is being used, including 'objective' surveys, but what counts is the awareness and transparency of the researcher's standpoint or subject position and how it may affect the theoretical approach to observation, the data analysis and interpretation. This subject position is shaped by characteristics such as gender, sexuality, ethnicity, national and religious belonging, class, age, disability, accent and so forth.

Hammersley and Atkinson (2007: 16) feel that 'the fact that [...] researchers [...] are likely to have an effect on the people [they] study does not mean that the validity of [their] findings is restricted' (Hammersley and Atkinson, 2007: 16), and Boellstorff et al. (2012) argue that researchers' subject positions do not only provide constraints. They can equally create opportunities, for example when researchers can take advantage of and make connections due to their gender, sexuality or other identities, certain specialised language skills they may have, or, in the case of co-researchers, their familiarity with particular cultures and traditions.

One of the main criticisms of participant observation, and actually one of the main reasons why collaborative and participatory approaches to ethnography have developed is, as Hammersley and Atkinson (2007: 14) point out, its lack of impact on policy making and practice. Ethnographic studies would 'simply lie on library shelves gathering dust, and ... as a result they are worthless' (2007: 14). Evans (2012) agrees and states that participant observation usually generates academic articles or books which are often inaccessible to research participants and are only read by a small number of 'experts'.

Hammersley and Atkinson (2007: 14) point out that research is inevitably affected by values and 'always has political consequences'. They feel therefore that 'researchers must take responsibility for their value commitments and for the effects of their work'. Hammersley and Atkinson refer to the participatory and action research sentiment that demands an interventionist ethnography that should be informed by the desire to bring about change. However, they also warn that the desire to challenge the status quo can potentially 'increase the chances of the findings being distorted by ideas about how the world ought to be, or by what it would be politic for others to believe' (Hammersley and Atkinson, 2007: 18).

Common to all participatory research approaches is the general concern that collaboration ultimately produces only a small number of confident individuals who then have access to multiple opportunities for leadership. Therefore, whilst collaborative approaches set out to redress power relations they may paradoxically also create new hierarchies. Stacey (1988) points out another paradox, namely, that critical (feminist) approaches to ethnography traditionally set out to create an egalitarian, reciprocal relationship between researchers and study participants, but by facilitating voice they actually subject research participants to a greater risk of exploitation, betrayal and abandonment than much of the traditional positivist research practice does. Stacey reminds us that ethnographic fieldwork is an intrusion into the life world of participants and their system of existing relationships that the researcher can much more easily leave behind than participants can. Participatory ethnographic research practice therefore demands ethical reflections which were discussed in detail in Chapter 4.

Summary

Participant observation is not usually associated with participatory research approaches, but as I have attempted to show in this chapter, this is perhaps unwarranted. Researchers involved in collaborative research usually recognise the importance of rapport building, of getting to know the field, of learning about and addressing power relations, finding and collaborating with appropriate gatekeepers – all of which support the identification of suitable data collection strategies and the recruitment of research participants. Spending significant time in the field doing what was once generally called 'fieldwork' can contribute significantly to desired research outcomes and to more efficient strategies when it comes to promoting positive changes in the communities in which the research takes place. Perhaps it is the pressure of producing measurable outcomes in increasingly limited time periods and decreasing resources in today's research landscape that is responsible for the re-configuration of ethnographic research into time-limited and increasingly narrow-focused micro-ethnography. Whilst collaborative or action ethnography is also possible within these new parameters, arguably, spending more time with groups of participants and co-researchers in their physical or online communities is worth the effort.

──FURTHER READING──

Hammersley, M. and Atkinson, P. (2007). *Ethnography: Principles in Practice* (3rd edition). London: Routledge.

Lassiter, L. E. (2005). *The Chicago Guide to Collaborative Ethnography*. Chicago: University of Chicago Press.

PRACTISING OBSERVATION SKILLS

Successful observation requires practice, in particular in terms of keeping personal interpretations separate from observations. The most effective activity in my view is to spend periods of time in public places – whether this is in the real physical world or in the virtual world – and to practise unobtrusive observations. To improve the rigour in record keeping and also effectiveness in recording of information, participants and co-researchers could complete the same observation activities in small teams and then compare notes. Are there aspects that some observer noted, but not another? How do the observations by different observers vary? How are our observations and reflections informed by our individual knowledge (refer to Malinowski's concept of 'foreshadowed problems', if appropriate) and by our particular standpoints that we bring to the field? How can collaborative research address these?

Both structured and unstructured observations should be practised like this: 30 minutes in pairs or in small groups in a busy public space, such as an airport arrival hall, a bus or train station or a market or shopping mall are ideal places to undertake unobtrusive observations. The observation schedule should be drawn up in advance.

7

GROUP DISCUSSION METHODS IN PARTICIPATORY RESEARCH

What you will learn

In this chapter I will examine group discussion methods (also known as 'focus groups' or 'group interviews') – one of the most commonly used research methods in participatory approaches. I will briefly look at the history of focus groups as a research method and their key characteristics. I will then discuss the theoretical perspectives group discussion methods are particularly aligned to. Finally, I will turn to the practicalities of conducting group discussions and I will do so from the perspective of participatory research approaches.

Introduction

Group discussion methods are research methods during which mostly verbal data is collected from more than one participant at the same time – ideally at least five and no more than twelve selected participants. 'Focus groups' originated in the 1930s when they were developed as an alternative way of conducting interviews (Krueger and Casey, 2009). Since then, from 'the specialist knowledge of market research and a few innovative academic researchers' (Macnaghten and Myers, 2004: 65), they have evolved as one of the most commonly used methods of data collection. Their applications include commercial market research projects, academic research and research in the voluntary and non-governmental sector. Adapted group discussion methods are commonly used by government in policy consultations as part of public engagement exercises to inform decision making on various issues such as strategies, service design or delivery, programmes for government or legislation. Their application in the voluntary and community sector is of particular relevance to this volume as this is where their exceptional participatory potential is often utilised, for example when voluntary or community organisations team up with academic researchers to undertake action research projects, as discussed in Chapter 5.

Group discussion methods as a 'natural' method of data collection

The value of using group discussion as a research method is linked to the very nature of the data being collected. Group discussions reflect how most people form and exchange views on a daily basis and this makes group discussion methods a very 'natural' way of collecting data and one that many research participants feel very comfortable with. Many people spend a lot of their time as part of a small group of people – whether this is in their family, in their workplace or during leisure time activities. Every day, people use verbal exchanges in small groups to find out what other people really think and the dynamics and variations in the views expressed by others in group contexts help us to form and express our own views, test personal attitudes and take sides in a debate. These daily exchanges with other people greatly influence our own behaviour. The fact that focus groups can mimic these exchanges explains their growing popularity in social research. Unlike in many one-to-one interview situations, where the interviewer–interviewee hierarchy is rarely overcome, during group discussions it is not uncommon for dynamics to develop which resemble real-life exchanges. As the discussions develop, participants gradually assume greater autonomy over the process of data collection and the power may shift considerably from the researcher towards the participants. It is this dynamic which makes group discussion methods one of the most popular and at the same time most challenging methods of data collection. It also gives group discussion methods a participatory touch per se.

In this chapter I will allude to mechanisms and methods through which group discussions can be developed further to give a voice to participants. I will explain how participatory and interactive elements can be incorporated in group discussions to take full advantage of the capacity of this method to elicit people's views and experiences. This will illustrate why group discussion methods have become one of the favourite research instruments used in action research (e.g. Weeks and Roberto, 2003) and participatory ethnography.

'Focus groups' or 'group discussions'?

The terms 'focus group' or 'group interview', which have been predominantly used in the academic literature, have become partially contested by those advocating and using participatory research approaches; these terms can assume that the power to determine the direction of the group discussion lies firmly with the researchers – they are the ones providing the 'focus'; they are the (group) 'interviewers'. In research practice this can of course often be an accurate reflection of the actual process and the distribution of power in a project. In fact, when focus groups first emerged as a method of data collection (Bogardus, 1926), this was very clearly a researcher-led innovation trying to address practical issues and increase the effectiveness of the interview method. However, since then, group discussion methods have arguably diversified into one of the most dynamic, flexible and versatile means of data collection. In these often very open and collaborative research approaches, the focus may be directed by the group members and not the researcher. Although the 'focus' will often be determined as part of the research project, it may shift and change through this process of interactive group engagement. Increasingly, researchers therefore refer to the term 'group discussion methods' instead of 'focus groups'.

As this book is really concerned with participatory methods and the shift of power relations within the research process, I will also use the term 'group discussion methods' when I refer to literature on 'focus groups'. For this book, and its context and subject matter, 'group discussion methods' is a more appropriate term for the nature of the research method covered in this chapter. The use of the term 'group discussions methods' instead of 'focus groups' is not merely a semantic trick but a reflection of the fact that this chapter describes how group discussion methods can be organised in a way that actively involves participants and gives them a greater say in the direction of a given research project (Krueger and King, 1998). What really matters for this book is how researchers can involve participants in their projects so that they have a say in the focus of the research and how it is being conducted. However, before I discuss ways of involving participants actively in group discussions, I will briefly discuss their history as a research method, their principal characteristics and how they are methodologically connected to social theory.

The history of group discussions as a research method

There appears to be agreement that the sociologist Emery Bogardus' 1926 publication 'The group interview' is the first milestone in the emergence of focus group methods in academic research (Morgan, 1997; Liamputtong, 2011; Stewart and Shamdasani, 2015). According to Morgan (1997), some of the first applications of focus groups were related to efforts by the US military in the Second World War, namely attempts to study the effectiveness of propaganda material and the morale and productivity of troops (Merton, Fiske and Kendall, 1956).

It was around that time that focus groups also became a popular method for market researchers. Whilst this volume is not particularly concerned with the use of group discussion methods for market research purposes, it would be inappropriate to deny the important contribution that market research has made to the development of this particular research method. However, due to its commercial nature, participants have little or no influence on the way the research is conducted. As this volume focuses on models of group discussion methods where participants have some influence over the research questions or research design, market research is not discussed in more detail.

Morgan (1997) claims that initially focus groups were seen as a convenient way to reach more than one person at the same time and the author suspects that this predominantly practical rationale prevented many researchers from thinking of, and developing, group discussion methods as a research technique in their own right. Despite their initial popularity, group discussion methods then 'virtually disappeared from the social sciences during the next three decades' (Morgan, 1997: 4). Morgan attributes this to the fact that scholars who used group discussion methods in their research did not publish or advertise this very much but rather started to use other data collection methods and concentrated on these. The proliferation of group discussion methods in academia was perhaps also delayed and their popularity limited because they were too closely associated with commercial market research (Liamputtong, 2011).

According to Morgan (1997), it was not until the 1980s when group discussion methods were used more widely in the areas of demography, family planning and sexual health (Folch-Lyon, de la Macorra and Schearer, 1981; Joseph et al., 1984; Bhana, 2009), communication and media studies (Lunt and Livingstone, 1996). Their use then quickly diversified making them one of the most widely used research methods in a large number of contexts and research fields. Liamputtong (2011) maintains that focus groups are seen as a low-cost research method, which provide results very quickly and with a great variety of audiences. This may explain why they feature in many programme evaluations and public consultations. However, as Liamputtong (2011: 2) warns appropriately, if they are to be used to their full potential group discussion methods are 'not as cheap, easy and quick [to conduct] as has been claimed'.

Theoretical perspectives

In practice, group discussion methods are often used without reference to or guidance from specific theoretical perspectives. Nevertheless, for academically informed projects, it is noteworthy that, epistemologically, group discussions are better matched to some theoretical perspectives than others. *Symbolic interactionism*, for example, is concerned 'with the subjective meaning individuals attribute to their activities and environments' (Flick, 2014: 66). The three premises of social interactionism are that: (1) people behave towards things on the basis of the meaning these things have for them; (2) this meaning is acquired through social interaction with others; and (3) these meanings are managed and changed through an interpretive process that individuals employ in dealing with these things they experience (Liamputtong, 2011). Group discussion methods are a perfect match for interactionist approaches as subjective meaning and information about the process of collective sense making is essentially what group discussions elicit and what researchers can therefore observe and record. Group discussions help us to see how individuals interpret and understand their world and how people negotiate and renegotiate meaning during the social interactions they have with each other.

Liamputtong (2011) argues that group discussion methods are also a good fit with *feminist research approaches* as they can provide safe spaces for discussions with others. As already discussed in previous chapters in his volume, feminist researchers not only aim to study the world of women and disadvantaged people, but they take an emancipatory approach in order to change the world of their study participants for the better, both at a personal and societal level. Unlike standardised and positivist research, which often fails to capture the lived experiences of women and marginalised or disadvantaged people, group discussion methods can help to discover the characteristics of their lives. According to Liamputtong (2011), focus groups are not only a research method that allows women to communicate their experiences, but also a powerful tool that can contribute to consciousness-raising as part of the research methodology. Esther Madriz's work with Latina women from socio-economically deprived backgrounds is a good example of a feminist methodology utilising group discussion methods (Madriz, 1998).

Innovative and educative group work activities modelled on *theoretical critical pedagogical practice* as promoted and practised by scholars such as Paulo Freire and Jan Kozol have also been closely connected with the development of group discussion methods, particularly with social movements and the educational arena, especially in relation to their emancipatory approaches and their desire to change things for the better for disadvantaged individuals and communities. As already alluded to in Chapters 1 and 2, Freire's pedagogical practice combines research with education and action, thus using a critical pedagogical approach, group discussion methods are much more than mere data collection tools. Rather they are dialogic focus groups, which potentially become vehicles that facilitate a process of emancipation, where praxis and conscientisation lead to critical reflection and political action. Kozol (1985) argues that the invitation to the active participation and contribution of people and communities in planning processes is likely to be more fruitful than programmes where people are just informed what is happening. The following are examples of this from Freire's and Kozol's work:

- Study groups being used as collective critical literacy practices.
- Work with local oppressed people in order to speak about local politics and express their concerns about local politics and social justice.
- Mobilising local groups to work against their oppression through praxis.

According to Kozol, learning or study groups of this nature could produce their own leaders and people would be emancipated to take more control of their lives, potentially enabling them to change things for the better.

Potential strengths and weaknesses of group discussion methods

Ultimately, finding out what people *really* think is not just the intention of group discussion methods, but of much of social research generally. In order to elicit people's thoughts and experiences, participants need to feel comfortable in the research context and environment and they need to feel able to express socially less acceptable views and opinions. Group discussion methods should be designed to create such an environment. Also issues of disclosure, social conformity and desirability cannot ever be completely eliminated. The dynamic of group settings may enhance the outcome and insights of a research project and the social desirability bias is potentially weaker in group discussions because they are set up to replicate everyday communication and tap into authentic exchanges and conversations.

It is because of this group dynamic that group discussion methods are ideal vehicles to witness the co-construction of meaning and to uncover the way groups of people form opinions and come to decisions. With regard to practical applications, group discussions can therefore help aid decision-making processes, including deciding about the aims and objectives and direction of a project. This can make group discussions meaningful at the start of a project or at a point when progress has come to a halt or when important strategic decisions have to be taken about what to do next. Policy makers, including government, like to adapt group discussion methodologies with different sets of people and audiences for policy consultations and for the assessment of existing programmes or development of new ones. The involvement of diverse groups of people allows policy makers to capture a broad range of views, including the views of those who might be under-represented in surveys or written submissions.

At a community organisational level, group discussion methods allow for the internal elicitation of views and assessment of needs which are relevant to specific communities or organisations. This can lead to organisations deciding about the direction they will take or developing a better understanding of the issues and concerns that their target audience or membership has.

Morgan (1997: 13) argues that the strengths and weaknesses of focus groups are linked directly to their two defining characteristics, namely (1) the group dynamic and (2) the researcher's need to provide a focus. If managed well, group discussions can enable researchers to collect large and concentrated volumes of data, more quickly and easily than some other methods, e.g. individual interviews. The potential for efficiency is one of the main reasons why focus groups are such a popular method in market research.

The second main strength is the dynamic in a group discussion. The group dynamic facilitates the collection of data not just on *what* is being said, but also *how* it is said and how ideas are produced dynamically in a group context. Contributions can trigger further thoughts among other participants. As Morgan (1997: 46) states:

> Until they interact with others on a topic, individuals are often simply unaware
> of their own implicit perspectives. Moreover, the interactions in the group may

present the need to explain or defend one's perspective to someone who thinks about the world differently.

The arguments and discussions that will emerge give a deeper insight into what people think and do, and why. This is much more likely to happen in a group discussion than in an individual interview. The facilitator can foster such debates by posing challenging or thought-provoking questions, for example. In a one-to-one context this may lead to a breakdown in relationships, but in a group context this is unlikely to happen. At the same time, the dynamic may also lead to participants being less open or voicing more extreme views than they normally would. For that reason, researchers should allow for less depth and probing in their group discussions than during in-depth individual interviews.

Other strengths are that group discussions generally encourage more open exchanges than interviews would and that the thoughts and ideas are generated using everyday language. The group context changes power relations between facilitator and participants and creates as less 'threatening' group environment so usually the data that emerges from group discussions is not influenced as much by the researcher than it would be in one-to-one research contexts. As a result, it may be easier for participants to disclose less socially acceptable views, and some participants may feel too intimidated to speak, whilst others may dominate.

Conditions for successful group discussions

Whilst group discussions are very natural ways of collecting data, they can also be complex, and it takes a lot of effort and thoughtful preparation to create a natural environment where people feel comfortable and free to talk. The organisation of group discussion methods therefore poses some significant practical challenges for a research team. In general, group discussions are much harder to control for the researcher than face-to-face interviews. Key to successful discussions are a very experienced group discussion facilitator and very detailed preparation and planning. A lack of preparation is likely to result in a lack of depth in the data.

An important aspect to consider from the outset is whether a dynamic group context offers an appropriate environment to collect the desired data. Very sensitive subject areas are likely to be unsuitable for group discussions, for example, although Liamputtong (2006; 2011) argues that people may feel more relaxed talking about sensitive issues in a group setting. Sabbe et al.'s (2015) research project on women's perspectives on arranged marriages in Morocco suggests that this is indeed possible.

It is also easy for a researcher to be drawn into discussions and activities and to forget that the data also needs to be recorded and collected. In his classic book on focus group research, Merton, Fiske and Kendall (1956) lists four criteria (see Box 7.1) that characterise a successful focus group discussion. Whilst the group discussion method has of course moved on and diversified since then, it is still useful advice to consider when assessing the quality of the data captured.

BOX 7.1

MERTON, FISKE AND KENDALL'S (1956) FOUR CRITERIA FOR SUCCESSFUL GROUP DISCUSSION METHODS

1 A maximum range of relevant topics should be covered.
2 The data yielded from the group discussion should be as specific as possible.
3 They should foster the interaction that explores participants' feelings in depth.
4 They should take into account the personal context that participants use in generating their responses.

In order to produce the right setting for good-quality data collection (and fulfil Merton's criteria), a suitable environment has to be created, which is (1) comfortable, (2) non-judgemental and natural, and an environment where (3) participants feel free to express their opinions (Krueger and Casey, 2009). The venue for the discussion must be accessible and neutral, have a low noise level, and it should be relatively flexible with regard to seating and space.

According to Krueger and Casey (2009), other factors that influence the success of the group discussions are: (1) a clarity of purpose, (2) the recruitment of appropriate participants, (3) the availability of sufficient resources (e.g. room hire of a suitable venue and catering, travelling expenses, stationery, incentives for participants) and (4) skilful moderators who ask effective questions.

Regarding the group's composition, a fine balance has to be struck. On the one hand, a level of homogeneity can ensure that the debate does not get out of control due to very contradictory experiences or opinions. A level of homogeneity among participants means that they are likely to be more willing to share their views honestly as they would feel supported by the views of other participants. This homogeneity can be created using different personal criteria (e.g. age, gender, ethnicity, socio-economic background, common interests or experiences, geographic location). These factors will depend on the topic of the respective project.

On the other hand, a group discussion can be very dull if participants are too similar in their perspective. A modest level of diversity is arguably equally essential to foster a debate which is likely to generate a dynamic where participants feel compelled to argue their point of view and in which dominant and subordinate group norms can come to the surface.

Liamputtong (2011) describes some skills and characteristics that good group discussion facilitators should have. She states that gender, age, status and other background characteristics of the facilitators are important ingredients that can make a big difference to whether or not a group discussion succeeds. Whilst it would be ignorant to neglect the importance of these factors, from my experience there can be a tendency to over-exaggerate their relevance to data collection. I find it easier to agree with the author that facilitators need to be 'sensitive and respectful to the needs of the participants, non-judgemental, open-minded' and that they should possess 'adequate knowledge about the subject/project' (Liamputtong, 2011: 60).

Undeniably these are general skills that any empirical researcher should be expected to bring to the table of any research project involving human participants, not just when they conduct group discussions. 'Good listening and observation skills, leadership skills and patience and flexibility' (Liamputtong, 2011: 60) are perhaps skills that are particu-larly relevant for conducting group discussions. I would also agree with Liamputtong that a degree of 'humour' is an important asset to have as a facilitator. Krueger and Casey (2009: 102) also refer to humour as a 'powerful bonding agent', but I can equally imagine that some researchers would contest that this is an essential skill required to conduct group discussions. Some topics and contexts do lend themselves more to the use of humour than others. Most children and young people love humour. If used well, and in the right circumstances, humour can break down barriers and power relations and it can lighten up discussions. In other circumstances, for example when very serious or sensitive topics are being discussed, however, it may be more appropriate to take a sober approach. Therefore, I would suggest that humour is a good tool to have and to use if the conditions are right.

Liamputtong (2011) also refers to the need to share ideas, ideals and attitudes, and occa-sionally use self-disclosures as a tool to foster a dynamic conversation. Again, in my view these are tools that need to be used sensibly. As we will see below, confidentiality is one of the most difficult issues to negotiate in group discussion contexts. So, if used sensitively and carefully, self-disclosure may increase the trust of participants in the process and in the researcher, or it may be a good ice breaker which fosters a vibrant conversation. On the other hand, self-disclosure may steer the discussion in other directions, it may encourage further self-disclosures from other participants, which may put them at undue risk.

It is important to note that group discussions are often conducted by a group of facili-tators. So, for co-facilitators, note takers or peer researchers it is of equal importance that they are well prepared for the context in which the discussion takes place.

Fern (2001) produced a very useful graphic representation of what will influence the outcome of focus groups, which I have adapted (Figure 7.1). The context factors dis-cussed above by Krueger and Casey (2009), such as the research setting and the group composition and cohesion, are mainly summarised under the heading of 'group discus-sion process' and, as Figure 7.1 shows, they do have a direct impact on the outcome of group discussions. However, in his model Fern refers also more directly to the actual communication processes that take place in group discussions; these are, of course, a crucial ingredient and can be managed only to some extent. Participants arrive with a certain social background and with a limited level of knowledge about the topic and the researcher's influence on this. In participatory approaches, it would be quite com-mon to provide information (capacity building, education) on the respective topic to the participants in the first instance before the actual discussion commences. The social background of participants can be taken into consideration only to a limited extent and some unknown factors will always remain.

However, there are also factors inherent to the group process which cannot be simply excluded or switched off. One of these Fern calls *production blocking*. This refers to the inability to listen to other people's contributions and to prepare one's own contribution at the same time. Focus group facilitators too are not exempt from the effects of production blocking. If anything it may be even harder to concentrate on what is being said by multiple participants, and at the same time facilitate the continuing discussion effectively. Both voice recording and the keeping of fieldnotes are much more testing tasks than in interviews, and they require careful planning. A useful step, for example, is to let people introduce themselves at the start of the voice recording to make it easier to identify individual contributions during transcription. It is also helpful as part of the note keeping to draw a visual representation of who is sitting where. Generally, the running of group discussions normally requires at least two facilitators, in some cases more, to capture the data.

The other important factor is called *free riding*, and this refers to some participants' tendency to pool their own thoughts with those of other contributions. This term is sometimes used to describe the behaviour of inactive participants. One of the reasons for this could be that other people have already expressed the same views that they have and there is no need to repeat this.

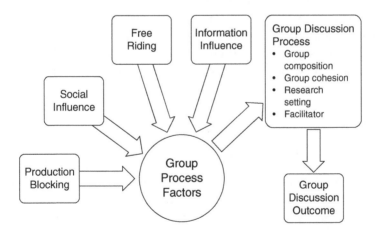

Figure 7.1 Factors that affect the group discussion process

Source: adapted from Fern (2001: 98)

Both production blocking and free riding can be partially addressed by agreeing **ground rules** with the participants on how contributions are to be made during the discussion, e.g. only one person speaks at a time, but this can ultimately create a more staged research setting, which could have detrimental effects on the dynamic and therefore the type of data generated.

Characteristics of group discussions

As discussed above, the main feature of group discussion methods is that they help us to understand how the thinking on a topic develops from a group perspective. Finch and Lewis (2003: 171) therefore describe them as 'synergistic' in the sense that the group works consciously or unconsciously together to produce data. Group discussions can therefore help us to monitor how ideas and opinions emerge in a group context and how language is used to communicate these views. This also helps us to understand how social constructions and norms play out as a part of this process.

The number of participants in group discussions is typically between five and ten people, and Krueger and Casey (2009) warn that focus groups with twelve or more people potentially create situations where participants disperse and the focus group facilitator can lose control. Whilst acknowledging this warning, there are situations where researchers may find themselves in a position where they have to deal with larger than the ideal number of participants, for example if they feel the need to accommodate gatekeepers in order to be given access to a specific target group. This can commonly be the case when existing and established groups are being utilised for the research, for example school classes or community groups, and in these situations group sizes can exceed twelve people. Researchers may find themselves having to accommodate a school by taking out a whole class for a group discussion rather than just six to ten pupils. In reality, researchers may sometimes feel under pressure to accommodate gatekeepers or may indeed have no choice but to accept less than ideal conditions if they want to collect any data at all. In these situations, the use of participatory interactive small group exercises as part of the group discussion is important as they can help researchers manage larger groups. How these activities can be incorporated into group discussions is discussed in detail below.

Uses of group discussion methods

Group discussions mirror everyday interactions where people can exchange views and opinions and are used to collect data for different purposes in multiple contexts and on a large variety of topics. As Morgan (1997: 2) points out, focus groups can be used as part of different methodological designs, namely:

1   As a self-contained method, i.e. as a principal way of collecting data.
2   As a supplementary or additional method, for example to either inform the design of a survey questionnaire or as a follow-up to explore information gathered in surveys in more detail.
3   As part of a multi-method or mixed methods study in which they are used as one of multiple primary data collection methods, for example alongside participant observation (see Chapter 6), or individual interviews.

Self-contained group discussions

There is no reason why group discussions should not be used as self-contained or self-sufficient sources of social data. However, as discussed above, it is a particular type of data that is being collected and whilst group discussions have strengths – such as the excellent way in which they can reveal group dynamics and the reasons why people think and act the way they do – methodologically they also have limitations. However, if used in combination with other methods to generalise findings they can mutually enhance each other.

Virtual focus groups

Online focus groups have emerged as a relatively new way of conducting group discussions. Many of the issues discussed here so far still apply to virtual group discussions but there are some obvious advantages and disadvantages, which Bloor et al. (2001) attempt to summarise. Virtual group discussions potentially reduce the effort and cost of organising these groups and the development of technology and software is likely to make it progressively easier, not just to link up virtually but also to communicate with younger generations who are increasingly IT literate and competent. The familiar social networking environment hosting virtual group discussions creates a more natural environment for data collection. Computer developments also mean that data can be transcribed more easily and subsequent contributions can be attributed to the correct person. So, in general, as long as the equipment works reliably, virtual group discussions have the potential to provide a high level of convenience for researchers and participants. I refrain from naming programs, platforms or apps that can be used to conduct virtual group discussions as inevitably, due to the speed of IT development, by the time this book goes to print there might be new and better products available.

Virtual group discussions also potentially enable the participation in research of people in hard to reach areas and they facilitate international encounters with significant cost savings (Abrams and Gaiser, 2017). One of the criticisms of social research is that it tends to take place in locations which are convenient to access for the researcher and virtual group discussions can counter this criticism. Bloor et al. (2001) argue that virtual discussions reduce interviewer effects although I am not so certain that this is inevitably the case. Abrams and Gaiser (2017) also feel that participants in virtual group discussions may be less inhibited than they are in face-to-face encounters but, as Bloor et al. (2001) correctly state, the higher convenience and greater reach might be outweighed by difficulties in developing the essential level of rapport with and between the participants. From the perspective of participatory researchers, for whom rapport is a crucial ingredient in a research project, this is a major concern. The other main concern in online focus groups is data security. It is almost impossible to guarantee confidentiality in the virtual world, so there are obvious limitations in relation to what projects or topics would be suitable for virtual group discussions, with sensitive and personal topics being potentially ethically problematic.

Linking group discussions with other methods of data collection

As Morgan (1997: 23) points out, 'the goal of combining research methods is to strengthen the total research project' and this is the same for any participatory project. As discussed above, group discussion methods tend to be one of the methods participants are most content with due to the nature of these discussions. They are also very flexible and can be easily combined with or incorporated into research designs based on other methods. The rationale for this can be varied.

Group discussions can be used as a method to plan participatory research projects together with participants, for example to inform the sampling and data collection methods, including theoretical sampling procedures for studies that draw on grounded theory (Glaser and Strauss, 1967; Strauss and Corbin, 2015) or social constructionist grounded theory methods (Charmaz, 2005), although the latter is not very common for participatory projects. They can be used for design and sample planning purposes at the very start, to take stock throughout the project and to undertake a preliminary analysis, or at the very end as part of data analysis.

Group discussions can easily be incorporated into fieldwork using *participant observation* (see Chapter 6). This can be done in quite an informal way, especially with very small groups of participants as part of the actual observations. This plays to the strength of group discussions in the way they foster, encourage and mimic comfortable everyday conversations.

One of the most common and fruitful ways to link group discussions is with a mixed method project incorporating *survey research*. Again, there are a variety of options for doing this depending on its purpose of the project. Group discussions would be a very suitable method to initially explore topics that will be the subject of a survey questionnaire. They can be used as part of the preliminary work on the survey design to help identify what participants are likely to know about a topic and what their attitudes and experiences are, so that survey questions can be written in a way that they will capture this in a broader population. Emerson and Lloyd (2014) have used interactive group discussions with children to develop questions for a survey on children's rights. However, alluding to the different nature and purpose of these two methods, Morgan (1997: 27) warns that using group discussions to develop survey instruments is 'not without its dangers', as isolated incidents in focus groups can have a powerful effect. Certain group members can be very dominant and may impose their views and experiences on the group. Focus group participants also tend to be more homogeneous in relation to their background and experiences than the general population, so a variety of group discussions should be used, and other pre-test mechanisms, such as survey pilots, cannot be neglected. On the other hand, group discussion can be used to explore survey findings in more depth and draw conclusions for necessary actions or interventions.

Focus groups and *one-to-one interviews* are also commonly combined, as their nature is really quite different. Interviews can, for example, help to inform the design of a group discussion guide, whilst on the other hand group discussions can equally help to inform an interview schedule. However, interviews and focus groups can also be used as complementary methods as they tend to yield different data.

Using group discussion methods within collaborative and participatory approaches

The rationale for involving co-researchers or volunteers in research projects, and the challenges to this, were discussed in Part I of this book. The flexibility of group discussion methods makes them ideal methods for participatory approaches as it is comparatively easy to involve participants actively in the running of group discussions. However, group discussions are also socially complex occasions, so Krueger and King's (1998) advice that it is sensible to have some experience in planning and conducting group discussions before attempting to involve co-researchers or community members in this is sound.

Evidence suggests that, if they are run well, people involved in participatory projects utilising group discussions profit collectively and individually from this, for example as a result of capacity building, increased confidence and the gaining of new skills and new friends. Weeks and Roberto (2003), for example, undertook a PAR study in Canada, which utilised group discussions and examined the perceived causes of falling among older women. The authors found that women who participated in group discussions took some ownership of preventing falls in their lives when the project was completed, so there were clear health benefits to this.

As detailed in the previous chapters, in collaborative, participatory approaches the aim is to maximise the different types of expertise and experience that different people bring to the project. Co-researchers or peer researchers who come from the organisations or communities where the research takes place have valuable background and context knowledge, and are often better equipped to frame questions. As Krueger and King (1998) state, collaborative studies often also have a more powerful impact. Their dynamism and versatility makes group discussion methods particularly suitable for use in participatory research projects, community-based participatory projects (see Liamputtong, 2011) or participatory action research projects. Group discussion methods lend themselves to the co-facilitation of interactive exercises, and the combination of data collection, project planning and the agreement of action or intervention.

As Liamputtong (2011) recounts, interactive group discussion methods were used historically by some of the founders and advocates of engaged and participatory methods, although they may not have used the term 'focus group' or 'group discussion'. Paulo Freire (1971) established so called 'study circles' in order to work with people from disadvantaged backgrounds and communities. Marxist and feminist activists have likewise used study circles for a similar purpose. One of the aims of these settings was always to initiate collective action to improve the position of those oppressed or marginalised in society.

Involving co-researchers in participatory group discussions

There are three main purposes for the use of group discussions in participatory research projects. Firstly, they can be used as exploratory brainstorming sessions to identify a project, determine its aims and objectives and design the project as a whole. Secondly, they can be used to explore a topic in more detail. According to Fern (2001: 5) the research purpose of exploratory group discussions includes: creating, collecting, identifying, discovering, explaining and generating thoughts, feelings and behaviours. Fern states that the purpose of exploratory group discussions is to discover all the thoughts that different people have and not just the thoughts they have in common. Thirdly, exploratory group discussions can also be used to aid the analysis of data collected for this or other projects, including focus group data itself, but also data derived from other means of data collection, such as survey data or documents.

Figure 7.2, which is adapted from Krueger and King's (1998) book on the involvement of community members in group discussion methods, is a visual representation of the different levels of participant involvement in group discussions and how this impacts on the power relations. The figure presents a continuum from researcher-led and initiated projects where the influence of the participants on the research process remains marginal, to community-led research, where the researcher has little more than an advisory status. Most participatory projects lie between the two poles.

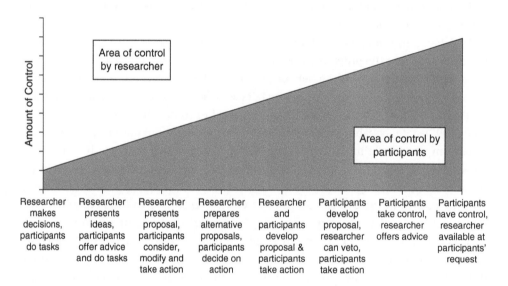

| Researcher makes decisions, participants do tasks | Researcher presents ideas, participants offer advice and do tasks | Researcher presents proposal, participants consider, modify and take action | Researcher prepares alternative proposals, participants decide on action | Researcher and participants develop proposal & participants take action | Participants develop proposal, researcher can veto, participants take action | Participants take control, researcher offers advice | Participants have control, researcher available at participants' request |

Figure 7.2   Levels of control between researchers and participants

Source: adapted from Krueger and King (1998: 3)

Running participatory group discussions

As revealed in the introduction to this chapter, one of the reasons why the focus group methodologies emerged was the desire to conduct interviews more effectively. Time-saving was one of the main motivations for choosing focus groups over one-to-one interviews. However, as Krueger and King (1998) warn, taking a collaborative approach to group discussions will ultimately take much more time than the organisation of interviews and I would reiterate this strongly. Genuine participatory approaches require that professional researchers are prepared to surrender some control to co-researchers as shown in Figure 7.2. Making this work, agreeing the roles and responsibilities, and preparing co-researchers for their roles, just takes time.

In principle, the aim of facilitators of any group discussion would be to achieve a free-flowing natural, but focused, communication. Conventional focus groups do not differ significantly from participatory group discussions in that respect. If anything, participatory approaches take a somewhat more open and less structured approach.

Organising the fieldwork requires care, regardless whether a participatory approach is taken or not. Practical arrangements in relation to the venue have to be made, participants have to be recruited, recording equipment checked, and so forth.

When working with co-researchers, they will take on some of these roles. They may, for example, recruit participants, community groups can provide the venue for the discussion and co-researchers may facilitate or co-facilitate all or part of the discussions, including interactive activities or taking notes. It is not only feasible, but appropriate and desirable to involve people with different skills and abilities in participatory research projects; however, the roles they take within these projects should play to their strengths.

When working with peer researchers or co-researchers who are not experienced in facilitating group discussions, it is really important to provide some training before group discussions are run and this should involve some practice for group discussion moderation.

Group contract

A good idea at the start of each group discussion is to establish a set of 'ground rules' or a 'group contract' with the participants – see Exercise 5.1. If the discussions take place as part of action research or CBPR or similar, an agreement or contract is likely to cover the entire project. In this case, the ground rules should cover issues such as the commitment of the research team to the study, their tasks, training, incentives and remunerations (if these are available), the research plan including budgeting requirements. A basic contract for one-off group discussions should contain some rules that the researchers agree with the participants on how the discussion should be run. This will contain important ethical agreements on issues such as confidentiality, consent, voluntary participation or protocols for disclosures, but it can also contain more practical issues, e.g. about giving feedback, or what breaks will be taken. An inherent ethical issue of group discussions is that information will be shared with the researchers *and* with other group participants as well; the implications of this need to be discussed from the outset. A good rule is also to encourage participants to be appreciative of everyone's contribution, even though one might personally disagree with this. It is important that participants have some meaningful and not tokenistic involvement in the agreement of the contract, although ultimately it is the researcher's responsibility to make sure that sensible rules are agreed.

Sampling strategies and recruitment

Sampling strategies in participatory group discussions are not fundamentally different from strategies used in traditional focus group research. The main variation is that in participatory projects, co-researchers may have insider knowledge that can help to identify participants who may otherwise be difficult to recruit. However, questions such as who is the target audience, how many groups and participants are needed to answer the questions, and how diverse these groups have to be apply as with any conventional research project using focus groups. Recruitment will often be purposive, whilst sometimes attempting maximum difference sampling techniques, with the aim of capturing as many different viewpoints as possible. Morgan proposes that the groups themselves should be reasonably homogeneous – he uses the term 'homogeneous strangers' (Morgan, 1997: 34), and he advocates a common-sense approach to sampling, which is a useful rule of thumb:

> Try asking whether these participants could easily discuss this topic in normal day-to-day interaction. Participants must feel able to talk to each other, and wide gaps in social background or lifestyle can defeat this requirement. (Morgan, 1997: 36)

Shared life experience enables participants to talk freely with each other. This is much less problematic when pre-existing or naturally occurring groups are being recruited for group discussions. As Liamputtong (2011: 39) states, 'friends and colleagues find it easier to connect to each other – this may lead to richer discussion, or to revoking of experiences that were half-forgotten'. However, the potential disadvantage of working with pre-existing groups is that they may already have discussed the research topic informally at an earlier stage. One of the potential consequences is a less detailed and less rich discussion. Established hierarchies and patterns of communication can also mean that particular views or statements which may divert from these group norms may not be vocalised.

Whether participants are recruited through face-to-face contact or other means of communication (e.g. email, phone, website) will depend on each individual project. Occasionally gatekeepers will have to give consent, such as school principals, in order to access pupils (see the example below in Figure 7.3). When planning for individual group discussions with participants who do not come from established groups, an over-recruitment (c. 25 per cent) may be advisable to offset the inevitable drop-outs. These drop-outs are likely to be significantly smaller if incentives can be offered to participants (e.g. gift vouchers, access to services), although incentives or compensations for expenses are also no guarantee that all recruited participants will actually show up.

The decision about the size of each group will be informed by a number of factors which include the purpose of the study and the complexity of the topic. As stated elsewhere in this chapter, a common position is that there should be no fewer than five and no more than twelve participants in a group discussion. However, factors such as the practicality, location and size of the venue, the nature and characteristics of participants, and the conditions set by gatekeepers are all factors that may influence the size of each group. For each project, there is a minimum and a maximum number below or beyond which it becomes simply impractical to conduct group discussions, but this number varies. In my view, a successful sampling strategy tends to be purposeful but opportunistic, as accommodating as possible towards participants and gatekeepers and flexible within the project team. Recruitment mechanisms include purposeful sampling, 'piggy-backing' other studies or services, follow-up recruitment based on previous data collection (e.g. surveys in mixed methods studies), advertisements in newspapers, posts in internet fora or chat rooms, recruitment via gatekeepers and snowball sampling.

Available resources and feasibility can be limiting factors in relation to saturation, but as Krueger and Casey (2009: 25) aptly put it, using a common-sense rather than theoretical rationale is often inevitable:

> Although theoretical saturation is a great concept and useful in academic work, as a consultant you won't land many contracts if you say you plan to conduct groups until you reach theoretical saturation.

A sampling grid can be a good tool to ensure that different views, experiences and perspectives are considered in group discussions. In participatory projects, these sampling grids can be developed and agreed with co-researchers or the community or group in which the study takes place. Figure 7.3 is an example of such a purposive sampling grid. I drafted this for a participatory mixed methods research project on the involvement of children and young people in policy making on school bullying (Schubotz et al., 2006). The sample takes account of different regional and school settings and school management types. Whilst it is in no way representative, this multiple category design reflects the diversity of the school landscape in Northern Ireland where the research took place, and it creates a variety of internally homogeneous groups (Morgan 1997: 37).

Focus group schedule and question development

One of the main planning tasks when preparing group discussions is to assess whether or not the participants are likely to be able to answer the questions asked. Overly complicated or complex issues are not really suitable for one-off group discussions. Questions should be straightforward, one-dimensional and suitable for the range of participants involved. One of the strengths of group discussion methods is that they to some extend mimic everyday language and communications, so this is good guidance for the level at which they should take place. In participatory approaches, co-researchers can help drafting questions and planning activities, and this is can be one their main contributions. Often co-researchers are familiar with, or affected by the issues discussed, so they will have a very good understanding at what level this

		School type		
		Primary	**Post-Primary**	**Special**
Belfast				
	Management Type	Catholic maintained	Voluntary grammar, (single sex male, with boarding section), predominantly Protestant intake	Catholic maintained
South Eastern				
	Management Type	Controlled	Catholic maintained secondary (single-sex female)	Controlled, primary
Southern				
	Management Type	Controlled	Controlled secondary	Controlled
North Eastern				
	Management Type	Controlled planned integrated	Voluntary grammar, predominantly Catholic intake	Alternative education provider
Western				
	Management Type	Catholic maintained	Grant maintained integrated	Controlled, post-primary

Left axis label: Education Authority and School Management Type

Figure 7.3 Purposive sampling grid for a study on school bullying

Source: Schubotz et al. (2006)

topic can be approached. A possible drawback is the risk for co-researchers to 'develop overrapport', but their responsibility as researchers can be addressed in the preparatory work and training that takes place before the actual group discussions commence.

The rule of thumb is that group discussions should last no more than 90 minutes to two hours. This can be extended if interactive activities are used and participants get a break. If participants have to travel a significant distance or from various different locations to attend the group discussion, it may well be more practical to organise one longer discussion only. Ideally, however, once the schedule exceeds four hours, one should seriously consider splitting the group discussion into two separate encounters, as poor concentration levels are likely to have an adverse effect on the group outcome. At the other extreme, group discussions in schools or with patients or youth groups may need to be limited to one hour or less if timetabling needs demand this. Again, there is no definite right or wrong, and this is something that co-researchers or community groups can advise on. Flexibility is key!

In general, participatory group discussions tend to take a less structured and a more open approach than conventional focus groups. Although this unstructured approach is not a mandatory feature of participatory group discussions, it is a common one. Part of the reason for this is that the group facilitator seeks to assume a less dominant role, so greater flexibility means greater variance between the discussions. A less structured approach potentially results in more dynamic exchanges and interactions between the facilitator and the participants and between the participants themselves. However, sometimes the schedule of interactive, participatory group discussions can be quite firm, in order to facilitate inter-group comparisons. A typical schedule of a participatory group discussion is shown in Figure 7.4.

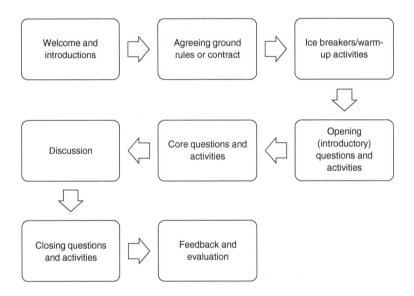

Figure 7.4 Common process and schedule of activities in group discussions

The ice-breaker activities and opening interactions are designed to develop a level of rapport between the participants and the research team. Some of the activities, including the ice breaker, may contain humorous aspects to create a relaxed and friendly atmosphere. The core questions and activities address the main topic and are usually designed to look at different aspects of this. The discussion and closing activities are geared towards generating main findings. It is at this point that participatory designs are most similar to conventional focus groups. The discussion allows the facilitator to ask participants probing and specifying questions, to follow up what has been communi-cated before and to invite interpretations from contributions from interactive activities conducted during the discussion. The feedback and evaluation should contain options for both group and individual feedback. This affords the less dominant participants an opportunity to make a contribution, if they have not done so before. It also allows for more sensitive and confidential issues to be raised privately. An example of a detailed interactive group discussion schedule can be found in Exercise 7.2.

Participatory and interactive activities in group discussions

The range of interactive group activities that can be embedded into group discussions is vast. The main purpose of these activities is to stimulate and encourage debate and discussion. Often group discussions start with ice breakers that do not necessarily generate relevant data but are designed to get people talking, to create a relaxed atmosphere or to help strangers to get to know each other before the actual discussion starts. Chambers (2002) provides a long list of various dynamic activities for participatory workshops and research. Other examples of interactive activities designed to support data collection include: the elicitation of views and experiences using photos or videos; vignettes; drama performances and role play; newspaper or magazine clippings, or everyday articles. Other activities to consider are anonymous voting, item sorting activities (e.g. Q Methodology), graffiti wall or walking decisions. Exercise 7.2 gives an example of a schedule for a participatory interactive group discussion and some of these activities are included in more detail there.

Photovoice, for example (e.g. Streng et al., 2004; Gant et al., 2009), is a visual method where participants take photographs which represent their understanding and meaning of the aspects of life under investigation and these photographs are then used as the basis for discussion. Often Photovoice is used with participants who find it difficult or unable to communicate verbally about a topic, for example people with intellectual disabilities (Povee, Bishop and Roberts, 2014) – see also the discussion of this and more examples in Chapter 3.

Other activities include the production of drawings and collages, educative activities, such as sharing information and statistics, for example on health-related matters, or other types of small group work. Views and opinions on issues can be written on sticky notes and pinned to graffiti walls or maps, or the room can be divided into areas which signify agreement or disagreement with statements or opinions and participants can be asked to walk to these different points in the room to indicate whether or not they agree with statements or viewpoints.

Although the facilitation of discussion and discourse is the primary aim of these interactive activities they also have other benefits. Usually not all participants in group discussions are equally engaged or able to verbalise their thoughts and activities like this provide opportunities for the quieter participants to express their views and, by doing so, shift the power relations between group members. Making collages or drawing can provide alternative ways of expression that suit participants who otherwise would be reserved. Some of these activities also break the group up into smaller groups which again can lead to some participants making contributions who in the larger context might not.

When faced with very large groups, for example school classes or existing community groups, small group activities facilitate a process where more participants can be involved in the process of knowledge generation than would be typical for traditional focus group designs.

The final advantage of these activities is that some of them produce data that the facilitator does not need to record separately. This frees up the facilitator to concentrate more on the content of the discussion. The accurate recording of data in focus groups is perhaps one of the hardest parts of group discussion methods and any support in this is very helpful. In one example from a project we undertook on behalf of the British Council (Schubotz and McCartan, 2016) on the internationalisation aspirations of young people, we asked participants to put stickers on a large world map to indicate where they had already travelled and asked them what the purpose of that journey was and where they could imagine living in future. It was very easy to take a photo of these maps with their stickers and they gave a good representation of young people's travelling experiences. The same would apply to drawings, collages, work sheets and even notes made on sticky notes that can then be taken away as data.

Stewart and Shamdasani (2015) also describe whole group discussion methods which differ from traditional focus group settings and some of these are also very suitable for participatory projects, for example brainstorming, synectics, and what they call 'leaderless discussion groups'.

Brainstorming is a very familiar method and does not require formal moderation throughout the discussion although differences are made between unguided and guided brainstorming. It is supposed to be a free-flowing creative activity during which participants explore solutions to particular questions. In practice, brainstorming hardly works without some guidance or leadership from someone who takes control over the process, including the timing and the conclusion of this. Most brainstorming sessions are therefore facilitated and guided. Ideally, participants should not feel constrained by specific conditions or perhaps a status quo, which makes brainstorming a very suitable method for participatory approaches, especially at the start of a project when research issues and questions are being distilled.

Synectics is a closer match with original focus group design. It is basically a facilitated brainstorming session and this is perhaps what we have come to associate with the term 'brainstorming'. Synectics is a technique that originated in business organisations and market research, but is also increasingly used in community organisations. According to Stewart and Shamdasani (2015), the five basic underlying principles of synectics are:

1   *Deferment* – looking for viewpoints and perceptions first before looking for solutions.
2   *Autonomy* – let the object of discussion take on its own life without setting boundaries at first.
3   *Use of commonplace* – trying to use the familiar as a way of gaining perspective on the strange.

4   *Involvement/detachment* – alternating between the general and the specific.
5   *Use of metaphors* – analogies.

In *leaderless discussion groups* the group is given a task to solve or questions to answer but the researcher does not facilitate this process. Instead, the researcher observes how the group solves the problem and how the group dynamic of this process unfolds. Again this is a useful technique that can be adapted to participatory group discussion methods, for example small group activities within a group discussion.

Facilitation challenges

Group discussion methods entail facilitation challenges that are inevitably much more complex than those for one-to-one research encounters. When organising groups, multiple needs and requirements that participants may have need to be considered. This is easier in existing group contexts, for example when regular meeting points and times can be used for a group discussion; however, established groups themselves pose other challenges related to their existing group dynamic or hierarchy which can be inhibiting for some participants. Managing the group dynamic is in my view and experience the single most important challenge in a group discussion. This includes different aspects, such as: restraining dominant participants whilst encouraging those who are reserved; reminding participants that *all* views are invited, whilst equally assuring that the discussion contributions are always respectful towards other views; making sure that contributions are not cut short whilst at the same time monitoring time and preventing people from rambling or getting distracted. Finally, the recording of information poses challenges, and technical equipment that works perfectly well for one-to-one interviews will often not suffice for group discussions. Specialised equipment or several recording devices may be required; however, if the group discussion contains interactive activities where participants move around or work in smaller groups, voice recording may not produce the desired results.

Types of participants

One issue that deserves special attention and needs to be addressed in groups with an existing group membership, but occasionally also with new groups, is that some participants may be very domineering. They may impose their own views on other group participants, intimidate them and inhibit others from expressing their own, alternative views. In established group settings, for example in community groups or youth groups, this is more likely to be the case. However, even if participants don't know each other, there is always the likelihood that some participants will find it easier than others to verbalise their views and experiences whilst others will tend to be quiet. On the one hand, very vocal participants can be vital in getting a group discussion started; on the other hand, they it may negatively affect the group dynamic and the outcome of the research overall. Macnaghten and Myers (2004: 69) describe as 'moderators' worst memories' situations where 'participants of a focus group saw themselves representing some group that is under threat in some way'.

Managing difficult, shy or unco-operative participants can be equally difficult although it may be a less common issue. Generally, participants have to consent to taking part in group discussions and, if they are failing to contribute anything meaningful, the facilitator should offer the option of withdrawal from the project without any consequences attached. It is possible that participants sign up for group discussions if incentives are on offer, although the modest incentives that are typically available are usually not the only reason why people take part in research.

Liamputtong (2006) describes in detail the challenges of doing research projects with vulnerable people, hidden populations or those at the margins of society (e.g. children and young people, people with dementia, sex workers, ethnic minorities, refugees, the homeless or people with disabilities). Whilst this is a challenge throughout all parts of the research process, it is one of the achievements of participatory approaches that they have been reasonably successful in giving a voice to such groups and communities.

Ethical issues in participatory group discussions

Group discussion methods come with a set of very particular ethical challenges in addition to the general issues already discussed in Chapter 4. The main challenge is that group discussions involve more than one participant at a time, and this ultimately creates limitations for confidentiality. Essentially, if personal information is revealed and discussed this does not just happen in front of the researcher who is professionally obliged to keep information confidential, but also in front of other participants who may not be tied to a professional code of conduct with regard to data security and information. Normally, research participants can expect that their right to confidentiality is respected and that what is being said during group discussions is not repeated outside of the group context. Realistically, in group discussions this is almost impossible to guarantee.

Some people feel uncomfortable discussing issues in a group setting and are naturally reluctant to share personal information, whilst other people may be less shy. However, if personal or sensitive information is shared, participants may later regret giving this information. If personal or intimate details are being revealed in public, this can also be to the disadvantage of individuals or whole communities. Even within established groups or among participants from close-knit communities things may be said about other people which may affect the relationships within these established groups or institutional settings.

The best way to tackle ethical issues in group discussions is to raise awareness about the implications of doing research in a group from the onset of the study and to provide contact and helpline numbers to participants in case they want to discuss some issues that affect them. There are effective learning activities available which can be incorporated into training programmes to help raise awareness among participants about confidentiality (see Exercise 4.2 for this). However, ultimately the only solution is to state very clearly that confidentiality can only be upheld if every participant plays his or her part in this. This is harder to do in one-off group discussions where there is little time to explore issues around confidentiality and anonymity. In participatory and action research projects, where regular meetings and relationship building are an integral part of the research, this should be routine. However, although it may not be very common for disclosures to be made, there is just no guarantee that it does not happen, regardless of how 'innocent' or benign the subject area appears to be. If disclosures are made about past or present abusive relationships, the default course of action for the researcher, in countries where research is regulated through strict ethical procedures, is to explore whether this has been reported or dealt with and, if not, to support the participant in doing this. Again, awareness of this should be raised from the outset and should ideally be covered in the research contract with the participants. Good practice would be to have a distress protocol in place for research projects which deals with sensitive subjects or vulnerable people. Liamputtong (2006; 2011) argues that focus groups are a good method to discuss sensitive topics because they reduce the power imbalance between the researcher and the participants who may therefore feel more relaxed about talking about these issues. A good example for this may be group discussions with young people about sexual health-related issues, who may enjoy being given an opportunity to discuss among their friends what is often construed as an awkward topic (Wellings, Branigan and Mitchell, 2000; Schubotz, Rolston and Simpson, 2004). Another study is that of Jordan et al. (2007) about nursing during violent conflicts, however, ultimately, it is important to recognise that not all topics are suitable for group discussions, and very sensitive, personal subject areas which may potentially involve disclosures are perhaps better researched using one-to-one interviews.

In principle, smaller groups are better to manage than larger ones so it is easier to monitor respondents' stress and comfort levels. In larger groups, there must be enough facilitators present that individual group members can be withdrawn from the discussion if stressful situations arise.

Ultimately, the researchers must prioritise participants' safety over academic curiosity. This may mean that quotes and contributions from group participants are not used, regardless of how insightful or important they seem for the research project, if there is a chance that this puts participants at risk. Providing individual feedback options after the group discussions and generous cooling-off periods during which participants can withdraw their consent to participate, as well as organising debriefing sessions, could all be part of an ethics package for group discussions. In general, of course, group discussions tend to pass as positive events for researchers and participants, but good practice is to prepare for the occasions where this may not be the case.

Analysing group discussion data

How group discussion data is analysed is largely determined by the aims and objectives of the research in general and the use of group discussions within it in particular. As alluded to above, group discussions can take place at different stages of a project and with varied rationales. For example, if they are used as part of a mixed methods project in order to inform the design of a study, to define its aims and objectives or to establish a research plan, then the analysis of the data is often part of the discussion itself. A group discussion may then quite likely end with the group agreeing a rationale for the research, or research aims or questions, and further analysis is largely unnecessary. The approach to data analysis would be completely different in research projects where group discussion methods are used as the only or main data collection instruments. In that case, the analysis of data from group discussion material, broadly speaking, follows the principles of qualitative text or content analysis, as described by Strauss and Corbin (2015), Coffey and Atkinson (1996) or Huberman and Miles (1994) for example, although the group dynamic as the core ingredient of the group discussions must be considered.

The basic rule is that group discussions produce group data. Thus, core to the analysis of group discussion data is to recognise that three levels of analysis – individual level, group level and group dynamic – have to be integrated. The contributions that participants make in a group discussion context must be understood and analysed with that context in mind. Extracting individual quotes without considering the context in which these contributions were made would be ignoring the complexity of the group dynamic and the environment in which the contribution was made. Potentially this can lead to a misinterpretation of the data.

A good way of taking account of the group dynamic when analysing the data is the knowledge mapping approach (Pelz, Schmitt and Meis, 2004). Knowledge mapping is essentially a simple, but effective, visualisation tool which can help to categorise contributions made during conversations and discourses, as Figure 7.5 illustrates. The figure represents a simple knowledge map on the basis of one hypothetical question. In this case, three arguments are being made by eight different contributors. An analysis like this for a whole group discussion eventually makes group dynamics visible, similar to sociograms. For example, two participants could always disagree with each other, or one participant may emerge as the person who dominates the discourse overall in relation to how often a contribution is being made, and in terms of the weight it carries. Were there dominant and less dominant participants? Did the opinions expressed by these participants vary significantly? But also: were the questions by the facilitator leading? Did this result in socially accepted opinions and norms being expressed and were honest opinions perhaps suppressed?

The knowledge mapping analysis usually takes place after the completion of the group discussion on the basis of fieldnotes or transcripts. Alternatively, however, a simple knowledge map, which records the main arguments and counter-arguments can be kept whilst a discussion takes place. The condition for this would be that a facilitator or co-facilitator writes down the gist of the contributions immediately. This could happen on a flip chart or white board, for example. This approach to knowledge mapping is perhaps more appropriate during brainstorming discussions, for example when a group wants to decide about the next steps in a research project.

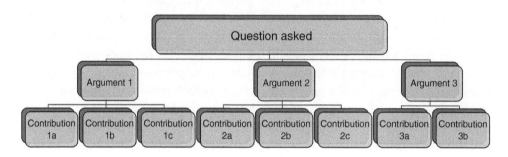

Figure 7.5 Knowledge mapping

Analysing group discussions as social enactments

Halkier (2010) describes how group discussions can be understood as social enactments and she offers four useful theoretical frameworks for their analysis, namely: Goffman-inspired interaction analysis; Garfinkel-inspired conversation analysis; discourse psychology; and positioning theory. The aim of this is to integrate the analysis of group interaction with content analysis.

Interaction analysis is based on the notion of the performative nature of social life in general and people's self-narratives in particular. So, the assumption is that people's interactions with others in everyday life are strategic communication encounters. Conversations can then be seen as social rituals which are based on silent assumptions about oneself and others. Phrases like 'I think we all know that ...' or 'I think most people would agree that ...' are indicative of such strategic communications which assume certain social norms, but are also designed to assume commonalities where they may not exist. Once someone has voiced an opinion in a way that assumes it is a majority view, it is much harder for another contributor to disagree with this and to offer a different perspective.

For conversation analysis on the other hand, in addition to *what* is being said, it is important in what way the social setting is organised. For example, in a heteronormative group discussion environment, it is likely to be much harder for someone who identifies as non-heterosexual to share views and experiences. This reminds us of the need to carefully choose, if this is possible, how the membership of a group is constituted. A very homogeneous group is likely to result in similar and less controversial responses. The venue, too, is of equal importance to conversation analysis. Group discussions about school experiences are likely to have a very different outcome if these take place in school – perhaps even with a teacher sitting at the back of the room.

According to Halkier (2010: 80), discourse psychology goes beyond conversation analysis in that it is 'interested in analysing how situational interaction draws upon but also negotiates, moderates and changes the larger discursive repertoires'. As already alluded to above when introducing knowledge mapping, discourse psychology is interested in how participants use strategies in conversations to present personal experiences and narratives or personal norms as fact, for example by stating, 'This is how things are'. Over-generalisations like that are very common in everyday conversations and their use in group discussion contexts helps us to understand how social norms are affecting people in certain contexts.

Finally, positioning analysis is concerned with contextual conditions and space for performance and multiple self-positionings in relation to other participants' views, but also perceived social norms. Again, the knowledge mapping analysis style above provides a good basis to capture these positionings.

Participatory approach to the analysis of group data

Krueger and King (1998) usefully differentiate between four levels of co-researcher involvement in the analysis of empirical data. At the basic level, a minimal involvement requires co-researchers to comment on the data analysis and research reports. The second level affords co-researchers some control in the data analysis; for example, they may take part in group analysis sessions. At a third level, where co-researchers are likely to have conducted at least parts of the group discussions themselves, they can take a more active role in writing up and analysing fieldnotes. At this level co-researchers will have received some research methods training on how to do this.

At the fourth level, the projects are likely to be participatory action research projects or community-based participatory research projects, where communities or organisations assume the main responsibility for the direction of a research project. At this level, academic researchers may just provide guidance and assistance in the data analysis to the community researchers.

In any of these cases, the analysis of group discussion data is likely to start with the writing up of fieldnotes, observations, memos, some transcripts and activity worksheets, etc. for the purpose of the production of a summary report for each discussion. The more structured the various discussion schedules are, the more scope there is to produce comparative reports which will address inter-group and within-group comparisons, also accounting for the various group facilitation styles and variations in the groups' composition. More detailed analysis usually follows the production of the summary reports. If there are detailed transcripts, they will be analysed following the mechanisms of qualitative thematic or content analysis. Throughout this process the research team must remember that it is the group and not the individual which is the main unit of analysis.

Group discussion methods are not really quantitative methods of data collection and there are much better methods that can deal with the quantification of issues. However, there is a limited remit for quantification, when it comes to decision-making processes or particular interactive activities, such as walking decisions (see group discussion schedule below).

Software packages for computer-assisted qualitative data analysis (CAQDAS), such as QSR NVivo or Atlas/ti, can be useful for the management of data as they allow for data linkage with documents, word searches, coding, and provide data visualisation tools, such as word clouds or tree nodes. In the context of a participatory project, where co-researchers are only marginally involved in the data analysis, this can work well as they can be presented with print-outs from the software packages. However, if co-researchers are more fundamentally involved in the data analysis, flip charts and markers, paper and pen, scissors and glue are probably more useful tools.

Findings can be translated into different outputs and multiple reporting strategies tailored to different audiences are common. These include oral presentations, written reports and summary reports, policy briefing papers, roundtables, dramatisations and videos, posters and websites, to name but a few.

Summary

As I have demonstrated, group discussion methods are a versatile and dynamic mechanism that allows us to collect data from a diverse range of participants. They are an ideal vehicle for interactive work with a large variety of groups and well suited for participatory projects. Group discussions are the closest equivalent to everyday conversations. Participants will be used to the group dynamic that can arise when discussing any topics in small groups, which is an activity that most people undertake most days. Group discussions can be adapted to suit different topics, different sizes of groups and explorative data collections as well as more strategic planning meetings. They provide therefore various opportunities for the involvement of community groups and co-researchers.

FURTHER READING

Chambers, R. (2002). *Participatory Workshops: A Sourcebook of 21 Sets of Ideas & Activities*. London: Earthscan.

Krueger, R. A. and Casey, M. A. (2015). *Focus Groups: A Practical Guide for Applied Research* (5th edition). London: Sage

Krueger, R. A. and King, J. A. (1998). *Involving Community Members in Focus Groups*. Focus Group Kit 5. Thousand Oaks: Sage.

Liamputtong, P. (2011). *Focus Group Methodology: Principles and Practice*. London: Sage.

ICE BREAKER – WHAT WORDS DO YOU USE?

Ice-breaker activities are very important in participatory and collaborative research, as they contribute to team building. Even if the research is undertaken within an existing institution or organisation with an established group dynamic, it is important to incorporate ice breaker or warm-up activities which sensitise participants for the research topic. One of the initial tasks is, for example, to agree a vocabulary that participants and researchers are comfortable and familiar with, and the activity suggested here is a good example on how to do this. This is a really good activity at the start of a group discussion as it 'kills two birds with one stone'.

Here we are focusing on sensitive topics where people tend to use slang in order to avoid 'technical' or 'official' terms, so they just talk 'around' an issues. I have used this activity in interactive group discussions that I undertook as part of my own sexual health research with young people. Often young people use slang words for body parts (e.g. vagina, breasts, penis), but also for sexual practices and preferences (e.g. oral or anal sex).

Ask participants to call out as many names they use as possible for a certain behaviour or body part and so forth. Write these down on a flip-chart sheet or board for everyone to see. Encourage people's competitive nature and ask participants to come up with as many terms as they can think of, and ask them specifically to include terms that they may deem colloquial, rude or inappropriate. This works best when done in a light-hearted way, which it is likely to result in some laughter, but it may also cause some embarrassment and tension.

When all terms and phrases are called out, agree with the participants those terms that are acceptable to use and the context(s) in which these are okay to use. For example, some terms may be okay in internal team discussions, but not in presentations or publications. Make sure that all participants feel happy to agree these terms and do not feel that these are derogatory towards themselves or others.

DESIGNING A PARTICIPATORY GROUP DISCUSSION SCHEDULE

Below is a schedule of a participatory project that utilised interactive group discussion methods (NCB NI and ARK YLT, 2010). The study focused on attitudes among young people to minority ethnic groups. Think about other interactive activities that can be meaningfully incorporated into this schedule to explore this topic with children and young people.

(Continued)

ATTITUDES TO DIFFERENCE: YOUNG PEOPLE AND MINORITY ETHNIC GROUPS

GROUP DISCUSSION SCHEDULE

Background Information

School: _____

No. of pupils (f/m) participating: _____

Date and time of discussion: _____

Facilitator 1 (F1): _____ Facilitator 2 (F2): _____

Young Researcher 1 (YR1): _____ Young Researcher 2 (YR2): _____

Schedule and responsibilities

Activity	Duration	Facilitators	Fieldnotes
Introduction + definition	10–15 min	F1	F2, YR1, YR2
Ground rules	10 min	YR1, F1	F2, YR2
Graffiti wall	10–15 min	YR1, F1	F2, YR2
Personal circle	10–15 min	YR1, F1	F2, YR2
Walking decisions	15–20 min	YR2, F2	F1, YR1
Revisiting graffiti wall	10–15 min	YR2, F2	F1, YR1
Feedback	5–10 min	YR2, F2	F1, YR1
1-2-1 interviews*	2 x 10–15 min	YR1, YR2	YR1, YR2

* If appropriate (i.e. if young people from minority ethnic backgrounds take part in discussions), interviews are to take place parallel with the last two activities. We need a maximum of four volunteers, and each YR will interview two minority ethnic pupils for 10–15 min each. In this case, F1/F2 *only* to facilitate/record graffiti wall and feedback activities with remaining pupils. YR to give each interviewee record card for feedback after interview, to make sure they complete one card as well.

Introduction (10–15 min)

Purpose: Introduction, defining subject area.

Material needed: Flip chart, markers, blue tack.

How it works:

Facilitators introduce themselves and explain briefly the aim and objectives of the research.

1   Ask participants if they know why they are here and how they were selected for the discussion.
2   Ask participants if they have ever taken part in a research project/group discussion in school before.

3   Tell participants about the project and include information on organisations involved, funder, number of schools involved and about our approach of working with young co-researchers.
4   Say that the purpose is to directly inform government policy making on these issues.
5   Ask participants what they think minority ethnic groups are and if they have ever talked about this in school or elsewhere?

At this point establish a definition of minority ethnic group – hopefully completely based on responses of young people. Do this by asking things like:

Do you think Travellers are a minority ethnic group?
Do you think Catholics/Protestants are a minority ethnic group? Etc.

We are interested in three groups:

a)   Migrant workers (people who came to the UK to seek work).
b)   People whose ethnic origins lie outside the UK or Ireland, regardless of whether or not they have lived here all their life (e.g. people with Chinese, Pakistani, Indian background).
c)   Irish Travellers.

Record the agreed definition on a flip chart and display.

Ground rules (10 min)

Purpose: Setting agenda and framework for discussions.

Material needed: Flip chart, markers.

How it works:

Explain that this will form the terms of reference/contract for the day to which everyone adheres.

1   Start off by making a suggestion yourself, e.g. on confidentiality.
2   Ask other YR or researchers to make another suggestion.
3   Then ask pupils ...
4   Record all of this on flip chart.

Ground rules should include the following issues:

•   Confidentiality and anonymity.
•   Right to withdraw consent at any time.
•   Respect for each other's opinions.
•   No right or wrong answers – just opinions/experiences.
•   Truthfulness since research would be worthless otherwise.
•   Participants' right to receive feedback.
•   Practical arrangements, e.g. break times (if any).

(Continued)

Activity 1: Graffiti wall (10–15 min)

Purpose: To collect initial thoughts about living in multi-ethnic society. To collate initial thoughts and views from participants on living in a multi-ethnic society.

Material needed: Coloured Post-it notes (two different colours), graffiti wall decoration, blue tack and/or masking tape to attach to 'wall', pens/pencils.

How it works:

1   Hand out two Post-it notes per person, one colour each.
2   Ask participants to write on one Post-it note one good thing/advantage that comes to their mind when they think about 'living in a multi-ethnic society'. One the other Post-it note they write one bad thing/disadvantage about living in a multi-ethnic society. Make sure that people do *not* write their names on these notes.
3   Ask students to attach their notes onto the respective graffiti walls.
4   Whilst they are writing, explain that during the group discussion they can add more notes with good things/bad things to the wall.
5   We will revisit the notes at the end of the group discussion.

Activity 2: Personal circle (15–20 min)

Purpose: To establish the level and nature of contact that participants have with (young) people from other ethnic backgrounds.

Material needed: Worksheets, printed off in two different colours – one for males, one for females, pens/pencils.

How it works:

1   Participants are separated into pairs and given a personal circle worksheet each with themselves ('Me') in the middle. Give males and females differently coloured sheets and remind them that we don't want names on the sheets.
2   Ask participants to write the initials of 20 people (max.) in their circles, depending on where they think they belong. We would want at least one name in each circle.
3   After 5–7 minutes ask participants to circle those names of people who have a different ethnic background from themselves and to discuss this briefly in pairs.
4   After 10 minutes ask for a feedback from the whole group.
5   In the feedback round, ask participants to discuss how many contacts/friends they have from the same background and how many of other backgrounds, and why this may be.

Ask some participants questions like this:

•   Can you tell me about one person that you have put in the red/yellow/green circle, please. How did you meet this person?

- Is there anyone in your circle who has a different ethnic background from you? What part of the circle is she/he in? How did you meet her/him?
- Ask why some people may have people from other ethnic backgrounds in the circle whilst others don't and why this may be.

Finally, collect the worksheets.

Activity 3: Walking decisions (15–20 min)

Purpose: To encourage discussion about attitudes held by young people about minority ethnic and ethnic mixing.

Material needed: One worksheet each with statements for facilitators and young researchers; pieces of paper representing the choices (Agree, Disagree, Not sure); timer (egg timer or mobile phone app).

How it works:

Each end of the room represents polar opposites of a continuum ranging from 'Agree' to 'Disagree'. A middle point in this imaginary continuum represents 'Not sure'. Up to 10, but at least the first 6 statements are read aloud by one of the Facilitators, and young people are asked to walk to the point in the room according to whether they agreed, disagreed or weren't sure about specific statements. After that ask for comments and views (2–3 minutes for each statement).

Note: Explain that these are genuine statements taken from a survey of 16-year-olds.

1. 'The sectarian hatred is now being directed towards minority ethnic communities, especially foreign workers coming into the UK.'
2. 'A lot of local jobs are being taken by other ethnic groups, which is unfair to locals.'
3. 'There's a lot to be learned from other races and religions. It's fascinating, not intimidating.'
4. 'People are very wary of other races because of the terrorism in mainland UK.'
5. 'At the moment I feel there is little chance of being able to become friends with people of different races and religions unless they attend your school.'
6. 'It doesn't matter what colour, creed or religion you are. Everyone is the same underneath.'
7. 'I don't mind working alongside people of different race and religion but I don't want to work with people that are racist or sectarian.'
8. 'All the foreigners should get out of the UK and go back to where they come from.'
9. 'I think people should be able to get on, no matter what religion/race they are.'
10. 'I think we should understand that those from different minority ethnic communities are not as well off as ourselves and need help to find jobs and support in this country to provide enough money for their family.'

(Continued)

Activity 4: Revisiting the graffiti wall (10–15 min)

Purpose: The collated initial views from participants expressed on the posted notes at the start of the group discussion should be discussed at this point. Participants sit in circle (or class room style arrangement, if necessary).

Material needed: no new material, but Post-it notes from Activity 1.

How it works:

1. Facilitators have collated information from the graffiti wall during the discussion, typically during the break.
2. They now read out some of the statements made. Participants are asked whether or not these issues had been discussed during the discussion or if they want to discuss, clarify or comment on these now.

Feedback (10–15 min)

Purpose: To evaluate the discussion and collect further opinions and views, to round up the discussion and thank pupils for participating.

Material needed: Pens, record cards.

How it works:

1. Thank participants for their input.
2. Remind participants about further steps in the research project and when the results will be out. Give them contact details in case anyone wants to get in touch with us.
3. Have a 10-minute feedback round and invite participants to express openly their feelings about how the group discussion went and if there is anything they would like to add.
4. Hand out one index card to each participant and ask them to write a brief comment on how they felt the discussion went on one side of card. One the other side of the card, ask them to write a personal key message in relation to the subject area. Say that this is something we want to do on a personal and private basis. No names, please!
5. Collect the cards.

8

PARTICIPATORY SURVEY METHODS

What you will learn

In this chapter I will discuss surveys, which are often regarded as the least likely method of data collection to include participatory elements. I will connect this to the perceived need of standardisation, to positivist approaches and laboratory-type 'testing'. However, I will argue that there are pros *and* cons of increasing participation in the design of surveys and in the collection and analysis of survey data. I will deal with the issue of statistical data analysis and to what extent it would be meaningful to take a participatory approach to this.

Introduction

This chapter explores how surveys can be used in participatory and collaborative research projects and which participatory mechanisms can be incorporated into the survey design, fieldwork and data analysis itself.

Surveys are one of the oldest and still most commonly used instruments in research and policy making. They are chiefly a means of collecting information systematically from a sample of respondents – usually individuals, although it can be entire households, groups of individuals, institutions or organisations – in order to generate quantifiable information of the matter under investigation. Censuses – a unique survey type – go back to biblical times.

Surveys with systematic and probability sampling procedures are a more recent development but have been used since societies started to systematically record population statistics. The development of systematic survey methodology and practice coincided with the emergence of welfare states, as did the rise in systematic evaluation methods. The systematic collection of data was required to develop and evaluate welfare state interventions.

Surveys are used to establish key population statistics, economic indicators, such as unemployment rates and economic growth, educational achievements and health outcomes, but also political preferences. They help to make sense of economic, political and social trends and they are used to evaluate all kinds of services. Surveys are designed with the aim of understanding and/or solving societal problems and, in order to do this, survey data is collected at all levels from the micro to the macro. Thus, as Groves et al. (2009: 3) put it: 'In a very real way, surveys are a crucial building block in a modern information-based society.'

Initially most surveys used a single, cross-sectional design (Wolf et al., 2016), whilst repeated cross-sectional surveys – sometimes with the development of time series, international surveys and longitudinal or panel surveys – developed much later and depended on significant resources in order to administer and maintain these survey programmes. Surveys these days can incorporate the collection of para-data, for example bio-markers, such as blood or saliva samples in health surveys. The British National Survey of Sexual Attitudes and Lifestyles (NATSAL), for example, tested survey respondents for sexually transmitted infections (STIs) (Erens et al., 2014). There are also increasing attempts to link survey data with administrative datasets, for example employment, education or health data (e.g. March, 2017). This can prevent the duplication of data collection and it certainly widens the scope of the survey data analysis, facilitating multi-level analyses.

The survey modes, i.e. the way they are administered, have also changed and diversified over time. When surveys first emerged as research instruments, the fieldwork consisted ultimately of face-to-face or door-to-door interviewing. Sampling, i.e. the selection of participants, was often not done systematically but purely opportunistically and the data analysis was basic and done by hand. With the increase of literacy among the population and the wider availability of paper and mail services, postal surveys became a feasible mode. Later, the development of communication technology and the expansion of phone networks led to the emergence of telephone surveys, whilst much more recently the computer and information technology has eventually resulted in the diversity of survey research that we see today (see Figure 8.1).

Now, all parts of the survey fieldwork from the design to data collection, processing and analysis, and dissemination have been computerised. Software packages that facilitate survey analysis, such as SPSS (originally an abbreviation for Statistical Package for Social Sciences), STATA, SAS, and recently R have been developed since the late 1960s and have increased in diversity and availability with technological developments and computer calculation power. It could be argued that survey methodology, which in the past was heavily reliant on academic expertise and capacity, has been democratised. Whilst face-to-face and paper-and-pen surveys still exist and have their merits, surveys can now be administered remotely in virtually all parts of the world using computer

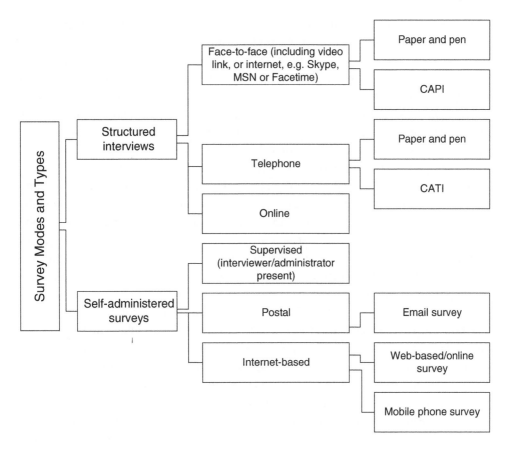

Figure 8.1 Survey modes and types

and mobile technology. Data entry is instant on remote servers as respondents answer survey questions. Analysing results can now basically be done from home or anywhere as long as there is internet access. This has created many opportunities for collaboration and participation by non-academics, although it cannot hide the fact that the construction of a good survey questionnaire, no matter how short, is a bit of an art (Payne, 1951).

I will now discuss the use of surveys as a tool in decision-making processes and some of the theoretical perspectives of survey research before I reflect on how participatory and collaborative processes can be embedded in the design of surveys and the analysis of survey results.

The survey as a tool in social research and the policy-making process

Although surveys are not without criticism, as a social research instrument, they are considered to be robust, rigorous tools. This is, in part, due to the fact that surveys enable researchers to capture data from a larger population than most qualitative research methods can. Many people find research results derived from larger and more diverse samples more convincing and trustworthy than findings based on smaller convenience samples and interpretive analysis. I am not going to rehearse the arguments for and against surveys here, I am simply making the point that their strength as a research tool may explain why they remain a popular instrument. One of the attractions of surveys is that they can help simplify cause–benefit associations on a macro-level. Policy indicators are therefore often developed and routinely monitored using regularly collected survey data. The assumption is that in order to make informed decisions about policy and practice, data from a large number of randomly selected participants need to be collected, and standardised surveys with generalisable outcomes and results have the capacity to deliver such data within an affordable budget. Equally, surveys are the most appropriate instrument to capture the attitudes, values and experiences of large population groups. Thus, surveys can be used descriptively, to explore particular issues and themes, or in an explanatory way, i.e. to test or develop theories and relationships.

Systematic approaches to the collection, review and analysis of evidence form the backbone to welfare state interventions in many, if not all, policy arenas, and surveys are at the core of these policy processes. Significant investments have been made by governments in many countries, but also cross-nationally, into large-scale longitudinal or cross-sectional survey programmes to aide their decision-making processes. However, surveys are also widely used in one-off projects in a large variety of fields, including health and health inequalities, education, farming, international development and employment. The use of surveys is often favoured due to the desire to access as many participants as possible within a reasonable budget, as well as the ability to collect comparable – ideally generalisable – information.

A typical model of the survey research process, which in the academic world commonly follows an objectivist approach, can be seen in Figure 8.2.

In an applied research context outside academia, the purpose of surveys is not typically to generate or test a theory or abstract hypothesis, but simply to assess the prevalence of a particular issue or capture the views and experiences of a community or neighbourhood. Rather than 'agreeing an underlying theory' and the related hypothesis, the first two steps in survey research in a practical context may be better described as 'Identifying the issue' and 'Agreeing the question focus/foci'. Nonetheless, even in a non-academic context, survey researchers are commonly interested in being able to make generalisable statements about their study population and this requires that surveys are standardised research instruments; i.e. everyone in a sample is asked the same questions and in the same order. This is also meant to reduce interviewer bias, as *how* a respondent answers survey questions should ideally not depend on *who* is administering the survey, when and in what circumstances. In fact, survey researchers go to great length to ensure that the way a question is worded and how answer options are presented do not influence the survey results.

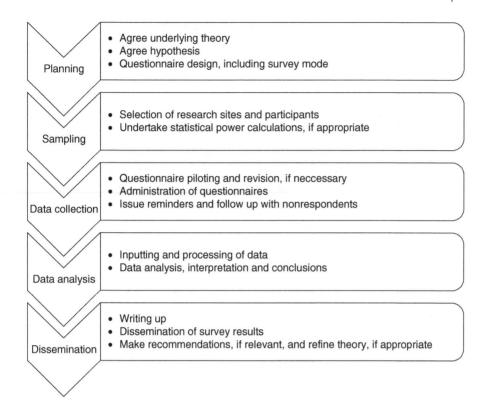

Planning
- Agree underlying theory
- Agree hypothesis
- Questionnaire design, including survey mode

Sampling
- Selection of research sites and participants
- Undertake statistical power calculations, if appropriate

Data collection
- Questionnaire piloting and revision, if neccessary
- Administration of questionnaires
- Issue reminders and follow up with nonrespondents

Data analysis
- Inputting and processing of data
- Data analysis, interpretation and conclusions

Dissemination
- Writing up
- Dissemination of survey results
- Make recommendations, if relevant, and refine theory, if appropriate

Figure 8.2 Ideal-typical survey research process in an academic context

Rigour in survey research

The rigour of survey results is measured by two main concepts, namely *reliability* and *validity*. In order to be reliable, findings should be consistent and therefore trustworthy. In survey research, consistency can be measured via time series or longitudinal research. Here, the same questions are asked repeatedly over time – either of the same respondents (in longitudinal research) or of different respondents (in cross-sectional time-series approaches), whilst the methodology remains constant. This helps to monitor changes in attitudes and/or experiences over time.

Validity, on the other hand, concerns the integrity of the results and conclusions of a research project – for detailed discussions of reliability and validity see specialised survey textbooks, e.g. de Vaus (1996), or more general research methods textbooks, e.g. Babbie (2015) or Bryman (2016).

A critical issue with rigour in surveys arises from the claim of objectivity and generalisability. At the end of the day, survey results not only have to be interpreted by survey researchers, but even after the very best design efforts, survey researchers have to trust and assume that all respondents interpret the questions and answer options in the same way, namely in the same way that researchers intended them to interpret the questions.

This, of course, may not always be the case. In self-administered (e.g. online or postal) surveys, the researcher is per se absent, so whilst this creates a level playing field for all respondents and significantly reduces interviewer bias, it also means that clarification questions cannot be asked by respondents if the question wording is unclear. However, if the survey mode means that there is interaction between the researcher or interviewer and the respondent, for example in face-to-face or phone surveys, there is potential for interviewer bias. In these survey modes, efforts are normally made to reduce interviewer-related bias and to minimise or neutralise the impact that the relationship between survey administrator and respondent has on how questions are answered, for example via interviewer training, a stringent researcher protocol or reducing the number of questions which could require additional explanations or probing. Nevertheless, as de Vaus (1996) puts it, the same behaviour or issue may mean different things to different people and this is a problem which is difficult or impossible to eliminate. Steps towards the clarity of research questions can be taken of course, for example by involving co-researchers in the survey design as we will see below.

Potential strength and weaknesses of survey research

As stated above, surveys are usually chosen as a research instrument with generalisability and representativeness in mind. The ambition is to be able to say something which applies to the respective population, whether that is a nation, a particular local neighbourhood, or a specific community. In order to do so, standard questions are used and interviewer bias is reduced as much as possible. In face-to-face surveys, the effect of the relationship between interviewer and interviewee is minimised as much as possible through interviewer training or the provisions of very prescriptive interviewer instructions.

However, the claim of representativeness does come with some serious problems. To start with, only if everybody in a representative (or probability) sample of the respective study population is asked the same questions, under broadly the same conditions, can claims be made that the findings apply generally to this population; but there are several weaknesses here. The first weakness is a potential sample bias. Even when a probability sample is drawn, it is unlikely that a fully representative number of people in the respective sample population will actually take part in the survey. There are several reasons why some people may feel more inclined to respond than others. People with more of an interest in the topic, for example, are more likely to take part. In many countries, females are more likely to respond to attitude surveys than males. People with busy lives are often also under-represented in surveys, as are people from minority groups. The under-representation of minority groups in population surveys is a serious issue and participatory methods are trying to help address this. However, if a particular group or community is small in proportion to the whole sample, to facilitate a reliable statistical analysis of their data, a very large sample or a specific booster sample is required – and both of these measures can be very expensive.

It is paradoxical that, from the point of view of a participatory researcher, the greatest appeal of surveys, namely the generalisability of results, is also the aspect which has attracted the most criticism. In turn, the focus on small-scale in-depth projects that often characterises participatory action research studies has also attracted repeated criticism. In fact, Chevalier and Buckles (2013) specifically challenge action and participatory action researchers to scale up their enquiry processes in order to contribute more to theoretical developments. In order to meet that challenge and to contribute to a better integration of theoretical and methodological advancements with community development and action, another look at survey methodology and how surveys can contribute to this would be useful.

One of the obstacles of survey research is that some elements of the methodology can be quite technical and 'scientific' and therefore require more of an expert input as regards the instrument design and the subsequent statistical data analysis. Although conducting group discussions or interviews also requires specific research skills, conversational methods with interpretive analytical frameworks come perhaps more naturally to us than statistical methods do.

Criticism of surveys

According to de Vaus (1996) criticism of survey research falls into three broad categories that encompass a range of issues: (1) philosophical, (2) technical and (3) political.

The philosophical criticism of surveys is levelled at their ability to establish causal relationships, their selective nature of questioning, the difficulties in eliciting the more intricate and meaningful aspects of social interaction and its context, and its empiricist, positivist and objectivist nature. Basically, critics hold that quantitative researchers treat people and institutions like nature, creating a perception that social life is somehow independent of people's lives and ignoring the fact that consciousness impacts on human behaviour and relationships and the way they reflect on these.

Critics of survey research also contest that it is possible to reduce or eradicate interviewer and researcher bias. Even the wording of questions, the inclusion or exclusion of answer items and their order will have an effect on the results of a survey. Viswanathan et al. (2004) remind us that knowledge development is never value-free but rather political in nature, even if standardisation and statistical abstraction in survey research sometimes give a sense of objectivity. According to de Vaus, critics also hold that many survey researchers assume that everything is measurable. Bryman (2016) adds that this gives a false sense of precision and accuracy.

The technical criticism of surveys focuses on two main aspects, namely that surveys are too restricted and highly structured. This ultimately reduces the complexity of the data gained from surveys. Qualitative researchers have criticised survey researchers for the tendency to sometimes arbitrarily applying quite crude categories to very complex forms of organisation (Smith and Atkinson, 2016). Further, according to de Vaus (1996), the focus on statistics leads to a reductionist reporting of study results which can also be too technical and therefore alienating to a large part of the audience. Bryman (2016) contends that an over-reliance on instruments and procedures may lead to a disconnect of researchers from everyday life.

The political criticism of survey research really focuses on how surveys can be used manipulatively, how the knowledge they produce can be abused by those in power, e.g. by oversimplifying questions, by asking leading questions or giving limited answer options and, by doing so, coercing respondents into responding in a way that can then be used in a manipulative manner.

Finally, regardless of the sampling frame and the issue researched, a focus on quantification means that surveys ultimately give priority to majority opinions and experiences. As we have already seen, this can start with a simple exclusion in demographic characteristics. Anyone who does not fit into one of the predetermined categories in a survey question (e.g. non-binary sex or gender categories, not listed minority religious or ethnic groups) falls into a 'statistical limbo' (Durand, 2016). Participatory researchers have criticised this and have taken a particular interest in those whose experiences get lost in the process of standardisation and generalisation. Durand's discussion shows that survey researchers themselves are not oblivious to the weaknesses of structured questionnaires. As Durand states, whilst standardisation simplifies questions in an attempt to create clarity, the results actually tend to be an oversimplification of issues.

Using surveys within collaborative and participatory research projects

As we have seen, survey research is not without criticism and weaknesses. Nonetheless, whilst acknowledging that surveys can be blunt instruments with very clear limitations, if their strengths are exploited appropriately as part of collaborative participatory project, they can also be very useful tools which carry the promise of the capacity to convince decision makers that change is necessary. This has often been the case in relation to attempts to make the voices of disadvantaged and marginalised people and communities heard. Lavelle, Larsen and Gundersen (2009), for example, argue that full and active participatory partnerships between American Indian communities and external researchers are required, not only in order for these communities to benefit from the research, but also to improve the quality of survey data collected among American Indian communities. Howe and McKay (2007). Lakwo (2008) and Cohen and Saisana (2014) describe the benefits of a participatory community-driven approach to develop suitable locally valid multi-dimensional poverty assessment tools in Africa and Asia. These included generating trust from the local population, but also the ability to survey people in their local languages.

In reality, there are very few elements of survey research which are out of bounds when it comes to co-design approaches, and surveys should not be regarded as unsuitable instruments for collaborative research designs. After all, the first time the term 'participatory research' was knowingly used in the academic context was in connection with a survey, namely an 'experimental pilot survey of skills' in rural Tanzania (Swantz, 1975). Indeed, there are many cases where surveys have been used to good effect in participatory and collaborative research projects, as the examples covered in this chapter show. Figure 8.3. shows the crucial ingredients in successful survey research, such as good timing, clarity, a suitable survey mode and respondents' trust. In all of these aspects, participatory approaches can make a meaningful contribution, as I will now discuss.

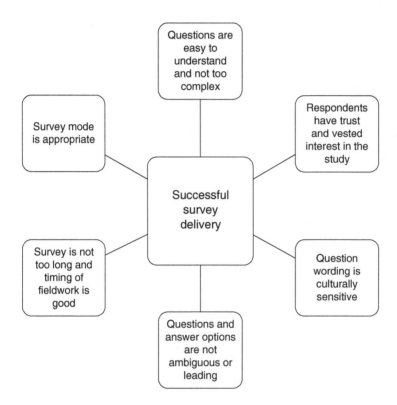

Figure 8.3 Ingredients for running a successful survey

However, I will start with a more general look at participatory survey design.

Objectives and potential benefits of participatory survey design

In traditional survey research there is a very clear power differential between the researchers and the participants. It is the researchers that decide what questions to ask, in what order and what answer categories to include or to exclude. Respondents are simply presented with these survey questions and answer options, and although survey piloting is normally one of the preparatory steps, which in principle provides some feedback from the participant cohort, it is often survey interviewers and researchers themselves that assess the success of the pilot. The focus on standardisation and generalisability in survey research ultimately means that the voices of those not captured by surveys or in insufficient numbers to be of statistical relevance, are potentially missing. Most participatory researchers will respond to this by privileging rather than ignoring, suppressing or neutralising participant voice and experience. This is perhaps best done in qualitative research practice which is more flexible and offers generally more contact time between researchers and participants. However, this does not mean that surveys are not suited to participatory and collaborative approaches, but rather that the challenge is to find ways and means to make survey research more inclusive. This could mean transferring agency to those individuals, communities or client groups who are often under-represented or marginalised in surveys. Participatory and collaborative survey approaches are therefore principally geared towards the following two *main aims*:

1   To redress this asymmetrical and hierarchical relationship between researcher and participants/respondents.
2   In collaboration with co-researchers or advisory groups, to improve the research instrument and therefore the kind of data that is being collected.

The *main potential benefits* of participatory approaches to survey research are:

1   Improved study robustness and rigour.
2   A closer connection between the study approach and outcomes and people's lived experiences.
3   An improved response rate to survey questionnaires.

Participatory approaches to survey research result in a fine balance between standardisation, which ultimately tries to neutralise relationships between researchers and participants, and fostering participation and the participant voice, consciously taking account of these relationships (Figure 8.4).

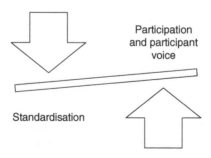

Figure 8.4   The balance between standardisation and participation in surveys

One of the main challenges of participatory survey research approaches is to preserve validity and reliability constructs in the survey instruments throughout the participatory design process. The need to standardise in survey research may also mean that some aspects of survey design are unsuitable for co-design approaches, as these would be impractical or tokenistic in nature, for example when standardised measures are being used in comparative research projects and the question wording or survey design is not negotiable, or if sophisticated statistical analysis may require significant capacity building and training beyond the remit or time frame of a project. However, many areas in survey research can still benefit from participatory design and input.

Addressing nonresponse with participatory means

One of the aspects that co-design approaches can help to address is nonresponse to surveys or to survey questions. Nonresponse is a much bigger issue in survey research than in qualitative research. In fact, Groves et al. (2009: 188–189) state that for decades 'the dominant goal of survey researchers was to minimise nonresponse rates'. The emphasis on the reduction of nonresponse is obviously related to the aim to achieve generalisable results and to reduce errors in the reporting of findings. Whether or not this has a scientific foundation, there is an underlying sense that it is much easier to trust survey results if three-quarters of eligible respondents completed a questionnaire or answered a question than if just one-quarter did. The higher the proportion of eligible respondents who co-operate, the more we feel that the study results are valid and reliable. However, as Fowler (2014) states, *how* problematic nonresponse really *is* largely depends on whether or not the respondents are systematically different from the nonrespondents in a survey. In fact, Groves et al. (2009: 191) encourage us to think about nonresponse 'in a more casual way' and show that an increase in response rate does not automatically result in a reduction of nonresponse errors. Instead, we need to work out what the key variables or questions are in a survey where we need to increase our response and who the missing respondents are that we need to encourage more to respond to a survey. In both cases of nonresponse participatory means can help to address this.

The first issue is item nonresponse. We talk about item nonresponse when study participants disproportionately fail to respond to a specific question or a specific set of questions. Typical reasons for this could be that questions are too sensitive, that the wording cannot be understood, the answer options do not capture people's experiences or simply that the survey is too long, too repetitive or too demanding.

The second issue is unit nonresponse, i.e. when only some members of the sample respond to the survey. Generally, with some exceptions, survey response rates are declining internationally (Stoop, 2016). The reasons for this vary and include: scepticism about research and its value; concerns about data security and more rigorous consent procedures; lack of time; but also survey-administrative reasons, such as inaccurate contact details or, in face-to-face or telephone surveys, inappropriate contact times.

As Groves et al. (2009) highlight, unit nonresponse is not problematic per se but it can become problematic if the sample is biased towards a particular group of respondents. As many people are probably more likely to take part in a study if they are interested in its topic, this is not unusual. However, if people with a vested interest in a study topic, or with particular characteristics or experiences directly related to the study topic, are more likely to complete a survey, bias is likely to skew the result and reduce the reliability of findings. In these circumstances, a probability or random sample can quickly become a non-probability sample. Bryman (2016), for example, reports that a study on the weight of primary school children commissioned by the Department of Health in England was likely to underestimate the prevalence of obesity as children (and their parents and carers) who knew or suspected that they were overweight, simply refused to take part in the study. Paradoxically, as Groves et al. (2009) report, efforts to improve the response rate in a survey may actually increase rather than decrease response bias, for example if the measures taken, such as incentives, reminder letters in postal surveys or repeat visits in door-to-door surveys, maximise the participation of already over-represented groups of participants.

Co-design approaches in collaborative research projects typically attempt to increase the participation of individuals and communities who are less likely to be taking part in surveys. Reasons could be that the instruments are unsuitable, they don't trust the research project and processes, or they are not asked to take part in the first place. Some of the factors associated with nonresponse are not under the control of the research team but others can be addressed. The latter include: the design of the survey questionnaire, including the language(s) used; the way the fieldwork is organised, including survey mode, timing and duration; the sampling frame; interviewer selection and training in phone and face-to-face surveys; and the use of incentives. Co-researchers can assist with the recruitment of under-represented/hard-to-reach communities. They can also help to build trust between respondents and their communities if they share similar experiences. However, as with anything in participatory approaches, this does not happen automatically, and the flipside is that there could be a risk that the familiarity between interviewer and respondent may lead to an increase in socially expected responses. Familiarity and common backgrounds may also increase sensitivities and highlight conflict, for example if there is conflict between neighbours or if community members want to hide certain attitudes or behaviours from other community members. The potential advantages and disadvantages of the involvement of community surveyors, for example, need to be worked out clearly.

Implementing participatory designs

As discussed throughout this book, participatory approaches are characterised by shared decision-making processes, co-learning and mutual ownership of a project and its methods. According to Formea et al. (2014) this sense of ownership of the research process helps to develop a shared vision of the eventual impact of the work. Davis and Whittington (1998) also feel that collaborative approaches to survey research may mean that stakeholders are more willing to spend resources on a project if they feel that they have some involvement and say in its development and design. According to Foster and Young (2015), the main themes emerging in relation to the group dynamics in collaborative co-design processes in large-scale surveys are legitimation, expertise, experiential knowledge, a different episte-mology, and power and control. Before embarking on a participatory approach to survey research, it is therefore important to stress that the negotiation of all of these issues can be a time-consuming undertaking, especially if the collaborative approach is to include all stages of the study from the design to the dissemination and communication of findings. As Garcia et al. (2008: 109) remarks, unlike traditional university-driven or professional research-driven studies that usually follow very tight and predictable timelines, in par-ticipatory projects 'flexibility of timelines is critical. When power is truly shared, the [...] process is time intensive because it is dependent on collaborative decision-making through extensive communication and mutual trust.'

In principle, there are two different kinds of participatory survey projects. Surveys can be embedded in larger participatory projects, for example CBPR projects. In this case, other means of data collection may also be used, such as group discussions, interviews or observations. However, participatory approaches have also been used in projects where surveys may be the only research instrument, for example in service user-led studies in the health and social care sector. In both embedded mixed methods designs and single-survey designs, and similar to all other participatory approaches, the levels of participation and different roles for co-researchers can vary, as Table 8.1 shows.

Table 8.1   Responsibilities and remits in collaborative survey research projects

Governing Board	The governing board makes decisions about the research study. It usually involves the funders of the study and the research team.
Research Advisory Groups	An advisory group is often made up of the same people who could be represented on a governing board, but their role is to give advice rather than to make decisions. Advisory groups can also look at particular aspects of a study only. An example for this could be a technical advisory committee which deals with technical and measurement issues in relation to a survey or a cultural advisory group that might advise researchers on the use of language or on particular local and cultural issues.
Stakeholders	A stakeholder is someone with a vested interested in the research project. There are different kinds of stakeholders. They could be representative of funding bodies of local government institutions or health care providers, charity representatives, but also representatives of community organisations, local neighbourhoods or clients of services.
Project Champions	Project champions are mainly responsible for the publicity and promotion of a study.
Consultants	A consultant is someone who is brought in to advise on specific aspects of a study. This tends to be someone with particular experience in an area of work.
Research Assistants	Someone working in the project and qualified and paid to do so.
Co-researchers	Someone who is involved actively in any or all of the stages of the research project but who may not be a paid member of the research team.
Advocacy Organisations	Advocacy organisations may be consulted about the research, for example as part of the advisory group or at the design stage of the survey, or they may be tasked with the dissemination and implementation of the findings.

According to Biggs (1989), there are four main modes of participation in collaborative research projects: 1) contractual, 2) consultative, 3) collaborative and 4) collegiate. One of these participation modes is likely to be used in participatory and collaborative projects:

1   The *contractual* mode relates to projects where people become involved as, usually paid, contracted co-researchers to provide certain services to the project. There are very clear line-management structures and the decision power remains firmly in the hands of the senior researchers. In relation to survey research, one of the most common examples would be that community members are employed as research assistants, to help with data collection or data processing for a survey. Having interviewers who are familiar with the neighbourhood can have many advantages, but also some disadvantages. Community members will understand the concerns of their community better, they speak their language, they may have the trust of their neighbours, or know the best time to call for an interview. However, neighbourhoods are not always harmonious places, so having familiar interviewers may also become a disadvantage.

2   A *consultative* mode implies that local people or members of the respective community where a study takes place are involved in a study as experts, as members of an advisory or advocacy group or a stakeholder forum, for example. Although the research team is seeking advice, the decision power remains with them, and advice can be taken or not taken. A consultative approach typically involves regular meetings at all stages of a project. In survey research, this might mean discussing the survey questionnaire and sampling techniques, and developing a draft of research findings or recommendations.

3   A *collaborative* mode implies that researchers and co-researchers, typically members of the respective community, work together on all elements of the study. They may identify the issue, initiate the research project and even help provide the financial and/or human resources to undertake the project, decide that a survey should be undertaken and help to collect and analyse survey data. In this mode the responsibility is shared between senior researchers and community co-researchers.

4   Finally, in a *collegiate* mode, senior researchers and local people work together as co-researchers. Everybody will have suitable roles to undertake making use of different skills and capacities. As in the collaborative mode, the responsibility and decision-making power is shared between the organisation or community and the researchers.

In collaborative or collegiate projects initiated by a community organisation, it is important to be aware of existing hierarchies and competing interests in these communities and to have a clear sense of the cultural and behavioural background in the respective community that is being studied (Parrado, McQuiston and Flippen, 2005). Mochmann (2017), for example, reports about the difficulties and sensitivities involved in researching the lives of children born of war (CBOW), i.e. children who have one parent who is a member of a local community and one who is a member of a foreign army. In her article she describes the collaboration between researchers in Norway and Denmark and the Norwegian War Child Association on a survey questionnaire.

Garcia et al. (2008) used a CBPR approach to undertake a bilingual study of mental health among Latino communities. They describe how they jointly defined the principles of their partnership work on the basis of open communication, mutual respect and shared ownership of, and access to, the survey data they were going to collect. CBPR projects are designed to ensure that 'insider' perspectives and worldviews of community members are taken into consideration. Especially in relation to the use of mainstream population survey questions this ensures that questions that may have no or only low cultural relevance among a target population can be amended or improved if necessary.

Smith, Christopher and McCormick (2004) undertook a CBPR project among native American communities during which community members helped to develop and implement a culturally sensitive survey on cervical cancer screening barriers.

In Parrado, McQuisten and Flippen's (2005) study on Hispanic migrant populations in the USA which were a high-risk group in relation to HIV, project aims and agendas were jointly developed on the basis of discussions with stakeholders, policy makers, community representatives, advocacy and peer-led organisations. They attended meetings and conferences. Before their survey took place, the authors also conducted focus groups and interviews with members of their target population.

Ostrow et al.'s (2017) work perhaps falls more into the category of a consultative project. They set up a 'consensus panel', which included advocates, programme directors and researchers, for their research on peer-run mental health organisations. Their consensus panel took the final decisions on their online questionnaire design. Stratford et al. (2003) also used an advisory panel approach to gain support for their rural health survey, which focused on HIV and tuberculosis. The authors reported that initially there was not very much community support for this project. However, they argue that their inclusive community-research partnership approach, which directly confronted the fears about the research, was an essential factor that contributed to the community mobilisation for the survey and the eventual success of this project. One of the positive outcomes of this research was the establishment and funding of a community-based organisation that provided HIV counselling and testing and HIV prevention case management.

A good example of a community-research partnership between university researchers and a professional community is Kuo et al.'s (2006) survey of licensed acupuncturists in California. A research management team consisting of practitioners, university researchers and representatives of professional organisations working in the field oversaw the whole survey process.

Scott et al. (2014) used a consultative participation model for their survey on attitudes towards gender norms and practices in South Sudan. They set up a community steering committee to inform the study design, survey development and data collection.

The process of participatory planning and co-design of surveys

The consultative, collaborative and collegiate modes of participatory survey design all require extensive group deliberation processes. One of the first steps in any participatory project, including those involving surveys, is to establish a common interest in the project, agree the target aims and objectives and, if necessary, to reconcile different interests among all partners involved. This means that guiding principles for decision-making processes should be established as early as possible and the level of participation and power-sharing should be agreed. Building and maintaining an effective team in which members have respect for each other's participation will take time and effort and requires frequent and regular information sharing. As Viswanathan et al. (2004) remind us, community-based participatory research approaches take the principal view that: (1) community members are uniquely qualified and capable to investigate their lived experiences; (2) they should therefore be given the opportunity to help generate relevant knowledge that is of immediate and direct benefit to them as individuals, but also collectively; and (3) they should therefore be given the opportunity to fulfil the role of the researcher and hold the respective status in relation to this. Decentralisation of power in decision-making processes is essential to facilitate the participation of people who have a stake in the process or are affected by the issue being studied, regardless of their status or prior experience in relation to the researched topic. Dialogue and divergent views are not a nuisance but are an integral part of research process and means of empowerment (Viswanathan et al., 2004).

Question development and wording

One of the main objectives of collaborative survey design is to develop questions that are relevant to the target population, whether that is in a mainstream probability sample or specific hard-to-reach or 'hidden' populations. As we have already seen, the actual questionnaire development has been described as an art form (Payne, 1951). Often quite diverse samples of respondents have to understand the questions in a survey and have to be willing to answer these honestly and accurately. This means:

- The question wording in a survey has to be clear, unambiguous and non-leading.
- Respondents have to be given appropriate answer options.
- The questions cannot be too sensitive, they must consider cultural norms and conventions and reflect people's lives.
- The survey should flow easily and should have an inherent logic.
- It must not take too long to complete a survey.
- Especially in face-to-face or phone surveys the timing of the survey fieldwork must be convenient for the respondents.

Clearly, there are lots of things that can go wrong in a survey if this is not planned properly. As surveys are standardised instruments and therefore much less flexible than semi-structured interviews or group discussions, once a survey is in the field errors are very difficult to correct. Survey design is therefore about being precise and meticulous. Even a simple design error in a paper survey, for example a tick box put in the wrong place, may result in answers being ambiguous and thus unusable.

In survey design pragmatic decisions are also made about the inclusion or exclusion of questions and answer options, and this is informed by issues such as:

- The time it would take to complete a survey.
- The survey flow and the uniformity and formats of questions.
- How meaningful it is statistically to include an answer option in a question.
- How likely is it that respondents co-operate in a survey, e.g. are questions too sensitive? Are respondents likely to know the answers to the questions?
- How difficult it is to analyse the survey data and how hard it would be to draw generalisable conclusions from the data.

Longitudinal, international or repeated cross-sectional surveys add more layers of design restrictions as comparability over time and across various jurisdictions may mean that there are limitations to the wording of questions and how these can be changed. Ideally, of course, questionnaires should be piloted in order to test whether or not questions work, but even piloting may not reveal all of the survey issues.

Whilst there is a great variety of question formats in surveys, over the years conventions have developed around what works well and what does not work so well in surveys. In principle, there are three different kinds of question formats: (1) closed (or closed-ended) questions; (2) open (or open-ended) questions; and (3) a hybrid variety where respondents

Open
• No standardised answer options are given to the respondent
• Response is not structured by researchers

Closed
• A limited number of answer options is given to the respondent who has to choose one or more responses from a given list, depending on instructions
• The response options are structured and determined by the survey researchers

Hybrid
• A list of suggested answer options is given, as in closed questions, but the respondent is given the opportunity to give an alternative answer or add their own 'other' answer in addition to choosing a given response from the list
• The responses are still structured by the researchers, but there is a level of openness

Figure 8.5 Main question formats in surveys

are presented with answer options to a question, but they may add their own options or explanatory comments (Figure 8.5). Within these three broad categories there are several sub-groups. Closed questions, for example, can utilise a Likert-scale (see Box 8.1).

The wording of closed questions is usually researcher-determined, as is the choice and order of answer options. However, in participatory survey designs, the design of closed questions should be discussed in order to make sure the survey works in the particular cultural or community context.

BOX 8.1

LIKERT SCALES

Likert scale-type questions are frequently used in surveys to capture attitudes and experiences, namely, the level of agreement with a particular statement or a set of statements. Likert scales present respondents with an answer range from strong agreement to strong disagreement. A 'neither' or 'undecided' answer option forms the middle point of each Likert scale. A Likert scale most commonly has five answer options (see examples below), but it can have as little as three – 'Agree' – 'Neither' – 'Disagree' – but equally seven, nine, or even more, although larger scales are less practical. The inclusion of 'Don't know' or 'Can't decide' responses in addition to the scale is optional and there are arguments for and against this. Supporters of their inclusion hold that a 'Don't know' option should be available for respondents who genuinely do not know how they feel about a statement. The counter argument is that a 'Don't know' or 'Can't decide' option can be a cop-out for respondents who do not want to think about a statement or who refuse to answer it. In a battery of statements, it is good practice to alter positive and negative statements to prevent satisficing, i.e. a respondent not reading and considering statements or questions properly.

	Strongly agree	Agree	Neither agree nor disagree	Disagree	Strongly disagree	I don't know
I'm given opportunities to do the sort of things I'd like to do	□1	□2	□3	□4	□5	□6
After a while I get bored and lose interest	□1	□2	□3	□4	□5	□6
I can cope with the things I'm asked to do	□1	□2	□3	□4	□5	□6
My efforts are appreciated by the organisation/people I volunteer for	□1	□2	□3	□4	□5	□6

Figure 8.6 Example Likert scale

Source: from ARK's annual Young Life and Times (YLT) survey of 16-year-olds in Northern Ireland

The example in Figure 8.6 of a Likert scale is taken from ARK's annual Young Life and Times (YLT) survey of 16-year-olds in Northern Ireland, in this case an extract from questions asked on volunteering experiences in 2009 and 2017 respectively (www.ark.ac.uk/ylt/quests).

A good example for a participatory survey design which also included Likert-scale type questions is that of Foster and Young's (2015) attitude survey among parents who had babies in neonatal care. When they designed their survey, Foster and Young consulted with a group of parents who had previously had this experience. The authors argue that their collaborative approach enabled those who had most direct experience to lead and influence the study design. This made the academic researchers accountable to the parent group. One of the outcomes of the co-design approach was that five-point Likert scale responses in the survey questionnaire were simplified into three-point responses. The authors also report that the parents had a good sense of what kind of questions were appropriate to ask and what wording should be used. Some questions that the academic researchers wanted to include were vetoed by the parent advisors. Foster and Young report that 'the benefits of the participatory approach to the study were mutual, with participants reporting that they had found it a worthwhile and enjoyable process' (2015: 97). The authors also note that parents felt that they had gained 'a sense of wellbeing', which was an additional positive outcome from their involvement in this study.

Webber et al.'s (2016) study aimed to improve the rigour in a household survey among a low-income Latino community in California. The authors engaged with a range of community partners but also survey experts to improve the design of a standardised survey. They found that the language of established survey instruments may not be appropriate or may be too difficult to understand. Academic survey researchers can be very protective of the established wording in survey questions but Webber et al. found that the simplification of survey language may actually improve their validity.

A very well-known and widely used example in which a standardised survey tool is combined with participatory survey design elements is Michael Ungar's Child and Youth Resilience Measure (CRYM) (Ungar and Liebenberg, 2005; Resilience Research Centre, 2016). CRYM is an internationally used standardised resilience screening tool, however, the CRYM manual (Resilience Research Centre, 2016) makes it very clear that this survey needs to be adapted for local use. In the first two steps of the application of CRYM, researchers are encouraged to conduct local focus groups to develop ten specific local questions to add to the standardised questions. This 'community input' can be achieved via a local advisory committee which is supposed to also suggest locally and contextually relevant and feasible ways of conducting the study. Researchers are also encouraged to reconvene the focus groups to discuss findings and make sure 'that interpretations of the data are given local context' (Research Resilience Centre, 2016: 9).

One of the largest surveys with participatory design input is the biannual California Health Interview Survey (Brown et al., 2005). Community organisations are involved in the planning and development of the survey sample design and content in each survey cycle. Brown et al. describe their participatory research model as a 'hybrid approach' as the survey development involves local policy making, public health and health care organisations working alongside advocacy groups and research organisations in an advisory board, to help shape survey topics, measures and sample design. The advisory group also decides which languages the survey needs to be translated into. The authors hold that this model 'ensures that 1) the survey is relevant to the communities that plan it, 2) the survey appropriately measures factors related to community needs, and 3) data and results are available and accessible to the relevant communities and their advocates' (Brown et al., 2005: 7).

Involving co-researchers in survey translations

Translations of surveys into different languages is one aspect of survey research that also benefits from the involvement of local speakers of these languages. According to Harkness, van de Vijver and Mohler (2002: 443), 'any cross-cultural survey project poses complex challenges regarding survey design, translation, sampling, and other matters'. Translations of question texts in survey research may indeed become an issue not just in international or multi-lingual studies, but also when it comes to the inclusion of people with disabilities, for example. It is the responsibility of survey researchers to ensure cultural and social relevance of their instruments (Garcia et al., 2008), but unless the respective communities are actively involved in the translation process, this may be difficult to achieve. Having said that, Behr and Shishido (2016) remind us that the background of the interpreters or translators will determine the outcome of the translation process. It is therefore not normally good practice to let friends, colleagues or partners who happen to be bilingual or multi-lingual undertake the translation. The project team needs to ensure that translators have an excellent command of the source and target languages, including dialectic nuances that may apply at a local level. However, the whole translation process requires a range of skills, including linguistic, cultural and methodological ones. Administratively, survey researchers need to check and see if standardised measures have been validated in the alternative language they wish to use. Formea et al. (2014: 331) summarise these challenges:

> Survey instruments with acceptable validity to answer questions that are important for partnerships are frequently not available for diverse languages and ethnicities. Beyond the challenges of semantic equivalence, simple translation of existing English-language surveys often lose conceptual equivalence with the original survey; likewise, translated surveys run the risk of ignoring differences in cultural norms that may impact participant reflection on a health topic.

Graybill et al. (2010) applied a participatory approach to adapting a survey for deaf individuals, a community traditionally under-represented in surveys due to a range of structural and socio-cultural barriers. The researchers established an advisory group – a 'Translation

Work Group' – consisting of representatives from the deaf community and specialised researchers specifically tasked with the adaptation of a health survey in English language into sign language. This included the technical adaptation of the survey, incorporating film clips and the use of a touch screen computer interface.

Formea et al.'s study (2014) focused on the participatory adaptation and translation of surveys for migrant and refugee populations, namely a survey about diabetes. Their CBPR approach initially explored the health literacy and the local relevance of the issue among the migrant population before they used a process of forward translation, group deliberation and back translation to adapt the survey and test its validity. During this process significant survey revisions took place to ensure semantic, cultural and conceptual equivalence with the original surveys. The authors stated that the group deliberation process is a crucial element of participatory and collaborative survey research even though it is very time-intensive. They felt that this process enhanced the community ownership of the project and acceptance of the survey when the fieldwork was undertaken. The authors concluded that a participatory process of survey translation 'has the potential to not only improve the survey product, but also to strengthen existing partnerships and eventual survey implementation' (Formea et al., 2014: 332).

Similarly, positive outcomes were reported by Tajik, Galvao and Siqueira (2010) from their survey among Brazilian immigrants living in Boston. They used a CBPR approach to develop a culturally appropriate and validated health survey in Portuguese, by translating the existing standardised health-promoting lifestyle profile II (HPLP-II) instrument. Their test of the Portuguese version showed good equivalence, consistency and reliability.

Involving co-researchers in data collection

A contractual mode (Biggs, 1989) in participatory survey research typically involves community residents working as interviewers in face-to-face or telephone surveys. This is often done to reduce nonresponse but also to approach hard-to-reach groups that may otherwise not take part in a survey. However, co-researchers can also be involved in other aspects of data collection, such as survey testing and piloting, which is an integral part of any survey-based research. The purpose of the questionnaire pilot is to make sure that the survey captures the data it is meant to capture, but also to get a sense of the time it takes to complete a survey and whether or not respondents might refuse to answer sensitive questions.

The engagement or employment of co-researchers in face-to-face household (or door-to-door) surveys and phone surveys is a common approach in development studies – and here notably in relation to farming, soil use, pest control and wildlife monitoring – but also in health studies undertaken among minority and native communities (e.g. Smith, Christopher and McCormick, 2004; Balcazar, Garcia-Iriarte and Suarez-Balcazar, 2009; Barrera-Bassols, Zinck and van Ranst, 2009; Hull et al., 2010; Kahindi et al., 2010; Msoffe et al. 2010; Cohen et al., 2012).

Face-to-face surveys

Hillier et al. (2014) argue that door-to-door surveys are particularly valuable when spending time in a community and building relationships are a central aim of a study. Usually community interviewers receive interviewer training, and sometimes household surveys may provide convenient short-term employment opportunities for people who may find it otherwise difficult to find jobs. Having said that, community interviewers will not always be paid.

Davis and Whittington (1998) argue that involvement of community interviewers in household surveys can have a positive effect on the social acceptability of a research project and in turn be more likely to benefit this community. Kaplan et al. (2004) also emphasise the benefit of capacity building among community survey interviewers. Another benefit, and the chief reason really for using this strategy, is that community interviewers can help to gain access to communities and individuals who might otherwise have been inaccessible or unwilling to participate in a survey. Co-residents may be more likely to trust fellow residents but also more likely to provide honest and open answers to the survey questions. Kaplan et al. (2004: 294) found that community interviewers 'would be savvy about how to reach potential respondents and [be] able to use their personal connections to pave the way for the survey'.

One of the challenges in household surveys is to look after the safety of interviewers. Arguably community interviewers may not be automatically safer because they know their community as there may also be conflict between the interviewers and some of the householders they interview.

Phone surveys

Telephone surveys might be chosen over face-to-face surveys which are expensive and time-consuming if large geographic distances have to be covered. They may also be appropriate if interviewer or respondent safety and anonymity might be a concern or if respondents are being surveyed on particularly sensitive topics. With telephone surveys, fewer community interviewers are required and those who are less mobile could be also be involved in data collection. Weiss et al.'s (2010) community-initiated action research project to promote safe sexual practices in light of increasing rates of HIV/AIDS and teenage pregnancy in a community in South Florida is such an example. The local community formed a research committee and undertook a telephone survey with over 1,000 residents. As a result of the phone survey, an education resource about the importance of HIV testing and prevention was developed and the local committee lobbied local education authorities to change the high school curriculum to include more comprehensive sex education.

Online and mobile surveys

Thanks to the emergence of new information and mobile technologies, online and mobile surveys, but also face-to-face surveys via video links, are now more common than ever before. Respondents in geographically remote locations are now more accessible. Technological advances have also simplified and revolutionised data processing and data analysis. A simple online or mobile survey can now be set up by anyone anywhere on any electronic device as long as there is access to the internet. Surveys can be promoted by emailing a survey link or by posting this on social networking sites. The costs to run such a short survey are very affordable. An added benefit of the new technological possibilities is that surveys have become more interactive. Surveys can be programmed to include audio-visual material, such as videos, or photographs or voice files. Questions and answer options can be read out, and interactive ways of responding to questions, such as drag-and-drop or sliding bars, can be incorporated. All this helps to adapt surveys to a variety of audiences and makes surveys more interesting and suitable to audiences, such as young children, for whom traditional survey modes could have been inaccessible or simply boring.

There is a now a large number of software packages and online survey tools – some of them very simple and free to use, others more complex and advanced with a more substantial licence fee, but also more customer support attached – which enable users to relatively easily design a professional looking online survey. Some online survey tools even incorporate basic data analysis tools. So, as an explorative mechanism many community organisations can utilise online surveys reasonably easily and quickly. Robust and rigorous online surveys do of course still require the respective systematic approaches discussed above, as well as the application of statistical knowledge when it comes to data analysis. Nevertheless, the availability of online surveys has contributed to a democratisation in survey research.

Orza et al. (2015) conducted an international online survey in a participatory project to explore violence experienced by women who live with HIV. Ostrow et al. (2017) followed a user-led research approach and undertook a national web survey among peer-led mental health organisations in the US. People with psychiatric histories were involved in this project from the survey design stage to the dissemination of its results. The co-design approach utilised a consensus panel consisting of advocates, representatives of mental health organisations and researchers who themselves had suffered episodes of poor mental health. Irwin et al. (2014) worked with members of the local LGBT community in Nebraska to develop and administer a survey on suicidal ideation among a convenience sample of LGBT people.

Mobile and internet technologies have been particularly useful in surveys used to record wildlife and agricultural crops, but also in citizen science projects, for example the location of stars and planets. Annual Garden Bird Watch Surveys, for example run by the RSPB or the German equivalent (NABU), every year attract tens of thousands of survey participants in just one weekend. Singla, Babbar and Kaur (2012) report how they utilised an online survey to investigate attitudes and practices of rodent control among farmers in India. Following the survey, farmers were involved in peer-led educational programmes in order to more effectively control rodents. Wang and Wang (2016) showed that a participatory survey involving local communities in China using mobile technology produced reliable data in terms of agricultural pest control.

Participatory approaches to data input and data analysis

Survey data input is increasingly computerised. In online and mobile surveys where both the survey questionnaire and dataset are held remotely on a server, data input is immediate. Phone and face-to-face surveys also increasingly utilise computer technology, namely computer-assisted personal interviewing (CAPI) and computer-assisted telephone interviewing (CATI), but in paper-based or phone surveys, data input has to be undertaken manually. This is an opportunity to employ co-researchers.

The availability of powerful computer technology means that survey data analysis, even of very large samples, only takes a fraction of the time it used to take and can be done without the significant statistical and mathematical skillset that was initially required of survey researchers. Having said that, in order to make meaningful use of surveys, some basic knowledge is still required.

The analysis of open questions is hardest from a statistical point of view, however, open questions transfer the most power and agency to respondents. Open questions are also a question type in which the involvement of co-researchers is not only easy to facilitate, but also meaningful. The thematic analysis of open responses requires an interpretive sense-making and coding process, and the lived experiences of co-researchers can be very beneficial in this. A collaborative approach to open answer coding would typically involve joint thematic coding and quantification of open survey responses. Alongside open coding, simple descriptive statistical analysis of data can also be undertaken in participatory projects. Simple frequency tables and crosstabulations are not only easy to understand, but also reasonably simple to produce without specialised statistical analysis software. Once basic statistical procedures are explained, co-researchers of all ages and capacities are able to comprehend survey results and can contribute to the interpretation of results, as the children's rights-based survey research of Emerson and Lloyd (2017) with primary school children in Northern Ireland shows (see Box 8.2. below). Like Emerson and Lloyd's study, Horsfield et al.'s (2014) survey of accessibility and youth-friendliness of pharmacies in New Zealand utilised a youth advisory group (YAG) throughout the research process, including the interpretation of survey data.

A good example of participatory survey data analysis is also Orza et al.'s (2015) international study on violence experienced by women living with HIV. This was a user-led mixed methods study which included an international survey element. The researchers established a global reference group with 14 women from different international backgrounds. They used a widely accessible online survey platform to collect data from nearly 1,000 women in 94 different countries. Some respondents were involved in the data analysis, namely the thematic coding of open responses and descriptive statistical analysis.

When working with co-researchers on the analysis and interpretation of data, pie and bar charts and other simple ways to visualise survey data will help in this process.

Involving co-researchers in the dissemination of survey results

Aside from the survey design stage and the support in data collection, perhaps the most common aspect of co-researcher involvement in collaborative survey projects is the dissemination of survey results and the respective advocacy work that commonly follows the completion of a survey project. The dissemination of survey findings can pose some challenges, as not all audiences, and not even the co-researchers themselves, may be familiar with and attuned to the use of survey statistics. However, computer programs and apps that can help with the visual representation and illustration of survey findings, for example via infographics, are becoming more easily available and can help with this.

BOX 8.2

INVOLVING CHILDREN IN A SURVEY ON THEIR RIGHTS TO PARTICIPATE IN SCHOOL AND COMMUNITY

In their study, Emerson and Lloyd (2014, 2017) have shown that participatory approaches are capable of facilitating the inclusion of primary school-aged children in the design of survey questions and in the subsequent analysis and dissemination of survey results. In 2013, the Centre for Children's Rights at Queen's University in Belfast commissioned a module in an annual survey of a primary school children (10 and 11 years old) in Northern Ireland. The aim of this survey module was to establish to what extent children felt their views were sought, listened to and acted upon in their schools and communities. A rights-based approach (Lundy and McEvoy (Emerson), 2012) was used for this project. A children's research advisory group (CRAG) was formed, and together with this CRAG the researchers developed and piloted the questions. The CRAG was also involved in the data analysis and presentation of the research findings. The children in the CRAG were the same age as the survey respondents.

The initial workshops with the CRAG were dedicated to the familiarisation with the topic. The children then generated a number of statements about school and community that they felt reflected environments that respected their rights. With support from the researchers, the children themselves chose the final set of statements that was included in the survey. In the online survey itself, it was made clear that this set of questions was co-designed by children and drawings that the children made of themselves were included. Once the data collection was complete, the researchers met the CRAG again and worked together on a descriptive and thematic analysis of the survey findings. The survey results were jointly launched by the academic researchers and the children from the CRAG in the school that the children attended.

One of the challenges is to adapt the presentation of survey results to different audiences – in Lloyd's and Emerson's project primary school children – whilst ensuring that co-authorship is handled sensibly in respective publications. As Emerson and Lloyd showed, statistically untrained co-researchers, such as children, can be skilled to an extent that they are capable of presenting key finding derived from survey research to a statistically untrained audience. With regard to the overall ambitions of collaborative research projects, survey results provide an excellent tool that can support advocacy and lobbying for change.

Ethical issues in participatory survey research

Surveys undertaken as part of participatory and collaborative research practice are subject to many of the ethical issues discussed in Chapter 4, but some specific issues also arise.

A risk assessment needs to be undertaken if co-researchers are involved in face-to-face data collection, for example in door-to-door surveys. Often this happens in neighbourhoods that they are familiar with, but this does not mean that this work is without risks. It is also important to be aware of cultural conventions. For example, in some cultures it is not acceptable for men to interview women or not appropriate for interviews to take place late in the evening or on Saturdays or Sundays.

Survey anonymity provides study participants with the option to share personal information or to make disclosures without the need to follow this up. Ethically, the research team must make a decision on how they want to handle these circumstances. There is a choice to facilitate personal disclosures, but this inevitably means that the confidentiality can no longer be guaranteed – see Chapter 4. On the other hand, it is possible to use a data minimisation strategy and to construct survey questionnaires in a way that disclosures of this nature are purposely blocked, for example by not including open text boxes. This arguably limits the agency of survey participants and the extent to which they can give additional information.

When using (commercial) internet survey tools, it is important to study the terms and conditions of the provider well to understand how that survey data will be stored and recorded, who has access to this, what it is used for and how the data can be deleted. Some online or mobile phone survey tool providers harvest personal information for their own use, such as the IP address, and may seek permission to use background data, such as the GPS location or search histories, for commercial purposes. Increasingly institutional research ethics review boards veto the use of these commercial tools if they do not comply with data protection legislation.

It is good practice to repeat occasionally in a survey questionnaire that the completion of questions is voluntary and that participants do not have to respond to questions if they do not want to. Providing space for feedback and offering feedback on survey results (e.g. via summary flier, seminar or website) is also good practice.

Small-scale surveys sometimes lack the statistical power to facilitate a detailed breakdown of results. If results are not used carefully, confidentiality could be compromised. As a rule of thumb, no results should be printed or reported where the cell count in a crosstabulation or frequency table is smaller than n = 5.

Typically, in participatory survey projects, data input is managed within the project team, as this is an activity that can easily be undertaken and participants and co-researchers can be trained in this. However, if data input companies are being used, it is important to let them sign confidentiality agreements.

Summary

I have tried to demonstrate that survey methods can be useful tools in participatory research projects. They have the capacity to give a study additional weight and rigour and they can be flexibly used for a range of purposes in a project, for example to establish baseline data, to evaluate progress, but also as a mechanism to include a wider audience in a study. Surveys are a versatile research instrument.

Whilst not dismissing the criticism of surveys as largely theory-driven positivist instruments, I hope to have demonstrated that it really is up to a research team to decide how they use surveys in a participatory project. In the opening of this chapter, but also at the very start of this book, I referred to Marja Liisa Swantz's original 'participatory research' study (1975), which did utilise a survey methodology. In my view, surveys, like the other methods discussed in this volume, provide opportunities, but also have limitations for participatory practice. As the many examples show, a collaborative survey research approach is feasible. Surveys may not be suitable to all participatory projects, but then neither are group discussions, interviews or observations. Perhaps surveys can go a long way to address one of the identified weaknesses of participatory research practice, namely its failure to have the desired and promised impact. It would almost be paradoxical if a participatory twist to the same research method that originally provided an impetus for the development of participatory and collaborative research practice also provided the solution to the original problem, namely the failure to include the voices of disadvantaged and disenfranchised communities and to convince policy makers that change is required.

FURTHER READING

Brown, E. R., Holtby, S., Zahnd, E. and Abbott, G. B. (2005). Community-based participatory research in the California Health Interview Survey. *Preventing Chronic Disease*, 2(4): 1–8.

de Vaus, D. A. (1996). *Surveys in Social Research*. London: UCL Press.

EXERCISE 8.1

CREATIVE DISSEMINATION OF SURVEY RESULTS

One of the difficulties of survey research is that survey results can be quite hard to digest and difficult to communicate to audiences that are not survey-skilled. In order to achieve the desired impact, survey results have to be communicated in an appropriate way to different audiences. This activity encourages you to think about how to do this.

Produce a survey results dissemination plan, and consider the following:

- What are the key results you want to communicate?
- In what format can these results be communicated?
- Can the results be linked to other study results from you project, such as arts-based material, visual material, documents, interviews or observation fieldnotes? Can a combination of these with your survey results enhance the impact of survey results?
- Can you use exhibitions or training manuals, etc. to utilise survey results?
- How can you visually (e.g. infographics), verbally or otherwise represent statistics?
- Who are the best people to present survey results to different audiences?

IN CONCLUSION

The main aim of this book was to introduce the reader to the history of participatory research methods, to critically showcase the main participatory and collaborative approaches, and to provide some practical guidance to researchers on how to approach participatory research, using some of the most commonly used research methods. Early in the book I also provided a theoretical lens to participatory approaches, which is something that is likely more of interest for academics and students than community researchers.

As I have demonstrated, there are now many participatory approaches and various versions of engaged research which do not necessarily encompass all elements of an all-inclusive PAR design, but would still come under the broad umbrella of participatory research or co-production. I made the point that research with a 'light' participatory touch applied to some parts of a project is okay too, for example when the constraints of a funding call or the commissioning of a particular piece of work determine the broad study design or pose the main research questions. Participatory purists may argue that the control over a study like this will then ultimately remain in the hands of professional researchers which would be in breach of a more egalitarian participatory ethos. We have indeed seen the publication of research studies which claim to be participatory in nature, but there is in reality very little evidence that participants had any say in how the study was undertaken or how the results are presented and to what end. Arguably, these studies are participatory in name only, but serve only the researcher.

From my practical experience in both youth and community work and empirical research, I feel that a little participation is better than none. In my view, a very important aspect in participatory research is honesty about the framework and boundaries within which co-production and participation can take place, and about realistic outcomes. I have worked with many children and young people in both community and academic settings who are quite happy to take on some responsibility in a research project, but would rather not take the lead, and I think that this is okay too. Working with young people and other groups of people who are not used to having a say in matters that affect them or who have been at the receiving end of broken promises about the value of their voices and participation means in my view that the level of participation can vary and is negotiable. This is not a bad thing, as even small contributions can foster self-confidence and provide skills on the basis of which more ambitious project ideas can grow.

The increasing expectation, and maybe also desire, among academics to demonstrate that their research has some societal 'impact' has certainly inspired and motivated many researchers to look more closely at opportunities to engage with study participants. In my view this has undoubtedly contributed to a participatory turn in the way we approach research. The endorsement of research findings by study participants and collaborators can be a very powerful experience even to those who think that unqualified 'lay researchers' have really very little to add to research design and methodology. Even though participatory and action research projects may face challenges in terms of institutional ethical review processes, there is no doubt that projects based on co-production with participants can be feel-good projects when it comes to ethical standards and the rapport with research participants. Nonetheless some important challenges remain.

Where next?

Throughout the chapters in this book I have highlighted some issues that particularly participatory researchers face. Notable challenges relate to the power relations in the field between researchers, participants and co-researchers; the *modus operandi* of institutional research ethics review boards, which are often not set up to accommodate the required flexibility in participatory research projects; but also more generally the ongoing debate about rigour and impact of participatory research.

Whilst the diversification and proliferation of participatory research practice would suggest that research based on collaboration and co-production is no longer a niche segment in social research, the debate about the purpose of co-production designs and the actual impact goes on. In my view, the mainstreaming of participatory and collaborative approaches presents both opportunities and challenges. As participatory research continues to develop and diversify, we continue to develop our vocabulary in relation to these approaches, as the short history of the term 'co-production' shows. At the same time what I called 'conventional research' has also developed and has made space for greater participation. Some researchers have warned strongly though that the mainstreaming of collaborative research practice potentially leads to a de-politicisation of participatory approaches. In my view, the risk to be participatory on just a tokenistic basis is real, and I think institutional review processes that have been heavily criticised for not being flexible enough to accommodate collaborative research practice, can actually play a positive role in spotting the risks of unethical tokenism at the planning stage of a project. As someone who has chaired an institutional ethics committee for a number of years, it is my view that there is strong evidence that developments in the research ethics framework have all but put an end to top-down exploitative approaches in research, and there is no reason why 'fake participation' could not be spotted at this stage.

The core question and challenge for me, however, is a much more serious one. As I pointed out in Part I of this book, the emergence of participatory research practice was closely connected to the failure of what I called conventional academic research to contribute sufficiently to positive social changes. Social, educational and health researchers have long been quite good at pointing the finger at social disadvantage, exploitation, inequality and disempowerment. However, despite more engagement, co-production and participation in research, certainly at the macro-level, very little has changed. If anything, macro-sociological data suggests that disadvantage and disempowerment are growing and inequality is increasing. The gap between the very rich and the very poor has never been bigger. The environmental changes brought about by our ruthless exploitation of the world's limited resources are now seriously threatening the livelihoods of some of the poorest and most disadvantaged people in the world, as well as those who are unfortunate enough to live in areas that are particularly affected by, for example, rising temperatures, droughts or rising sea levels. Paradoxically, some of the most damaging practices continue to exist because of poverty and social exclusion and the lack of alternatives to make a living.

The promise of participatory research practice was that, unlike conventional research, collaborative approaches would actively bring about positive social change. At this moment in time, we can perhaps see where some positive changes were brought about at community level with the help of participatory and action research, but at the global level, the evidence that this has actually happened is at best very underwhelming. So, are we again (or still) looking at broken promises?

Of course I am not promoting the abandonment of co-production approaches. The evidence is overwhelming that participation, volunteering and advocacy work all have really positive effects on individuals and communities. However, in order to fulfil the promises, it is time in my view to think more seriously about the up-scaling of participatory efforts and ambitions. Chevalier and Buckles (2013) point out correctly that the future challenges lie in the up-scaling of participatory enquiries and social actions. Only then can we tackle the urgent issues of our planet and keep the promise of meaningful social and sustainable change. This means that professional researchers also need to be more proactive in taking on the different roles that action research requires them to fulfil: being a researcher, but also an organiser and activist at the same time.

GLOSSARY

Below is a glossary of selected frequently used terms in this book. For further definitions of key theoretical and conceptual terms and descriptions of how they are connected to participatory research approaches, see Figure 2.2 (p. 39).

Constructivism (also Constructionism)   An ontological position according to which social phenomena and meaning is continuously constructed and re-constructed by social actors. In relation to collaborative research this is an important ontological perspective as it provides a theoretical rationale for a co-production approach.

Conventional research   In this volume the term 'conventional research' is used to describe research approaches that do not involve participants actively in decision-making processes at any stage of a research project (e.g. design and planning, data collection, analysis, decisions about dissemination).

Co-production   A relatively recent term, coined in in the first decade of this millennium, originally used in relation to stakeholder involvement in health research, but increasingly used as an umbrella term to describe a range of collaborative and participatory research approaches, in which communities are given greater control over research processes, including the determination of research questions and topics.

Empowerment   A term often used in connection with the objective to give people and communities more of a voice through participatory research practice. However, the term 'empowerment' has also been critically appraised due to the inherent paradox contained within it. The very fact that someone or a group can be in position to 'empower' or 'give' a voice to another suggests that one group or an individual holds and can potentially abuse power. So, the aim in participatory research practice is to set the project up in a way that the structures and processes of the project itself are ideally 'empowering' to everyone involved.

Epistemology (epistemological)   Epistemology is the study of the nature of knowledge, what origin it has, what methods are being used and what the limitations are. *How* do we know *what* we know? For participatory researchers the question arises to what extent the nature of knowledge varies between different study participants, such as professional, academically trained researchers, community or co-researchers, and study participants.

Ground rules   Ground rules in participatory research projects often refer to a 'group contract' – the way of working in a participatory project. These ground rules are determined and agreed by study participants. Ground rules may be drawn up to manage expectations and relationships between study participants. This may include aspects such as role distributions, responsibilities and agreements about confidentiality.

Objectivism   Objectivism is an ontological position that assumes that there is a meaningful reality which is independent from the operation of human consciousness. In participatory research objectivist ontological positions are not very common, as they are often associated with deductive, theory-led approaches which favour expert knowledge and research designs led by professional researchers who are regarded as best placed to scientifically discover and reveal a meaningful reality. People's everyday understanding of social phenomena would then consequently be seen as inferior to this scientific understanding, which is in contradiction to what co-production approaches are aiming to achieve.

Ontology   Ontology is concerned with the nature of existence or being and with the structure of reality. Like epistemological convictions, ontological standpoints impact on approaches to research and whether or not co-production is seen as beneficial for scientific endeavours.

REFERENCES

Abel, G. M. and Fitzgerald, L. J. (2008). On a fast-track into adulthood: an exploration of transitions into adulthood for street-based sex workers in New Zealand. *Journal of Youth Studies*, 11(4): 361–376.

Abrams, K. M. and Gaiser, T. J. (2017). Online focus groups. In N. Fielding, R. M. Lee and G. Blank (eds) *The Sage Handbook of Online Research Methods*. London: Sage (pp. 435–450).

Adams, K., Burns, C. Liebzeit, A., Ryschka, J., Thorpe, S. and Browne, J. (2012). Use of participatory research and photo-voice to support urban Aboriginal healthy eating. *Health and Social Care in the Community*, 20(5): 497–505.

Adato, M., Lund, F. and Mhlongo, P. (2007). Methodological innovations in research on the dynamics of poverty: a longitudinal study in KwaZulu-Natal, South Africa. *World Development*, 35(2): 247–263.

Alanen, L. and Mayall, B. (eds) (2001). *Conceptualizing Child–Adult Relations*. London: Psychology Press.

Aldiss, S., Horstman, M., O'Leary, C., Richardson, A. and Gibson, F. (2009). What is important to young children who have cancer while in hospital? *Children and Society*, 23(2): 85–98.

Aldridge, J. (2015). *Participatory Research: Working with Vulnerable Groups in Research and Practice*. Bristol: Policy Press.

Andrews, A. B., Motes, P. S., Floyd, A. G., Flerx, V. C. and Lopez-De Fede, A. (2005). Building evaluation capacity in community-based organizations: reflections of an empowerment evaluation team. *Journal of Community Practice*, 13(4): 85–104.

Archard, D. and Skivenes, M. (2009). Balancing a child's best interests and a child's views. *The International Journal of Children's Rights*, 17(1): 1–21.

Ardévol, E. (2012). Virtual/visual ethnography: methodological crossroads at the intersection of visual and internet research. In S. Pink (ed.) *Advances in Visual Methodology*. London Sage (pp. 74–93).

Argyris, C. and Schön, D. A. (1991). Participatory action research and action science compared: a commentary. In W. F. Whyte (ed.) *Participatory Action Research*. Newbury: Sage (pp. 85–96).

Arnstein, S. (1969). A ladder of citizen participation. *Journal of the American Institute of Planners*, 35(4): 216–224.

Ashwood, L., Harden, N., Bell, M. M. and Bland, W. (2014). Linked and situated: grounded knowledge. *Rural Sociology*, 79(4): 427–452.

Babbie, E. (2015). *The Practice of Social Research*. Boston: Cengage Learning.

Baker, L., Lavender, T. and Tincello, D. (2005). Factors that influence women's decisions about whether to participate in research: an exploratory study. *Birth*, 32(1): 60–66.

Balcazar, F. E., Garcia-Iriarte, E. and Suarez-Balcazar, Y. (2009). Participatory action research with Colombian immigrants. *Hispanic Journal of Behavioral Sciences*, 31(1): 112–127.

Banks, S. and Brydon-Miller, M. (eds) (2019). *Ethics in Participatory Research for Health and Social Wellbeing: Cases and Commentaries*. Abingdon: Routledge.

Baraldi, C. (2014). Children's participation in communication systems: a theoretical perspective. In M. N. Warehime (ed.) *Soul of Society: A Focus on the Lives of Children and Youth*. Sociological Studies of Children and Youth (Vol. 18). Bingley: Emerald (pp. 63–92).

Baraldi, C. and Iervese, V. (eds) (2012). *Participation, Facilitation, and Mediation: Children and Young People in Their Social Contexts*. Abingdon: Routledge.

Barnes, M. and Cotterell, P. (eds) (2012). *Critical Perspectives on User Involvement*. Bristol: Policy Press.

Barrera-Bassols, N., Zinck, J. A. and van Ranst, E. (2009). Participatory soil survey: experience in working with a Mesoamerican indigenous community. *Soil Use and Management*, 25(1): 43–56.

Baum, F., MacDougall, C. and Smith, D. (2006). Participatory action research. *Journal of Epidemiology and Community Health*, 60(10): 854–857.

Becker A. B. (2001). Community-based participatory research: policy recommendations for promoting a partnership approach in health research. *Education for Health*, 14(2): 182–197.

Beckett, H. and Warrington, C. (2015). *Making Justice Work: Experiences of Criminal Justice for Children and Young People Affected by Sexual Exploitation as Victims and Witnesses*. Luton: University of Bedfordshire.

Bela, G., Peltola, T., Young, J. C., Balázs, B., Arpin, I., Pataki, G. et al. (2016). Learning and the transformative potential of citizen science. *Conservation Biology*, 30(5): 990–999.

Bengtsson, T. T. and Mølholt, A. K. (2016). Keeping you close at a distance: ethical challenges when following young people in vulnerable life situations. *Young*, 24(4): 359–375.

Beresford, P. and Carr, S. (eds) (2012). *Social Care, Service Users and User Involvement*. London: Jessica Kingsley Publishers.

Berg, B. and Lune, H. (2014). *Qualitative Research Methods for the Social Sciences* (8th edition). Harlow: Pearson.

Berger, P. L. and Luckmann, T. (1966). *The Social Construction of Reality: A Treatise in the Sociology of Knowledge*. Garden City, NY: Doubleday.

Bernard, C. (2013). Ethical issues in researching Black teenage mothers with harmful childhood histories: marginal voices. *Ethics and Social Welfare*, 7(1): 54–73.

Bernard, M., Rickett, M., Amigoni, D., Munro, L., Murray, M. and Rezzano, J. (2015). Ages and stages: the place of theatre in the lives of older people. *Ageing & Society*, 35(6): 1119–1145.

Bernstein, R. J. (1976). *The Restructuring of Social and Political Thought*. Philadelphia: University of Pennsylvania Press.

Bhana, D. (2009). 'AIDS is rape!' Gender and sexuality in children's responses to HIV and AIDS. *Social Science & Medicine*, 69(4): 596–603.

Bicknell, J. (2014) Body of knowledge: a practice as research case study on the capacity for dance-theatre to promote wellbeing. *Working with Older People*, 18(1): 18–23.

Biggs, S. (1989). *Resource-poor Farmer Participation in Research: A Synthesis of Experiences from Nine National Agricultural Research Systems*. OFCOR Comparative Study Paper 3. The Hague: International Service for National Agricultural Research.

Biott, C. and Cook, T. (2000). Local evaluation in a national early years excellence centres pilot programme: integrating performance management and participatory evaluation. *Evaluation*, 6(4): 399–413.

Blair, T. and Minkler, M. (2009). Participatory action research with older adults: key principles in practice. *The Gerontologist*, 49 (5): 651–662.

Blake, M. K. (2007). Formality and friendship: research ethics review and participatory action research. *ACME: An International Journal for Critical Geographies*, 6(3): 411–421.

Blee, K. M. (1991). *Women of the Klan: Racism and Gender in the 1920s*. Berkeley: University of California Press.

Bloor, M., Frankland, J., Thomas, M. and Robson, K. (2001). *Focus Groups in Social Research*. London: Sage.

Blumer, H. (1986). *Symbolic Interactionism: Perspective and Method*. Berkeley: University of California Press.

Bock, J. G. (2001). Towards participatory communal appraisal. *Community Development Journal*, 36(2): 146–153.

Boellstorff, T. (2008). *Coming of Age in Second Life: An Anthropologist Explores the Virtually Human*. Princeton: Princeton University Press.

Boellstorff, T., Nardi, B., Pearce, C. and Taylor, T. L. (2012). *Ethnography and Virtual Worlds: A Handbook of Method*. Princeton: Princeton University Press.

Bogardus, E. (1926). The group interview. *Journal of Applied Sociology*, 10: 372–382.

Booth, D. (ed.) (1994). *Rethinking Social Development: Theory, Research and Practice*. Harlow: Longman.

Borland, M., Hill, M. Laybourne, A. and Stafford, A. (2001). *Improving Consultation with Children and Young People in Relevant Aspects of Policy-making and Legislation in Scotland*. Edinburgh: Scottish Parliament.

Boser, S. (2006). Ethics and power in community-campus partnerships for research. *Action Research*, 4(1): 9–21.

Bowers, H. and Wilkins, A. (2012). Co-production in evaluation and outcomes: lessons from working with older people in designing and undertaking research initiatives on older people's lives, independence and wellbeing. In P. Beresford and S. Carr (eds) *Social Care, Service Users and User Involvement*. London: Jessica Kingsley Publishers (pp. 96–119).

Boyden, J. and Ennew, J. (1997). *Children in Focus: A Manual for Participatory Research with Children*. Stockholm. Rädda Barnen.

Bradbury, H. and Mainemelis, C. (2001). Learning history and organizational praxis. *Journal of Management Inquiry*, 10(4): 340–357.

Brady, B. (2007). Developing children's participation: lessons from a participatory IT project. *Children and Society*, 21(1): 31–41.

Brady, L. M., Davey, C., Shaw, C. and Blades, R. (2012). Involving children and young people in research: principles into practice. In P. Beresford and S. Carr (eds) *Social Care, Service Users and User Involvement*. London: Jessica Kingsley Publishers (pp. 226–242).

Braithwaite, R., Cockwill, S., O'Neill, M. and Rebane, D. (2007). Insider participatory action research in disadvantaged post-industrial areas. The experiences of community members as they become Community Based Action Researchers. *Action Research*, 5(1): 61–74.

Braun, K., Browne, C., Ka'opua, L. S., Kim, B. J. and Mokuau, N. (2014). Research on indigenous elders: from positivistic to decolonizing methodologies. *The Gerontologist*, 54(1): 117–126.

Brodie, E., Hughes, T., Jochum, V., Miller, S., Ockenden, N and Warburton, D. (2011). *Pathways Through Participation: What Creates and Sustains Active Citizenship?* Summary report. London: Pathways Through Participation. Available online at: www.sharedpractice.org.uk/Downloads/Pathways_final_report.pdf (accessed May 2019).

Brown, E. R., Holtby, S., Zahnd, E. and Abbott, G. B. (2005). Community-based participatory research in the California Health Interview Survey. *Preventing Chronic Disease*, 2(4): 1–8.

Brown, L. D. and Tandon R. (1983). Ideology and political economy in inquiry: action research and participatory research. *The Journal of Applied Behavioral Science*, 19: 277–294.

Browne, K., Bakshi, L. and Lim, J. (2011). 'It's something you just have to ignore': understanding and addressing contemporary lesbian, gay, bisexual and trans safety beyond hate crime paradigms. *Journal of Social Policy*, 40(4): 739–756.

Brownlie, J. (2009). Researching, not playing, in the public sphere. *Sociology*, 43(4): 699–716.

Brydon-Miller, M. (2001). Education, research, action: theory and methods in participatory action research. In D. Tolman and M. Brydon-Miller (eds) *From Subjects to Subjectivities: A Handbook of Interpretive and Participatory Methods*. New York: New York University Press (pp. 77–89).

Brydon-Miller, M. and Greenwood, D. (2006). A re-examination of the relationship between action research and human subjects review processes. *Action Research*, 4(1): 117–128.

Bryman, A. (2012/2016). *Social Research Methods* (4th/5th edition). Oxford: Oxford University Press.

Buettgen, A., Richardson, J., Beckham, K., Richardson, K., Ward, M. and Riemer, M. (2012). We did it together: a participatory action research study on poverty and disability. *Disability and Society*, 27(5): 603–616.

Burgess, R. G. (ed.) (1982). *Field Research: A Sourcebook and Field Manual*. London: George Allen & Unwin.

Burgess, R. G. (1993). *In the Field: An Introduction to Field Research*. London: Routledge.

Burke, J. (2012). 'Some kids climb up; some kids climb down': culturally constructed play-worlds of children with impairments, *Disability and Society*, 27(7): 965–981.

Burke, J., Hess, S., Hoffmann, K., Guizzetti, L., Loy, E., Gielen, A. et al. (2014). Translating Community-Based Participatory Research (CBPR) principles into practice: building a research agenda to reduce intimate partner violence. *Progress in Community Health Partnerships: Research, Education, and Action*, 7(2): 115–122.

Burke, T. (2010). *Listen and Change: An Introductory Guide to the Participation Rights of Children and Young People* (2nd edition). London: Participation Works.

Burns, D., Hyde, P., Killett, A., Poland, F. and Gray, R. (2014). Participatory organizational research: examining voice in the co-production of knowledge. *British Journal of Management*, 25(1): 133–144.

Carey, P. and Sutton, S. (2004). Community development through participatory arts: lessons learned from a community arts and regeneration project in South Liverpool. *Community Development Journal*, 39(2): 123–134.

Cargo, M. and Mercer, S. L. (2008). The value and challenges of participatory research: strengthening its practice. *Annual Review of Public Health*, 29: 325–350.

Carney, G. M., Dundon, T. and Léime, Á. N. (2012). Participatory action research with and within community activist groups: capturing the collective experience of Ireland's Community and Voluntary Pillar in social partnership. *Action Research*, 10(3): 313–330.

Carpenter, J. (1995). Involving users and carers in the care programme approach, *Integrate News*, 67: 19–21.

Carr, S. (2012). Participation, resistance and change. examining influences on the impact of service user involvement. In P. Beresford and S. Carr (eds) *Social Care, Service Users and User Involvement*. London: Jessica Kingsley Publishers (pp. 37–51).

Castleden, H., Garvin, T. and Huu-Ay-Aht First Nation (2008). Modifying Photovoice for community-based participatory indigenous research. *Social Science & Medicine*, 66(6): 1393–1405.

Centre for Social Justice and Community Action & National Co-ordinating Centre for Public Engagement (2012). *Community-based Participatory Research: A Guide to Ethical Principles and Practice*. Durham University & University of Bristol.

Chambers, R. (1994). The origins and practice of participatory rural appraisal. *World Development*, 22(7): 953–969.

Chambers, R. (1997). *Whose Reality Counts? Putting the First Last*. London: Intermediate Technology Publications.

Chambers, R. (1998). Beyond 'Whose reality counts?' New methods we now need. *Studies in Cultures, Organizations and Societies*, 4(2): 279–301.

Chambers, R. (2002). *Participatory Workshops: A Sourcebook of 21 Sets of Ideas & Activities*. London: Earthscan.

Charmaz, K. (2005). Grounded theory in the 21st century: applications for advancing social justice studies. In N. K. Denzin and Y. S. Lincoln (eds) *The Sage Handbook of Qualitative Research*. Thousand Oaks: Sage (pp. 507–535).

Chevalier, J. M. and Buckles, D. J. (2013). *Participatory Action Research: Theory and Methods for Engaged Inquiry*. London: Routledge.

Chisholm, R. F. and Elden, M. (1993). Features of emerging action research. *Human Relations*, 46: 275–298.

Chopel, A. M. (2014). Reproductive health in indigenous Chihuahua: giving birth 'alone like the goat'. *Ethnicity & Health*, 19(4): 270–296.

Clark, A., Holland, C., Katz, J. and Peace, S. (2009). Learning to see: lessons from a participatory observation research project in public spaces. *International Journal of Social Research Methodology*, 12(4): 345–360.

Clark, A. and Moss, P. (2011). *Listening to Young Children: The Mosaic Approach*. London: NCB (National Children's Bureau).

Cloutier, G., Joerin, F., Dubois, C., Labarthe, M., Legay, C. and Viens, D. (2015). Planning adaptation based on local actors' knowledge and participation: a climate governance experiment. *Climate Policy*, 15(4): 458–474.

Coffey, A. and Atkinson, P. (1996). *Making Sense of Qualitative Data: Complementary Research Strategies*. Thousand Oaks: Sage

Coghlan, D. and Brannick, T. (2014). *Doing Action Research in Your Own Organization* (4th edition). London: Sage.

Cohen, A., Lopez, A., Malloy, N. and Morello-Frosch, R. (2012). Our environment, our health: a community-based participatory environmental health survey in Richmond, California. *Health Education & Behavior*, 39(2): 198–209.

Cohen, A. and Saisana, M. (2014). Quantifying the qualitative: eliciting expert input to develop the multidimensional poverty assessment tool. *The Journal of Development Studies*, 50(1): 35–50.

Cole, S. (2005). Action ethnography: using participant observation. In B. W. Ritchie, P. Burns and C. Palmer (eds) *Tourism Research Methods: Integrating Theory with Practice*. Wallingford: CABI Publishing (pp. 63–72).

Collins, K. J. (1997). Participatory process in the construction of a model for organisational change in South African welfare. *Social Work Maatskaplike Werk*, 33(2): 98–109.

Conder, J., Milner, P. and Mirfin-Veitch, B. (2011). Reflections on a participatory project: the rewards and challenges for the lead researchers. *Journal of Intellectual and Developmental Disability*, 36(1): 39–48.

Cooperrider, D. and Whitney, D. D. (2005). *Appreciative Inquiry: A Positive Revolution in Change*. San Francisco: Berrett-Koehler Publishers.

Corbin, J. and Morse, J. M. (2003). The unstructured interactive interview: issues of reciprocity and risks when dealing with sensitive topics. *Qualitative Inquiry*, 9(3): 335–354.

Corman, M. K. (2018). Titrating the rig: how paramedics work in and on their ambulance. *Qualitative Health Research*, 28(1): 47–59.

Cornish, F. and Ghosh, R. (2007). The necessary contradictions of 'community-led' health promotion: a case study of HIV prevention in an Indian red light district. *Social Science and Medicine*, 2 (64): 496–507.

Cornwall, A. (1996). Towards participatory practice: participatory rural appraisal (PRA) and the participatory process. In K. de Koning and M. Martin (eds) *Participatory Research in Health: Issues and Experiences*. Johannesburg: Zed Books (pp. 95–107).

Cornwall, A. and Jewkes, R. (1995). What is participatory research? *Social Science & Medicine*, 41(12): 1667–1676.

Council for Disabled Children (2012). *The VIPER Project: How We Did the Qualitative Research*. London: Council for Disabled Children.

Council for Disabled Children (2013). *The VIPER Project: Hear Us Out*. London: Council for Disabled Children.

Cousins, J. B. and Earl, L. M. (1992). The case for participatory evaluation. *Educational Evaluation and Policy Analysis*, 14(4): 397–418.

Crabtree, J. L., Wall, J. M. and Ohm, D. (2016). Critical reflections on participatory action research in a prison setting: toward occupational justice. *OTJR: Occupation, Participation and Health*, 36(4): 244–252.

Craig, Y. J. (1997). *Elder Abuse and Mediation: Exploratory Studies in America, Britain and Europe*. Aldershot: Avebury.

Crishna, B. (2007). Participatory evaluation (II) – translating concepts of reliability and validity in fieldwork. *Child: Care, Health and Development*, 33(3): 224–229.

Crotty, M. (1998). *The Foundations of Social Research. Meaning and Perspective in the Research Process*. London: Sage.

Daniel, B., Cross, B., Sherwood-Johnson, F. and Paton, D. (2014). Risk and decision making in adult support and protection practice: user views from participant research. *British Journal of Social Work*, 44(5): 1233–1250.

Davis, J. and Whittington, D. (1998). 'Participatory' research for development projects: a comparison of the community meeting and household survey techniques. *Economic Development and Cultural Change*, 47(1): 73–94.

de Freitas, C. and Martin, G. (2015). Inclusive public participation in health: policy, practice and theoretical contributions to promote the involvement of marginalised groups in healthcare. *Social Science & Medicine*, 135: 31–39.

Delamont, S., (2007). Ethnography and participant observation. In C. Seale, G. Gobo, J. F. Gubrium and D. Silverman (eds) *Qualitative Research Practice*. London: Sage (pp. 205–217).

Department of Health (2007). *Putting People First: A Shared Vision and Commitment to the Transformation of Adult Social Care*. London: Department of Health

de Vaus, D. A. (1996). *Surveys in Social Research*. London: UCL Press.

Dorsner, C. (2004). Social exclusion and participation in community development projects: evidence from Senegal. *Social Policy and Administration*, 38(4): 366–382.

Durand, C. (2016). Surveys and society. In C. Wolf, D. Joye, T. W. Smith and Y. C. Fu (eds) *The Sage Handbook of Survey Methodology*. London: Sage (pp. 57–86).

Durham Community Research Team (2011). *Community-based Participatory Research: Ethical Challenges*. Durham: Centre for Social Justice and Community Action, Durham University.

Durkheim, E. (1982 [1938]). *The Rules of Sociological Method: And Selected Texts on Sociology and Its Method*. New York: The Free Press.

Durkheim, E. (1995 [1912]). *The Elementary Forms of the Religious Life*. New York: The Free Press.

Dwyer, P. and Hardill, I. (2012). Promoting social inclusion? The impact of village services on the lives of older people living in rural England. *Ageing and Society*, 31(2): 243–264.

Edwards, M. (1989). The irrelevance of development studies. *Third World Quarterly*, 11(1): 116–135.

EKOS Ltd (2007). *Evaluation of the Rural Voices Action Research Competition*. Edinburgh: Scottish Executive Social Research.

Elwood Martin, R., Murphy, K., Hanson, D., Hemingway, C., Ramsden, V., Buxton, J. et al. (2009). The development of participatory health research among incarcerated women in a Canadian prison. *International Journal of Prisoner Health*, 5(2), 95–107.

Emerson, L. and Lloyd, K. (2014). *Are Children's Views Being Sought, Listened to and Taken Seriously?* ARK Research Update 94, Belfast: ARK.

Emerson, L. and Lloyd, K. (2017). Measuring children's experience of their right to participate in school and community: a rights-based approach. *Children and Society*, 31(2): 120–133.

Erdtman, E. (2012). Research initiation based on idea-circles: from research object to co-actor. *Disability and Society*, 27(6): 879–882.

Erens, B., Phelps, A., Clifton, S., Mercer, C. H., Tanton, C., Hussey, D. et al. (2014). Methodology of the third British National Survey of Sexual Attitudes and Lifestyles (Natsal-3). *Sexually Transmitted Infections*, 90(2): 84–89.

Eriksson, C. C., Fredriksson, I., Fröding, K., Geidne, S. and Pettersson, C. (2014). Academic practice–policy partnerships for health promotion research: experiences from three research programs. *Scandinavian Journal of Social Medicine*, 42(15_suppl): 88–95.

Evans, D. H., Bacon, R. J., Greer, E., Stagg, A. M. and Turton, P. (2015). 'Calling executives and clinicians to account': user involvement in commissioning cancer services. *Health Expectations*, 8(4): 504–515.

Evans, R. (2012). Towards a creative synthesis of participant observation and participatory research: reflections on doing research with and on young Bhutanese refugees in Nepal. *Childhood*, 20(2): 169–184.

Eylon, D. (1998). Understanding empowerment and resolving its paradox: lessons from Mary Parker Follett. *Journal of Management History*, 4(1): 16–28.

Fals-Borda, O. (2001). Participatory (action) research in social theory: origins and challenges. In P. Reason and H. Bradbury (eds) *Handbook of Action Research: Participatory Inquiry and Practice*. London: Sage (pp. 27–37).

Farquhar, S. A. and Dobson, N. (2005). Community and university participation in disaster-relief recovery: an example from eastern North Carolina. *Journal of Community Practice*, 12(3/4): 203–217.

Fenge, L.-A. (2010). Striving towards inclusive research: an example of participatory action research with older lesbians and gay men. *British Journal of Social Work*, 40(3): 878–894.

Fenge, L.-A., Fannin, A., Armstrong, A., Hicks, C. and Taylor, V. (2009). Lifting the lid on sexuality and ageing: the experiences of volunteer researchers. *Qualitative Social Work*, 8(4): 509–524.

Fern, E. F. (2001). *Advanced Focus Group Research*. Thousand Oaks: Sage.

Fetterman, D. M., Kaftarian, S. J. and Wandersman, A. (2014). *Empowerment Evaluation: Knowledge and Tools for Self-assessment and Accountability*. London: Sage.

Fieldhouse, J. (2012). Mental health, social inclusion, and community development: lessons from Bristol. *Community Development Journal*, 47(4): 571–587.

Finch, H. and Lewis, J. (2003). Focus groups. In J. Ritchie and J. Lewis (eds) *Qualitative Research Practice: A Guide for Social Science Students and Researchers*. London: Sage (pp. 170–198).

Finch, J. (1984). It's great to have someone to talk to: the ethics of interviewing women. In C. Bell and H. Roberts (eds) *Social Researching: Politics, Problems. Practice*. London: Routledge (pp. 70–87).

Fine, M. and Torre, M. E. (2006). Intimate details: participatory action research in prison. *Action Research*, 4(3): 253–269.

Fiske, S. T. and Taylor, S. E. (2016). *Social Cognition: From Brains to Culture* (3rd edition). London: Sage.

Flick, U. (2014). *An Introduction to Qualitative Research*. London: Sage

Flicker, S., Travers, R., Guta, A., McDonald, S. and Meagher, A. (2007). Ethical dilemmas in community-based participatory research: recommendations for institutional review boards. *Journal of Urban Health*, 84(4): 478–493.

Folch-Lyon, E., de la Macorra, L. and Schearer, S. B. (1981). Focus group and survey research on family planning in Mexico. *Studies in Family Planning*, 12(12): 409–432.

Follett, M. P. (1919). Community is a process. *The Philosophical Review*, 28(6): 576–588.

Fonow, M. M. and Cook, J. A. (1991). Back to the future: a look at the second wave of feminist epistemology and methodology. In M. M. Fonow and J. A. Cook (eds) *Beyond Methodology: Feminist Scholarship as Lived Research*. Bloomington: Indiana University Press (pp. 1–15).

Formea, C. M., Mohamed, A. A., Hassan, A., Osman, A., Weis, J. A., Sia, I. G. and Wieland, M. L. (2014). Lessons learned: cultural and linguistic enhancement of surveys through community-based participatory research. *Progress in Community Health Partnerships: Research, Education, and Action*, 8(3): 331.

Foster, V. (2007). Ways of knowing and showing: imagination and representation in feminist participatory social research. *Journal of Social Work Practice: Psychotherapeutic Approaches in Health, Welfare and the Community*, 21(3): 361–376.

Foster, V. and Young A. (2015). Reflecting on participatory methodologies: research with parents of babies requiring neonatal care. *International Journal of Social Research Methodology*, 18(1): 91–104.

Fowler, F. J. (2014). *Survey Research Methods*. Thousand Oaks: Sage.

Fox, J. (2009). A participatory action research project evaluating a carers' representation group – carers against stigma. *Mental Health Review Journal*, 14(4): 25–35.

Fox, M. and Fine, M. (2013). Accountable to whom? A critical science counter-story about a city that stopped caring for its young. *Children and Society*, 27(4): 321–335.

Fox, R. (2013) Resisting participation: critiquing participatory research methodologies with young people. *Journal of Youth Studies*, 16(8): 986–999.

Francisco, V. (2014). 'Ang Ating Iisang Kuwento' our collective story: migrant Filipino workers and participatory action research. *Action Research*, 12(1): 78–93.

Franks, M. (2011). Pockets of participation: revisiting child-centred participation research. *Children and Society*, 25(1): 15–25.

Franz, N., Piercy, F., Donaldson, J., Richard, R. and Westbrook, J. (2010). How farmers learn: implications for agricultural educators. *Rural Social Sciences*, 25(1): 37–59.

Freeman, M. D. (1992). Taking children's rights more seriously. *International Journal of Law, Policy and the Family*, 6(1): 52–71.

Freire, P. (1971). *Pedagogy of the Oppressed*, trans. M. B. Ramos. New York: Seabury Press.

Friedman, V. J. (2008). Action science: creating communities of inquiry in communities of practice. In P. Reason and H. Bradbury (eds) *Handbook of Action Research*. London: Sage (pp. 131–143).

Fry, C. and Dwyer, R. (2001). For love or money? An exploratory study of why injecting drug users participate in research. *Addiction*, 96(9): 1319–1325.

Fulcher, J. and Scott, J. (2003). *Sociology*. Oxford. Oxford University Press.

Gallagher, L. A. and Gallagher, M. (2008). Methodological immaturity in childhood research? Thinking through participatory research. *Childhood*, 15(4): 499–516.

Gant, L. M., Shimshock, K., Allen-Meares, P., Smith, L., Miller, P., Hollingsworth, L. A. et al. (2009). Effects of photovoice: civic engagement among older youth in urban communities. *Journal of Community Practice*, 17(4): 358–376.

Garcia, C. M., Gilchrist, L., Campesino, C., Raymond, N., Naughton, S. and de Patino, J. G. (2008). Using community-based participatory research to develop a bilingual mental health survey for Latinos. *Progress in Community Health Partnerships*, 2(2): 105–120.

Garcia-Iriarte, E., Kramer, J. C., Kramer, J. M. and Hammel, J. (2009). 'Who did what?': A participatory action research project to increase group capacity for advocacy. *Journal of Applied Research in Intellectual Disabilities*, 22(1): 10–22.

Gardner, K. and Mand, K. (2012). 'My away is here': place, emplacement and mobility amongst British Bengali children. *Journal of Ethnic and Migration Studies*, 38(6): 969–986.

Garfinkel, H. (1967). *Studies in Ethnomethodology*. Englewood Cliffs, NJ: Prentice-Hall.

Garfinkel, H. (2002). *Ethnomethodology's Program: Working out Durkheim's Aphorism*, edited and introduced by Anne Rawls. Lanham, MD: Rowman & Littlefield.

Geertz, C. (1973). *The Interpretation of Cultures: Selected Essays* (Vol. 5019). New York: Basic Books.

Ghaffar, A., Khan, M. Q and Ullah, N. (2007). Integrated approach for improving small scale market oriented dairy systems in Pakistan: participatory rural appraisal and economic opportunity survey. *Tropical Animal Health and Production*, 39(8): 593–601.

Gilchrist, F., Rodd, H. D., Deery, C. and Marshman, Z. (2013). Involving children in research, audit and service evaluation. *British Dental Journal*, 214(11): 577–582.

Girodo, M. (1991). Drug corruption in undercover agents: measuring the risk. *Behavioral Sciences and the Law*, 9(3): 361–370.

Gitonga, P. N. and Delport, A. (2014). Exploring the use of hip hop music in participatory research studies that involve youth. *Journal of Youth Studies*, 18(8): 984–996.

Giulianotti, R. (1995). Participant observation and research into football hooliganism: reflections on the problems of entree and everyday risks. *Sociology of Sport Journal*, 12(1): 1–20.

Glaser, B. G. and Strauss, A. L. (1967). *The Discovery of Grounded Theory: Strategies for Qualitative Research*. London: Weidenfeld & Nicholson.

Glass, K. C. and Kaufert, J. (2007). Research ethics review and aboriginal community values: can the two be reconciled? *Journal of Empirical Research on Human Research Ethics*, 2(2): 25–40.

Gleason-Comstock, J., Streater, A., Calhoun, C. B., Simpson, H. L., Rolack, R. and Norman Jr, S. (2006). Development of a community-based participatory research effort to evaluate conventional HIV testing (CHT) and HIV rapid testing (HRT). *Journal of HIV/AIDS and Social Services*, 5(3/4): 201–219.

Godin, P., Davies, J., Heyman, B., Reynolds, L., Simpson, A. and Floyd, M. (2007). Opening communicative space: a Habermasian understanding of a user-led participatory research project. *The Journal of Forensic Psychiatry and Psychology*, 18(4): 452–469.

Goffman, E. (1959). *The Presentation of Self in Every-day Life*. Harmondsworth: Penguin.

Gold, R. L. (1958). Roles in sociological field observations. *Social Forces*, 36: 217–223.

Goodfellow-Baikie, R. L. and English, L. M. (2006). First Nations and community economic development: a case study. *Community Development Journal*, 41(2): 223–233.

Gotschi, E., Delve, R. and Freyer, B. (2009). Participatory photography as a qualitative approach to obtain insights into farmer groups. *Field Methods*, 21(3): 290–308.

Gough, K. V., Langevang, T. and Namatovu, R. (2014). Researching entrepreneurship in low-income settlements: the strengths and challenges of participatory methods. *Environment and Urbanization*, 26(1): 297–311.

Gowen, L. K., Bandurraga, A., Jivanjee, P., Cross, T. and Friesen, B. J. (2012). Development, testing, and use of a valid and reliable assessment tool for urban American Indian/Alaska native youth programming using culturally appropriate methodologies. *Journal of Ethnic and Cultural Diversity in Social Work*, 21(2): 77–94.

Grassau, P. (2009). Resilience and 'turning it out': how the arts engage with relational and structural aspects of oppression. *Canadian Social Work Review*, 26(2): 249–265.

Graybill, P., Aggas, J., Dean, R. K., Demers, S., Finigan, E. G. and Pollard Jr, R. Q. (2010). A community-participatory approach to adapting survey items for deaf individuals and American Sign Language. *Field Methods*, 22(4): 429–448.

Groeben, N. (1990). Subjective theories and the explanation of human action. In G. R. Semin and K. J. Gergen (eds) *Everyday Understanding: Social and Scientific Implications. Inquiries in Social Construction*. Thousand Oaks: Sage (pp. 19–44).

Groves, R. M., Fowler Jr., F. J., Couper, M. P., Lepkowski, J. M., Singer, E. and Tourangeau, R. (2009). *Survey Methodology* (2nd edition). Hoboken: John Wiley & Sons.

Gubrium, A. C., Hill, A. L. and Flicker, S. (2014). A situated practice of ethics for participatory visual and digital methods in public health research and practice: a focus on digital storytelling. *American Journal of Public Health*, 104(9): 1606–1614.

Habermas, J. (1972). *Knowledge and Human Interest*. London: Heinemann.

Habermas, J. (1984). *Communication and the Evolution of Society*. Cambridge: Polity Press.

Habermas, J. (1985). *The Theory of Communicative Action*. Boston: Beacon Press.

Hacking, S., Secker, J., Spandler, H., Kent, L. and Shenton, J. (2008). Evaluating the impact of participatory art projects for people with mental health needs. *Health and Social Care in the Community*, 16(6): 638–648.

Halkier, B. (2010). Focus groups as social enactments: integrating interaction and content in the analysis of focus group data. *Qualitative Research*, 10(1): 71–89.

Hall, B. L. (1975). Participatory research: an approach for change. *Convergence*, 8(2): 24.

Hall, B. L. (2001). 'I wish I were a poem of practices of participatory research'. In P. Reason and H. Bradbury (eds) *Handbook of Action Research*. London: Sage (pp. 171–178).

Hall, B. L., Jackson, E. T., Tandon, R., Fontan, J. and Lall, N. (eds) (2013). *Knowledge, Democracy and Action: Community University Research Partnerships in Global Perspectives*. Manchester: Manchester University Press.

Hall, B. L., Tandon, R. and Tremblay, C. (eds) (2015). *Mainstreaming Community University Research Partnerships: Global Perspectives*. Victoria: University of Victoria.

Hammersley, M. and Atkinson, P. (2007). *Ethnography. Principles in Practice* (3rd edition). London: Routledge.

Hampshire, K., Porter, G., Owusu, S., Mariwah, S., Abane, A., Robson, E. (2012). Taking the long view: temporal considerations in the ethics of children's research activity and knowledge production. *Children's Geographies*, 10(2): 219–232.

Haney, C., Banks, C. and Zimbardo, P. (1972). *Interpersonal Dynamics in a Simulated Prison* (No. ONR-TR-Z-09). Stanford: Stanford University, Department of Psychology.

Harding, S. G. (1986). *The Science Question in Feminism*. Ithaca: Cornell University Press.

Harding, S. G. (ed.) (1987). *Feminism and Methodology*. Bloomington: Indiana University Press.

Harkness, J. A., van de Vijver F. J. R. and Mohler, P. P. (2002). *Cross-Cultural Survey Methods*. Hoboken: John Wiley & Sons.

Hart, E. and Bond, M. (1995). *Action Research for Health and Social Care: A Guide to Practice*. Buckingham: Open University Press.

Heinonen, P. (2013). Participant observation versus participatory research: voices from the field. *DADA Rivista di Antropologia post-globale*, 3(1): 37–42.

Hemment, D., Ellis, R. and Wynne, B. (2011). Participatory mass observation and citizen science. *Leonardo*, 44(1): 62–63.

Heron, J. (1996). *Co-operative Inquiry: Research into the Human Condition*. London: Sage.

Hesse-Biber, S. N. (2007). *Handbook of Feminist Research: Theory and Praxis*. London: Sage

Hill, R. P., Rapp, J. M. and Capella, M. L. (2015). Consumption restriction in a total control institution: participatory action research in a maximum security prison. *Journal of Public Policy and Marketing*, 34(2): 156–172.

Hillier, A., Cannuscio, C. C., Griffin, L., Thomas, N. and Glanz, K. (2014) The value of conducting door-to-door surveys. *International Journal of Social Research Methodology*, 17(3): 285–302.

Hilsen, A. I. (2006). And they shall be known by their deeds: ethics and politics in action research. *Action Research*, 4(1): 23–36.

Hine, C. (2000). *Virtual Ethnography*. London: Sage.

Hodge, S. (2005). Participation, discourse and power: a case study in service user involvement. *Critical Social Policy*, 25(2): 164–179.

Hoff, L. A. (1988). Collaborative feminist research and the myth of objectivity. In K. Yllö and M. Bograd (eds) *Feminist Perspectives on Wife Abuse*. Newbury Park: Sage (pp. 269–281).

Hogg B. and Schur H. (1998). Using research as a tool for change in a residential setting. *Care – The Journal of Practice and Development*, 6(4): 17–35.

Honneth, A. (1995). *The Struggle for Recognition: The Moral Grammar of Social Conflicts*. Cambridge: Polity.

Horsfield, E., Kelly, F., Clark, T. and Sheridan, J. (2014). How youth-friendly are pharmacies in New Zealand? Surveying aspects of accessibility and the pharmacy environment using a youth participatory approach. *Research in Social & Administrative Pharmacy*, 10(3): 529–538.

Howe, G. and McKay, A. (2007). Combining quantitative and qualitative methods in assessing chronic poverty: the case of Rwanda. *World Development*, 35(2): 197–211.

Huberman, A. M. and Miles, M. B. (1994). Data management and analysis methods. In N. K. Denzin, and Y. S. Lincoln, Y. S. (eds) *Handbook of Qualitative Research*. Thousand Oaks: Sage (pp. 428–444).

Hull, P. C., Canedo, J. R., Reece, M. C., Lira, I., Reyes, F. and Garcia, E. et al. (2010). Using a participatory research process to address disproportionate Hispanic cancer burden. *Journal of Health Care for the Poor and Underserved*, 21: 95–113.

Humphreys, L. (1970). Tearoom trade. *Society*, 7(3): 10–25.

Hyde, C. A. and Meyer, M. (2004). A collaborative approach to service, learning and scholarship: a community-based research course. *Journal of Community Practice*, 12(1/2): 71–87.

Irwin, J. A., Coleman, J. D., Fisher, C. M. and Marasco, V. M. (2014). Correlates of suicide ideation among LGBT Nebraskans. *Journal of Homosexuality*, 61(8): 1172–1191.

Jacobson, M. and Rugeley, C. (2007). Community-based participatory research: group work for social justice and community change. *Social Work with Groups*, 30(4): 21–39.

James, A. (2009). Agency. In J. Qvortrup, W. A. Corsaro, M. S. Honig and G. Valentine, G. (eds) *The Palgrave Handbook of Childhood Studies*. Basingstoke: Palgrave (pp. 34–45).

Johnson, M. A. (2010). Teaching macro practice through service learning using participatory photography. *Journal of Community Practice*, 18(2–3): 297–314.

Johnson-Agbakwu, C. E., Helm, T., Killawi, A. and Padela, A. I. (2014). Perceptions of obstetrical interventions and female genital cutting: insights of men in a Somali refugee community. *Ethnicity & Health*, 19(4): 440–457.

Jones, B. L., Pomeroy, E. C. and Sampson, M. (2009). University-community partnerships and community-based participatory research: one community's approach to enhance capacity in end-of-life and bereavement practice, research, and education. *Journal of Social Work in End-of-life & Palliative Care*, 5(1–2): 94–104.

Jones, V., Northway, R., Stamp, J. and Evans, L. (2010). Staying on TRAC. *Learning Disability Today*, 34–36.

Jordan, J., Lynch, U., Moutray, M., O'Hagan, M. T., Orr, J., Peake, S. et al. (2007). Using focus groups to research sensitive issues: insights from group interviews on nursing in the Northern Ireland 'Troubles'. *International Journal of Qualitative Methods*, 6(4): 1–19.

Joseph, J. G., Emmons, C. A., Kessler, R. C., Wortman, C. B., O'Brien, K., Hocker, W. T. et al. (1984). Coping with the threat of AIDS: an approach to psychosocial assessment. *American Psychologist*, 39(11): 1297.

Joseph Rowntree Foundation (2008). *Engaging and Empowering Women in Poverty*. York: Joseph Rowntree Foundation.

Jupp Kina, V. (2012). What we say and what we do: reflexivity, emotions and power in children and young people's participation. *Children's Geographies*, 10(2): 201–218.

Kahindi, O., Wittemyer, G., King, J., Ihwagi, F., Omondi, P. and Douglas-Hamilton, I. (2010). Employing participatory surveys to monitor the illegal killing of elephants across diverse land uses in Laikipia-Samburu, Kenya. *African Journal of Ecology*, 48(4): 972–983.

Kaplan, S. A., Dillman, K. N., Calman, N. S. and Billings, J. (2004). Opening doors and building capacity: employing a community-based approach to surveying. *Journal of Urban Health*, 81(2): 291–300.

Kawulich, B. B. (2005). Participant observation as a data collection method [81 paragraphs]. *Forum Qualitative Sozialforschung/Forum: Qualitative Social Research*, 6(2): Art. 43, http://nbnresolving.de/urn:nbn:de:0114-fqs0502430.

Kellett, M. (2005). Children as active researchers: a new research paradigm for the 21st century? *NCRM Methods Review Papers*, NCRM/003. Southampton: ESRC National Centre for Research Methods. Available at: http://eprints.ncrm.ac.uk/87/1/MethodsReviewPaperNCRM-003.pdf (accessed March 2019).

Kelly, G. A. (1955). *The Psychology of Personal Constructs* (Vol. I, II). New York: Norton.

Kemmis, S. (2001). Exploring the relevance of critical theory for action research: emancipatory action research in the footsteps of Jürgen Habermas. In P. Reason and H. Bradbury (eds) *Handbook of Action Research: Participative Inquiry and Practice*. London: Sage (pp. 91–102).

Kendall, E. and Barnett, L. (2015). Principles for the development of Aboriginal health interventions: culturally appropriate methods through systemic empathy. *Ethnicity & Health*, 20(5): 437–452.

Kershaw, G. G., Castleden, H. and Laroque, C. P. (2014). An argument for ethical physical geography research on indigenous landscapes in Canada. *The Canadian Geographer/Le Géographe canadien*, 58(4): 393–399.

Kim, M. M., Calloway, M. O. and Selz-Campbell, L. (2004). A two-level community intervention model for homeless mothers with mental health or substance abuse disorders. *Journal of Community Practice*, 12(1/2): 107–121.

Koskinen, I. (2014). Critical subjects: participatory research needs to make room for debate. *Philosophy of the Social Sciences*, 44(6): 733–751.

Kozol, J. (1985). *Illiterate America*. New York: Random House

Kramer, J. M., Kramer, J. C., García-Iriarte, E. and Hammel, J. (2011). Following through to the end: the use of inclusive strategies to analyse and interpret data in participatory action research with individuals with intellectual disabilities. *Journal of Applied Research in Intellectual Disabilities*, 24(3): 263–273.

Kreitzer, L., Abukari, Z., Antonio, P., Mensah, J. and Kwaku, A. (2009). Social work in Ghana: a participatory action research project looking at culturally appropriate training and practice. *Social Work Education (The International Journal)*, 28(2): 145–164.

Krueger, R. A. and Casey, M. A. (2009). *Focus Groups: A Practical Guide for Applied Research* (4th edition). London: Sage

Krueger, R. A. and King, J. A. (1998). *Involving Community Members in Focus Groups*. Focus Group Kit 5. Thousand Oaks: Sage.

Kuo, T., Christensen, R., Gelberg, L., Rubenstein, L. and Burke, A. (2006). Community-research collaboration between researchers and acupuncturists: Integrating a participatory research approach in a statewide survey of licensed acupuncturists in California. *Ethnicity & Disease*, 16(1): 98–106.

Ladkin, D. (2007). Action research. In C. Seale, G. Gobo, J. F. Gubrium and D. Silverman (eds) *Qualitative Research Practice*. London: Sage (pp. 478–490).

Lakwo, A. (2008). Poverty eradication dilemma: understanding poverty dynamics in Nebbi District, Uganda. *Africa Development*, 33(2): 117–140.

Lassiter, L. E. (2005). *The Chicago Guide to Collaborative Ethnography*. Chicago: University of Chicago Press.

Lather, P. (1991). *Getting Smart: Feminist Research and Pedagogy with/in the Postmodern*. New York: Routledge.

Lavelle, B., Larsen, M. D. and Gundersen, C. (2009). Strategies for surveys of American Indians. *Public Opinion Quarterly*, 73(2): 385–403.

Lengwiler, M. (2008). Participatory approaches in science and technology: historical origins and current practices in critical perspective. *Science, Technology, & Human Values*, 33(2): 186–200.

Lennie, J. (2005). An evaluation capacity-building process for sustainable community IT initiatives: empowering and disempowering impacts. *Evaluation*, 11(4): 390–414.

Lennie, J., Tacchi, J., Wilmore, M. and Koirala, B. (2015). A holistic, learning-centred approach to building evaluation capacity in development organizations. *Evaluation*, 21(3): 325–343.

Le Roy Ladurie, E. (1978). *Montaillou: Cathars and Catholics in a French Village, 1294–1324*. London: Scholar Press.

Letiecq, B. L. and Bailey S. J. (2004). Evaluating from the outside: conducting cross-cultural evaluation research on an American Indian reservation. *Evaluation Review*, 28(4): 342–357.

Leung, M. W., Yen, I. H. and Minkler, M. (2004). Community based participatory research: a promising approach for increasing epidemiology's relevance in the 21st century. *International Journal of Epidemiology*, 33(3): 499–506.

Lewin, K. (1946). Action research and minority problems. *Journal of Social Issues*, 2(4): 34–46.

Liamputtong, P. (2006). *Researching the Vulnerable*. London: Sage.

Liamputtong, P. (2011). *Focus Group Methodology: Principles and Practice*. London: Sage.

Little, R. M. and Froggett, L. (2010). Making meaning in muddy waters: representing complexity through community based storytelling. *Community Development Journal*, 45(4): 458–473.

Littlechild, R., Tanner, D. and Hall, K. (2015). Co-research with older people: perspectives on impact. *Qualitative Social Work*, 14(1): 18–35.

Looking into Abuse Research Team (2014). *Looking into Abuse: Research by People with Learning Disabilities*. Glamorgan: University of Glamorgan. Available at: http://udid.research.southwales.ac.uk/media/files/documents/2013-03-05/Final_report.pdf (accessed May 2019).

Lorenzo, T. (2003). No African renaissance without disabled women: a communal approach to human development in Cape Town South Africa. *Disability and Society*, 18(6): 759–778.

Lowe, C., Gaudion, K., McGinley, C. and Kew, A. (2014). Designing living environments with adults with autism. *Tizard Learning Disability Review*, 19(2): 63–72.

Luhmann, N. (1995). *Social Systems*. Stanford: Stanford University Press

Luhmann, N. (2000). *Problems of Reflection in the System of Education*. Münster: Waxmann Verlag.

Lundy, L. (2018). In defence of tokenism? Implementing children's right to participate in collective decision-making. *Childhood*, 25(3): 340–354.

Lundy, L. and McEvoy (Emerson), L. (2012). Children's rights and research processes: assisting children to (in)formed views. *Childhood*, 19(1): 1–16.

Lundy, P. and McGovern, M. (2006). Participation, truth and partiality: participatory action research, community-based truth-telling and post-conflict transition in Northern Ireland. *Sociology*, 40(1): 71–88.

Lunt, P. and Livingstone, S. (1996). Rethinking the focus group in media and communications research. *Journal of Communication*, 46(2): 79–98.

Lykes, M. B. and Coquillon, E. (2007). Participatory and action research and feminisms. In S. N. Hesse-Biber (ed.) *Handbook of Feminist Research: Theory and Practice*. Thousand Oaks: Sage (pp. 297–326).

Macaulay, A., Commanda, L. E., Freeman, W. L., Gibson, N., McCabe, M. L., Robbins, C. M. et al. (1999). Participatory research maximises community and lay involvement. *British Medical Journal*, 319(7212): 774–778.

MacFarlane, A. and Roche, B. (2019). Blurring the boundaries between researcher and researched, academic and activist. In S. Banks and M. Brydon-Miller (eds) *Ethics in Participatory Research for Health and Social Wellbeing: Cases and Commentaries*. Abingdon: Routledge (pp. 80–103).

MacKinnon S. (2011). Building capacity through participatory action research: the state of the inner-city report project. *Community Development Journal*, 46(2): 309–323.

Macnaghten, P. and Myers, G. (2004). Focus groups. In C. Seale, G. Gobo, J. F. Gubrium and D. Silverman (eds) *Qualitative Research Practice*. London: Sage (pp. 65–79).

Maconochie, H. and McNeill, F. (2010). User involvement: children's participation in a parent–baby group. *Community Practitioner*, 83(8): 17–20.

Madden, R. (2017). *Being Ethnographic. A Guide to the Theory and Practice of Ethnography*. London: Sage.

Madriz, E. I. (1998). Using focus groups with lower socioeconomic status Latina women. *Qualitative Inquiry*, 4(1): 114–128.

Maguire, P. (1987). *Doing Participatory Research: A Feminist Approach*. Amherst: The Centre for International Education, University of Massachusetts.

Maiter, S., Simich, L., Jacobson, N. and Wise, J. (2008). Reciprocity: an ethic for community-based participatory action research. *Action Research*, 6(3): 305–325.

Malik, N. M., Ward, K. and Janczewski, C. (2008). Coordinated community response to family violence: the role of domestic violence service organisations. *Journal of Interpersonal Violence*, 23(7): 933–955.

Malinowski, B. (2013 [1922]). *Argonauts of the Western Pacific: An Account of Native Enterprise and Adventure in the Archipelagoes of Melanesian New Guinea*. London: Routledge.

March, S. (2017). Individual data linkage of survey data with claims data in Germany – an overview based on a cohort study. *International Journal of Environmental Research and Public Health*, 14(12): 1543.

Marcus, M. T., Walker, T., Swint, J. M., Smith, B. P., Brown, C., Busen, N. et al. (2004). Community-based participatory research to prevent substance abuse and HIV/AIDS in African-American adolescents. *Journal of Interprofessional Care*, 18(4): 347–359.

Martin, R. E., Murphy, K., Chan, R., Ramsden, V. R., Granger-Brown, A., Macaulay, A. C. et al. (2009). Primary health care: applying the principles within a community-based participatory health research project that began in a Canadian women's prison. *Global Health Promotion*, 16(4): 43–53.

Marx, K. and Engels, F. (1848). *Manifest der Kommunistischen Partei*. [Manifesto of the Communist Party]. London: Office der Bildungsgesellschaft für Arbeiter.

Marx, K. and Engels, F. (2001). *The German Ideology. Part 1. Edited and with an introduction by C. J. Arthur*. London: Electric Book Company.

Mason, J. (2002). *Qualitative Researching*. London: Sage.

McAlister, S. and Neill, G. (2009). 'The L Pack': addressing the sexual health needs of young lesbians. *Child Care in Practice*, 15(3): 209–226.

McCambridge, J., Witton, J. and Elbourne, D. R. (2014). Systematic review of the Hawthorne effect: new concepts are needed to study research participation effects. *Journal of Clinical Epidemiology*, 67(3): 267–277.

McCartan, C., Burns, S. and Schubotz, D. (2012). Recruitment and capacity-building challenges in participatory research involving young people in Northern Ireland. In L. Goodson and J. Phillimore (eds) *Community Research for Participation: From Theory to Method*. Bristol: Policy Press (pp. 283–297).

McCartan, C., Schubotz, D. and Murphy, J. (2012). The self-conscious researcher – post-modern perspectives of participatory research with young people [48 paragraphs]. *Forum Qualitative Sozialforschung/Forum: Qualitative Social Research*, 13(1), Art. 9, http://nbn-resolving.de/urn:nbn:de:0114-fqs120192.

McConnell, T., Best, P., Davidson, G., McEneaney, T., Cantrell, C. and Tully, M. (2018). Coproduction for feasibility and pilot randomised controlled trials: learning outcomes for community partners, service users and the research team. *Research Involvement and Engagement*, 4(1): 32

McDonnell, O., Lohan, M., Hyde, A. and Porter, S. (2009). *Social Theory, Health and Healthcare*. Basingstoke: Palgrave Macmillan.

McGee, R. (2004). Constructing poverty trends in Uganda: a multidisciplinary perspective. *Development and Change*, 35(3): 499–523.

McIntyre A. (2002). Women researching their lives: exploring violence and identity in Belfast, the North of Ireland. *Qualitative Research*, 2(3): 387–409.

McIntyre, A. (2008). *Participatory Action Research*. Qualitative Research Methods Series, No 52. London: Sage.

McTaggart, R. (ed.) (1997). *Participatory Action Research: International Contexts and Consequences*. Albany: State University of New York Press.

Mead, G. (2016). Muddling through: facing the challenges of managing a large-scale action research project. In P. Reason and H. Bradbury (eds) *Handbook of Action Research: Participatory Inquiry and Practice*. London: Sage (pp. 629–642).

Mead, G. H. (1934). *Mind, Self and Society*. Chicago: University of Chicago Press.

Mears, A. (2013). Ethnography as precarious work. *The Sociological Quarterly*, 54(1): 20–34.

Merton, R. K., Fiske, M. and Kendall, P. L. (1956). *The Focussed Interview*. New York: Free Press.

Messerli, S. and Abdykaparov, M. (2008). Participatory approaches in developing farmer education and community ownership of training in Kyrgyzstan. *Community Development Journal*, 43(3): 341–357.

Mezirow, J. (1991). *Transformative Dimensions of Adult Learning*. San Francisco: Jossey-Bass Wiley.

Milner, P. and Kelly, B. (2009). Community participation and inclusion: people with disabilities defining their place. *Disability and Society*, 24(1): 47–62.

Minkler, M., Blackwell, A. G., Thompson, M. and Tamir, H. (2003). Community-based participatory research: implications for public health funding. *American Journal of Public Health*, 93(8): 1210–1213.

Minkler, M. and Wallerstein, N. (eds) (2011). *Community-based Participatory Research for Health: From Process to Outcomes*. San Francisco: Jossey-Bass.

Minore, B., Boone, M., Katt, M., Kinch, P. and Birch, S. (2004). Addressing the realities of health care in northern aboriginal communities through participatory action research. *Journal of Interprofessional Care*, 18(4): 360–368.

Misgav, C. (2014). Memory and place in participatory planning. *Planning Theory and Practice,* 15(3): 349–369.

Mochmann, I. C. (2017). Children born of war: a decade of international and interdisciplinary research. *Historical Social Research,* 42(1): 320–346.

Morawski, J. (2001). Feminist research methods: bringing culture to science. In D. Tolman and M. Brydon-Miller (eds) *From Subjects to Subjectivities. A Handbook of Interpretive and Participatory Methods.* New York: New York University Press (pp. 56–75).

Morgan, D. L. (1997). *Focus Groups as Qualitative Research* (2nd edition). Thousand Oaks: Sage.

Morgan, M. F., Moni, K. B. and Cuskelly, M. (2015). The development of research skills in young adults with intellectual disability in participatory research. *International Journal of Disability Development and Education,* 62(4): 438–457.

Mosavel, M., Simon, C., Van Stade, D. and Buchbinder, M. (2005). Community-Based Participatory Research (CBPR) in South Africa: engaging multiple constituents to shape the research question. *Social Science and Medicine,* 61(12): 2577–2587.

Moschitz, H. and Home, R. (2014). The challenges of innovation for sustainable agriculture and rural development: integrating local actions into European policies with the Reflective Learning Methodology. *Action Research,* 12(4): 392–409.

Msoffe, F. U., Ogutu, J. O., Kaaya, J., Bedelian, C., Said, M. Y., Kifugo, S. C. et al. (2010). Participatory wildlife surveys in communal lands: a case study from Simanjiro, Tanzania. *African Journal of Ecology,* 48(3): 727–735.

Mulder, H. A. and De Bok, C. F. (2006). Science Shops as university–community interfaces: an interactive approach in science communication. In D. Cheng, J. Metcalfe and B. Schiele (eds) *At the Human Scale: International Practices in Science Communication.* Beijing: Science Press (pp. 285–304).

NCB NI and ARK YLT (2010). *Attitudes to Difference: Young People's Attitudes to and Experiences of Contact with People from Different Minority Ethnic and Migrant Communities in Northern Ireland.* London: NCB. Available at: www.ark.ac.uk/ylt/results/Attitudes_to_difference_report.pdf (accessed October 2018).

Newbigging, K., Roy, A., McKeown, M., French, B. and Habte-Mariam, Z. (2012). Involving ethnically diverse service users in the research process: alliances and action. In P. Beresford and S. Carr (eds) *Social Care, Service Users and User Involvement.* London: Jessica Kingsley Publishers (pp. 120–141).

Niba, M. B. and Green, J. M. (2005). Major factors influencing HIV/AIDS project evaluation. *Evaluation Review,* 29(4): 313–330.

Novek, S. and Menec, V. H. (2014). Older adults' perceptions of age-friendly communities in Canada: a photovoice study. *Ageing and Society,* 34(6): 1052–1072.

O'Fallon, L. R. and Dearry, A. (2002). Community-based participatory research as a tool to advance environmental health sciences. *Environmental Health Perspectives,* 110(Suppl. 2): 155.

O'Hara, L. and Higgins, K. (2017). Participant photography as a research tool: ethical issues and practical implementation. *Sociological Methods & Research.* https://doi.org/10.1177/0049124117701480.

Ollerton, J. and Horsfall, D. (2013). Rights to research: utilising the Convention on the Rights of Persons with Disabilities as an inclusive participatory action research tool. *Disability & Society,* 28(5): 616–630.

O'Neill, M. (2010). Cultural criminology and sex work: resisting regulation through radical democracy and participatory action research (PAR). *Journal of Law and Society,* 37: 210–232.

O'Neill, M. (2012). Ethno-mimesis and participatory arts. In S. Pink (ed.) *Advances in Visual Methodology.* London: Sage (pp. 153–172).

O'Neill, M., Woods, P. A. and Webster, M. (2005). New arrivals: participatory action research, imagined communities, and 'visions' of social justice. *Social Justice*, 32(1): 75–88.

O'Reilly, K (2009). *Key Concepts in Ethnography*. London: Sage.

Ormrod, S. and Norton, K. (2003). Beyond tokenism in service users involvement: lessons from a democratic therapeutic community replication project. *Therapeutic Communities: The International Journal of Therapeutic Communities*, 24(2): 104–114.

Orza, L., Bewley, S., Chung, C., Crone, E. T., Nagadya, H., Vazquez, M. (2015). 'Violence. Enough already': findings from a global participatory survey among women living with HIV. *Journal of the International AIDS Society*, 18(Suppl. 5): 20285.

Osteria, T. S. and Ramos-Jimenez, P. (1988). Women in health development: mobilization of women for health care delivery in a Philippine community. *Sojourn*, 3(2): 217–235.

Ostrow, L., Penney, D., Stuart, E. and Leaf, P. J. (2017). Web-based survey data collection with peer support and advocacy organizations: implications of participatory methods. *Progress in Community Health Partnerships: Research, Education, and Action*, 11(1): 45–52.

Panek, J. (2015). How participatory mapping can drive community empowerment – a case study of Koffiekraal, South Africa. *South African Geographical Journal*, 97(1): 18–30.

Parrado, E. A., McQuiston, C. and Flippen, C. A. (2005). Participatory survey research integrating community collaboration and quantitative methods for the study of gender and HIV risks among Hispanic migrants. *Sociological Methods & Research*, 34(2): 204–239.

Parsons, T. (1949). *The Structure of Social Action*. New York: Free Press.

Patten, S., Mitton, C. and Donaldson, C. (2006). Using participatory action research to build a priority setting process in a Canadian Regional Health Authority. *Social Science and Medicine*, 63(6): 1121–1134.

Patton, M. Q. (2011). *Developmental Evaluation: Applying Complexity Concepts to Enhance Innovation and Use*. New York: Guilford Press.

Payne, S. (1951). *The Art of Asking Questions*. Princeton: Princeton University.

Pelletier, J.-F., Lesage, A., Delorme, A., Macaulay, A. C., Salsberg, J., Valle, C. (2011) User-led research: a global and person-centered initiative. *International Journal of Mental Health Promotion*, 13(1): 4–12.

Pelz, C. Schmitt, A. and Meis, M. (2004). Knowledge mapping as a tool for analyzing focus groups and presenting their results in market and evaluation research [in German] [68 paragraphs]. *Forum Qualitative Sozialforschung/Forum: Qualitative Social Research*, 5(2): Art. 35, http://nbn-resolving.de/urn:nbn:de:0114-fqs0402351.

Percy, R. (2005). The contribution of transformative learning theory to the practice of participatory research and extension: theoretical reflections. *Agriculture and Human Values*, 22(2): 127–136.

Petrie, S. Fiorelli, S. and O'Donnell, K. (2006). 'If we help you what will change?' Participatory research with young people. *Journal of Social Welfare and Family Law*, 28(1): 31–45.

Pink, S. (2012). Visual ethnography and the internet: visuality, virtuality and the special turn. In S. Pink (ed.) *Advances in Visual Methodology*. London: Sage (pp. 113–130).

Pinto, R. M., Schmidt, C. N., Rodriguez, P. S. and Solano, R. (2007). Using principles of community participatory research: groundwork for a collaboration in Brazil. *International Social Work*, 50(1): 53–65.

Poupart, J. Baker, L. and Horse, J. R. (2009). Research with American Indian communities: the value of authentic partnerships. *Children and Youth Services Review*, 31(11): 1180–1186.

Povee, K. Bishop, B. J. and Roberts, L. D. (2014). The use of Photovoice with people with intellectual disabilities: reflections, challenges and opportunities. *Disability and Society*, 29(6): 893–907.

Pratchett, L., Durose, C., Lowndes, V., Smith, G., Stoker, G. and Wales, C. (2009). *Empowering Communities to Influence Local Decision Making: A Systematic Review of the Evidence*. London: Department for Children, Schools and Families.

Puente-Rodríguez, D., van Slobbe, E., Al, I. A. and Lindenbergh, D. D. (2016). Knowledge co-production in practice: enabling environmental management systems for ports through participatory research in the Dutch Wadden Sea. *Environmental Science & Policy*, 55(3): 456–466.

Ramsden, V., Martin, R., McMillan, J., Granger-Brown, A. and Tole, B. (2015). Participatory health research within a prison setting: a qualitative analysis of 'Paragraphs of passion'. *Global Health Promotion*, 22(4): 48–55.

Reason, P. (1993). Sitting between appreciation and disappointment: a critique of the special edition of Human Relations on action research. *Human Relations*, 46(10): 1253–1270.

Reason, P. and Bradbury, H. (eds) (2016). *Handbook of Action Research: Participatory Inquiry and Practice* (3rd edition). London: Sage.

Reason, P. and Torbert, W. R. (2001). The action turn: toward a transformational social science. *Concepts and Transformation*, 6(1): 1–37.

Reese, D. J. (1999). Hospice access and use by African Americans: addressing cultural and institutional barriers through participatory action research. *Social Work (NASW)*, 44(6): 549–559.

Reinharz, S. (1992). *Feminist Methods in Social Research*. New York: Oxford University Press.

Rekalde, I., Vizcarra, M. T. and Macazaga, A. M. (2014). La observación como estrategia de investigación para construir contextos de aprendizaje y fomentar procesos participativos [Observation as a research strategy for building learning context and encouraging participatory processes]. *Educación XXI*, 17(1): 201–220.

Renold, E. (2013). *Boys and Girls Speak Out: A Qualitative Study of Children's Gender and Sexual Cultures (Age 10–12)*. Cardiff: Cardiff University School of Social Sciences.

Resilience Research Centre (2016). *The Child and Youth Resilience Measure (CYRM) Youth Version*. User's Manual. Halifax, Nova Scotia: Resilience Research Centre. Available at: www.resilienceresearch.org/files/CYRM/Youth%20-%20CYRM%20Manual.pdf (accessed May 2019).

Revans, R. W. (2011). *ABC of Action Learning*. Farnham: Gower Publishing.

Rhoades, R. E. and Booth, R. H. (1982). Farmer-back-to-farmer: a model for generating acceptable agricultural technology. *Agricultural Administration*, 11(2): 127–137.

Riecken, T., Strong-Wilson, T., Conibear, F., Michel, C. and Riecken, J. (2005). Connecting, speaking, listening: toward an ethics of voice with/in participatory action research. *Forum Qualitative Sozialforschung/Forum: Qualitative Social Research*, 6(1): Art. 25, http://nbn-resolving.de/urn:nbn:de:0114-fqs0501260.

Rimmer, A. (1998). Women, poverty and credit unions. *Social Action*, 3(3): 15–24.

Ringstad R., Leyva, V. L., Garcia, J. and Jasek-Rysdahl, K. (2012). Creating space for marginalized voices: re-focusing service learning on community change and social justice. *Journal of Teaching in Social Work*, 32(3): 268–283.

Roberto, K. A., Brossoie, N. and McPherson, M. C. (2013). Violence against rural older women. *Australasian Journal on Ageing*, 32(1): 2–7.

Robins, S. (2010). A participatory approach to ethnographic research with victims of gross human rights violations: studying families of the disappeared in post-conflict Nepal. In A. Özerdem and R. Bowd (eds) *Participatory Research Methodologies: Development and Post-disaster/Conflict Reconstruction*. London: Ashgate/Routledge (pp. 181–196).

Roethlisberger, F. J. and Dickson, W. J. (1939). *Management and the Worker*. Cambridge, MA: Harvard University Press.

Romero, D., Kwan, A. and Chavkin, W. (2013). Application of empirical research findings in public health advocacy: focus on maternal, child, and reproductive health. *Journal of Social Issues*, 69(4): 633–644.

Rose, G. (2014). On the relation between 'visual research methods' and contemporary visual culture. *The Sociological Review*, 62: 24–46

Rosenhan, D. L. (1974). On being sane in insane places. *Clinical Social Work Journal*, 2(4): 237–256.

Rosenthal, G. (2003). The healing effects of storytelling: on the conditions of curative storytelling in the context of research and counselling. *Qualitative Inquiry*, 9 (6): 915–933.

Ross, F., Donovan, S., Brearley, S., Victor, C., Cottee, M., Crowther, P. et al. (2005). Involving older people in research: methodological issues. *Health and Social Care in the Community*, 13(3): 268–275.

Ross, N. J., Renold, E., Holland, S. and Hillman, A. (2009). Moving stories: using mobile methods to explore the everyday lives of young people in public care. *Qualitative Research*, 9(5): 605–623.

Sabbe, A., Oulami, H., Hamzali, S., Oulami, N., Le Hjir, F. Z., Abdallaoui, M. et al. (2015). Women's perspectives on marriage and rights in Morocco: risk factors for forced and early marriage in the Marrakech region. *Culture, Health and Sexuality*, 17(2): 135–149.

Salmon, D. and Rickaby, C. E. (2014). City of one: a qualitative study examining the participation of young people in care in a theatre and music initiative. *Children and Society*, 28(1): 30–41.

Sample, P. L. (1996). Beginnings: participatory action research and adults with developmental disabilities. *Disability and Society*, 11(3): 317–332.

Sarri, R. and Sarri, C. (1992). Participatory action research in two communities in Bolivia and the United States. *International Social Work*, 35(2): 267–279.

Saurugger, S. (2010). The social construction of the participatory turn: the emergence of a norm in the European Union. *European Journal of Political Research*, 49(4): 471–495.

Scharlach, A. E. and Sanchez E. (2011). From interviewers to friendly visitors: bridging research and practice to meet the needs of low-income Latino seniors. *Journal of Gerontological Social Work*, 54(1): 73–91.

Schubotz, D. and Devine, P. (2005). *Lower Ormeau Training and Employment Survey 2005*. Belfast: ARK. Available at: www.ark.ac.uk/services/morningtonreport.pdf (accessed March 2019).

Schubotz, D. and McCartan, C. (2016). *Attitudes to Language Learning and Internationalisation. Evidence from 2015 Young Life and Times (YLT)*. Belfast: ARK. Available at: www.ark.ac.uk/pdfs/Researchreports/BC_Internationalisation2015.pdf (accessed March 2019).

Schubotz, D., Rolston, B. and Simpson, A. (2004). Sexual behaviour of young people in Northern Ireland: first sexual experience. *Critical Public Health*, 14(2): 177–190.

Schubotz, D., Sinclair, R., Burns, S., Busby, C. Cook D., Hanna, J. et al. (2006). *'Being Part and Parcel of the School': The Views and Experiences of Children and Young People in Relation to the Development of Bullying Policies in Schools*. Belfast: NICCY. Available at: www.ark.ac.uk/ylt/results/Being_Part_and_Parcel_of_the_School_report.pdf (accessed March 2019).

Schütz, A. (1944). The stranger: an essay in social psychology. *American Journal of Sociology*, 49(6): 499–507.

Schütz, A. (1962). *Collected Papers*, Vol. I, II. The Hague: Nijhoff.

Scott, J., Hacker, M., Averbach, S., Modest, A. M., Cornish, S. and Spencer, D. (2014). Influences of sex, age and education on attitudes towards gender inequitable norms and practices in South Sudan. *Global Public Health: An International Journal for Research, Policy and Practice*, 9(7): 773–786.

Scottish Human Services Trust (2002). *Real Choices: A Participatory Action Research Project Involving Young People with Learning Difficulties Who Are About to Leave School*. Edinburgh: Scottish Human Services Trust.

Seale, C. (2000). *The Quality of Qualitative Research: Introducing Qualitative Methods*. London: Sage.

Seale, J., Wald, M. and Draffan, E. A. (2008). Exploring the technology experiences of disabled learners in higher education: challenges for the use and development of participatory research methods. *Journal of Assistive Technologies*, 2(3): 4–15.

Seligman, M. E. P. (2002). *Authentic Happiness: Using the New Positive Psychology to Realize Your Potential for Lasting Fulfillment*. New York: Simon & Schuster.

Seligman, M. E. P. (2006). *Learned Optimism: How to Change Your Mind and Your Life*. New York: Vintage Books.

Shannon, K., Kerr, T., Allinott, S., Chettiar, J., Shoveller, J. and Tyndall, M. W. (2008). Social and structural violence and power relations in mitigating HIV risk of drug-using women in survival sex work. *Social Science and Medicine*, 66(4): 911–921.

Sherwood, J. and Kendall, S. (2013). Reframing spaces by building relationships: community collaborative participatory action research with Aboriginal mothers in prison. *Contemporary Nurse*, 46(1): 83–94.

Silver, C. (2008). Participatory approaches to social research. In N. Gilbert and P. Stoneman (eds) *Researching Social Life* (3rd edition). London: Sage (pp. 101–124).

Simmel, G. (1950 [1908]). The stranger. In K. Wolff (trans.) *The Sociology of Georg Simmel*. New York: Free Press (pp. 402–408).

Singla, N., Babbar, B. K. and Kaur, J. (2012). Farmers' participatory research on rodent control in Punjab state: Survey, education, impact assessment and sustainability. *Crop Protection*, 34: 25–31.

Siri, R. and Chantraprayoon, O. S. (2017). Local community participatory learning with a nature interpretation system: a case study in Ban Pong, Sansai district, Chiang Mai, Thailand. *Kasetsart Journal of Social Sciences*, 38(2): 181–185.

Skeggs, B. (2001). Feminist ethnography. In P. Atkinson, A. Coffey, S. Delamont, J. Lofland and L. Lofland (eds) *Handbook of Ethnography*. London: Sage (pp. 426–442).

Smith, A., Christopher, S. and McCormick, A. K. H. G. (2004). Development and implementation of a culturally sensitive cervical health survey: a community-based participatory approach. *Women and Health*, 40(2): 67–86.

Smith, D. E. (2005). *Institutional Ethnography: A Sociology for People*. Toronto: Altamira Press

Smith, R. J. and Atkinson, P. (2016). Method and measurement in sociology, fifty years on. *International Journal of Social Research Methodology*, 19(1): 99–110.

Smucker, T. A., Campbell, D. J., Olson, J. M. and Wangui, E. E. (2007). Contemporary challenges of participatory field research for land use change analyses: examples from Kenya. *Field Methods*, 19(4): 384–406.

Spinney, A. (2013). Safe from the start? An action research project on early intervention materials for children affected by domestic and family violence. *Children and Society*, 27(5): 397–405.

Srivastva, S. and Cooperrider, D. L. (1999). *Appreciative Management and Leadership: The Power of Positive Thought and Action in Organizations*. San Francisco: Jossey-Bass.

Stacey, J. (1988). Can there be a feminist ethnography? *Women's Studies International Forum*, 11(1): 21–27.

Stake, R. E. (2004). *Standards-Based and Responsive Evaluation*. London: Sage.

Steinhaus, N. (2014). With or without you: the development of Science Shops and their relations to higher education institutions in Europe. In R. Munck, L. McIlrath, B. Hall, R. Tandon, R. (eds) *Higher Education and Community-Based Research: Creating a New Vision.* Basingstoke: Palgrave Macmillan (pp. 71–83).

Stevenson, M. (2010). Flexible and responsive research: developing rights-based emancipatory disability research methodology in collaboration with young adults with Down syndrome. *Australian Social Work*, 63(1): 35–50.

Stewart, D. W. and Shamdasani, P. N. (2015). *Focus Groups: Theory and Practice.* Thousand Oaks: Sage.

Stickley, T., Rush, B., Shaw, R., Smith, A., Collier, R., Cook, J. et al. (2009). Participation in nurse education: the Pine project. *Journal of Mental Health Training Education and Practice*, 4(1): 11–18.

Stoecker, R. (1999). Are academics irrelevant? Roles for scholars in participatory research. *American Behavioral Scientist*, 42(5): 840–854.

Stoop, I. A. L. (2016). Unit nonresponse. In C. Wolf, D. Joye, T. W. Smith and Y. C. Fu (eds) *The Sage Handbook of Survey Methodology*. London: Sage (pp. 409–424)

Stratford, D., Chamblee, S., Ellerbrock, T. V., Johnson, R. J. W., Abbott, D., von Reyn, C. F. et al. (2003). Integration of a participatory research strategy into a rural health survey. *Journal of General Internal Medicine*, 18(7): 586–588.

Strauss, A. L. and Corbin, J. (2015). *Basics of Qualitative Research: Techniques and Procedures for Developing Grounded Theory* (4th edition). London: Sage.

Streng, J., Rhodes, S., Ayala, G., Eng, E., Arceo, R. and Phipps, S. (2004). Realidad latina: Latino adolescents, their school, and a university use photovoice to examine and address the influence of immigration. *Journal of Interprofessional Care*, 18(4): 403–415.

Strydom, H. (2003). A participatory action research approach to ageing in a particular community in the north-west province of South Africa. *Social Work Maatskaplike Werk*, 39(3): 240–250.

Susman, G. and Evered, R. (1978). An assessment of the scientific merits of action research. *Administrative Science Quarterly*, 23: 582–603.

Sutherland, C. and Cheng, Y. (2009). Participatory-action research with (im)migrant women in two small Canadian cities: using photovoice in Kingston and Peterborough, Ontario. *Journal of Immigrant and Refugee Studies*, 7(3): 290–307.

Sutton, L. (2008). The state of play: disadvantage, play and children's well-being. *Social Policy and Society*, 7(4): 537–549.

Swantz, M. L. (1975). Research as an educational tool for development. *Convergence*, 8(2): 44–52.

Tajik, M., Galvao, H. M. and Siqueira, C. E. (2010). Health survey instrument development through a community-based participatory research approach: health promoting lifestyle profile (HPLP-II) and Brazilian immigrants in greater Boston. *Journal of Immigrant and Minority Health*, 12(3): 390–397.

Tandon, R., Hall, B. L., Lepore, W. and Singh, W. (eds) (2016). *Knowledge and Engagement: Building Capacity of the Next Generation of Community Based Researchers*. Victoria: University of Victoria Press.

Taylor, J., Rahilly, T, Hunter, H, Bradbury-Jones, C, Sanford, K, Caruthers, B. et al. (2012). *Children Who Go Missing from Care: A Participatory Project with Young People as Peer Interviewers*. London: NSPCC (National Society for the Prevention of Cruelty to Children). Available at: www.research.ed.ac.uk/portal/files/12901332/K201207.pdf. (accessed May 2019).

Temple, B., Moran, R., Fayas, N., Haboninana, S., McCabe, F., Mohamed, Z. et al. (2005). *Learning to Live Together: Developing Communities with Dispersed Refugee People Seeking Asylum*. York: Joseph Rowntree Foundation.

Temu, A. E. and Due, J. M. (2000). Participatory appraisal approaches versus sample survey data collection: a case of smallholder farmers well-being ranking in Njombe District, Tanzania. *Journal of African Economies*, 9(1): 44–62

Ten Have, P. (2004). Ethnomethodology. In C. Seale, G. Gobo, J. F. Gubrium and D. Silverman (eds) *Qualitative Research Practice*. London: Sage (pp. 139–152).

Tetley, J. (2013). Using participatory observation to understand older people's experiences: lessons from the field. *Qualitative Report*, 18(45): 1–18.

Thomas, P., Seebohm, P., Henderson, P., Munn-Giddings, C. and Yasmeen, S. (2006). Tackling race inequalities: community development, mental health diversity. *Journal of Public Mental Health*, 5(2): 13–19.

Thomas, W. I. and Thomas, D. S. (1928). *The Child in America: Behaviour Problems and Programs*. New York: Knopf.

Tisdall, E. K. M. (2008). Is the honeymoon over? Children and young people's participation in public decision-making. *The International Journal of Children's Rights*, 16(3): 419–429.

Tisdall, E. K. M. and Davis, J. (2004). Making a difference? Bringing children's and young people's views into policy-making. *Children and Society*, 18(2): 131–141.

Tolman, D. and Brydon-Miller, M. (eds) (2001). *From Subjects to Subjectivities. A Handbook of Interpretive and Participatory Methods*. New York: New York University Press.

Tong, R. (1995). *Feminist Thought: A Comprehensive Introduction*. London: Routledge.

Torronen, M. L. and Vormanen, R. H. (2014). Young people leaving care: participatory research to improve child welfare practices and the rights of children and young people. *Australian Social Work*, 67(1): 135–150.

Townsend, A. and Cox, S. M. (2013). Accessing health services through the back door: a qualitative interview study investigating reasons why people participate in health research in Canada. *BMC Medical Ethics*, 14(1): 40.

Treseder, P. (2004). *Empowering Children and Young People: Promoting Involvement in Decision Making*. London: Save the Children.

Tritter, J. Q. and McCallum, A. (2006). The snakes and ladders of user involvement: moving beyond Arnstein. *Health Policy*, 76(2): 156–168.

Truman, C. (2003). Ethics and the ruling relations of research production. *Sociological Research Online*, 8(1). Available at: www.socresonline.org.uk/8/1/truman.html (accessed 29 April 2019).

Turnbull, H. R. and Turnbull, A. P. (1991). Participatory action research and public policy (unpublished manuscript). University of Kansas, Lawrence, Beach Center on Families and Disability.

Ungar, M. and Liebenberg, L. (2005). The International Resilience Project: a mixed methods approach to the study of resilience across cultures. In M. Ungar (ed.) *Handbook for Working with Children and Youth: Pathways to Resilience Across Cultures and Contexts*. London: Sage (pp. 211–226).

United Nations (2009) *Committee on the Rights of the Child: General Comment No. 12 – the Right of the Child to be Heard*. Geneva: United Nations.

Vandermause, R. K., Severtsen, B. and Roll, J. (2013). Re-creating a vision of motherhood: therapeutic drug court and the narrative. *Qualitative Social Work*, 12(5): 620–636.

Vermeulen, H. F. (2008). Early history of ethnography and ethnology in the German enlightenment: anthropological discourse in Europe and Asia, 1710–1808. Doctoral dissertation, Department of Cultural Anthropology and Development Sociology, Faculty of Social and Behavioural Sciences, Leiden University.

Viswanathan, M., Ammerman, A., Eng, E., Gartlehner, G., Lohr, K. N., Griffith, D. et al. (2004). *Community-based Participatory Research: Assessing the Evidence*. Rockville: Agency for Healthcare, Research and Quality (US) (AHRQ) Evidence Report. Available at: www.ncbi.nlm.nih.gov/books/NBK37280/ (accessed February 2018).

VOYPIC (2014). *Our Life in Care. VOYPIC's Third CASI Survey of the Views and Experiences of Children and Young People in Care*. Belfast: VOYPIC (Voices of Young People in Care).

Wacquant, L. (2009). The body, the ghetto and the penal state. *Qualitative Sociology*, 32(1): 101–129.

Walmsley, J. and Johnson, K. (2003). *Inclusive Research with People with Learning Difficulties: Past, Present and Future*. London: Jessica Kingsley.

Walmsley, J. and Mannan, H. (2009). Parents as co-researchers: a participatory action research initiative involving parents of people with intellectual disabilities in Ireland. *British Journal of Learning Disabilities*, 37(4): 271–276.

Wang, H. and Wang, C. (2016). An analysis of the feasibility of incorporating a mobile phone-based participatory field survey into satellite-based fall webworm monitoring. *Remote Sensing Letters*, 7(4): 388–396.

Ward, J., Bailey, D. and Boyd, S. (2012). Participatory action research in the development and delivery of self-harm awareness sessions in prison: involving service users in staff development. *Prison Service Journal*, 202: 20–25.

Ward, L., Barnes, M. and Gahagan, B. (2012). *Well-being in Old Age: Findings from Participatory Research*. Brighton: University of Brighton and Age Concern. Available at: www.brighton.ac.uk/_pdf/research/ssparc/wellbeing-in-old-age-full-report.pdf (accessed March 2019).

Ward, L. and Gahagan, B. (2010). Crossing the divide between theory and practice: research and an ethic of care. *Ethics and Social Welfare*, 4(2): 210–216.

Warming, H. (2012). Theorizing (adult's facilitation of) children's participation and citizenship. In C. Baraldi and V. Iervese (eds) *Participation, Facilitation, and Mediation: Children and Young People in Their Social Contexts*. Abingdon: Routledge (pp. 42–60).

Webb, B. (1926). *My Apprenticeship*. London: Longman.

Webber, W., Stoddard, P., Rodriguez, M., Gudiño, P., Chagoya, T., Jauregui, D. et al. (2016). Improving rigor in a door-to-door health survey: a participatory approach in a low-income Latino neighborhood. *Progress in Community Health Partnerships: Research, Education, and Action*, 10(1): 103–111.

Weber, M. (1947). *The Theory of Social and Economic Organisations*. New York: Free Press.

Weeks, L. and Roberto, K. (2003). The impact of falls on quality of life: empowering older women to address falls prevention. *Quality in Ageing*, 4(3): 5–13.

Weiss, J. A., Dwonch-Schoen, K., Howard-Barr, E. M. and Panella, M. P. (2010). Learning from a community action plan to promote safe sexual practices. *Social Work (NASW)*, 55(1): 19–26.

Wellings, K., Branigan, P. and Mitchell, K. (2000). Discomfort, discord and discontinuity as data: using focus groups to research sensitive topics. *Culture, Health & Sexuality*, 2(3): 255–267.

Whyte, W. F. (1955). *Street Corner Society: The Social Structure of an Italian Slum*. Chicago: Chicago University Press.

Whyte, W. F. (ed.) (1991). *Participatory Action Research*. Newbury: Sage.

Whyte, W. F., Greenwood, D. J. and Lazes, P. (1989). Participatory action research: through practice to science in social research. *American Behavioral Scientist*, 32: 513–551.

Williams, J. and Nelson-Gardell, D. (2014). Mentoring up-cycled: creating a community-based intervention for sexually abused adolescents. *Journal of Children's Services*, 9(3): 235–247.

Williamson, G. R. and Prosser, S. (2002). Action research: politics, ethics and participation. *Journal of Advanced Nursing*, 40(5): 587–593.

Windsor, L. C. and Murugan, V. (2012). From the individual to the community: perspectives about substance abuse services. *Journal of Social Work Practice in the Addictions*, 12(4): 412–433.

Winter, K. (2012). Ascertaining the perspectives of young children in care: case studies in the use of reality boxes. *Children and Society*, 26(5): 368–380.

Wolf, C., Joye, D., Smith, T. W. and Fu, Y. C. (eds) (2016). *The Sage Handbook of Survey Methodology*. London: Sage.

Wolff, K. H. (ed.) (1950). *The Sociology of Georg Simmel*. New York: The Free Press

Wrentschur, M. (2014). 'Stop: Now we are speaking!' a creative and dissident approach of empowering disadvantaged young people. *International Social Work*, 57(4): 398–410.

Zarb, G. (1992). On the Road to Damascus: first steps towards changing the relations of disability research production. *Disability, Handicap and Society*, 7(2): 125–138.

Zeitlyn, B. and Mand, K. (2012). Researching transnational childhoods. *Journal of Ethnic and Migration Studies*, 38(6): 987–1006.

INDEX

Abel, G.M., 57, 112
Aboriginal communities, 52, 64
Abrams, K.M., 159
abusive relationships, 58, 172
academic and non-academic contexts, 186–7
academic freedom, 71
academic theory, 29
Academy of Social Sciences, 71–2
access to the field of research, 133–4
action, theory of (Goffman), 29
action ethnography, 126, 142
action learning, 101
action research (AR), 3, 15, 26, 33, 36, 76, 84,
    88, 97–105, 109–10, 114–16, 149, 172, 213
  aims of, 101, 105
  critique of, 114–16
  differences from 'ordinary' research, 99–102
  five-tier concept of, 101–2
  participatory nature of, 100–2
  rationale for, 98
  research areas covered by, 109–10
  typology of, 99
action science, 48, 55
Adams, K., 52
Adato, M., 60
Adorno, Theodor, 34
agency, 35–40
Alanen, L., 36
Aldiss, S., 65
Aldridge, J., 12, 14–15, 73, 79
Althusser, Louis, 34
altruistic motives for engaging in research,
  18, 20
American Indian communities, 190
appreciative inquiry (AI), 114
Archard, D., 89
Ardévol, E., 140
Argyris, C., 48
arts-based approaches, 50, 55
Ashwood, L., 47
Atkinson, P., 121, 124, 128–9, 133–4, 145

Babbar, B.K., 205
Bailey, D., 64
Bakshi, L., 58
Balcazar, F.E., 111
Banks, S., 74

Baraldi, C., 35–7
Barnes, M., 24, 79
Beckett, H., 58
Bengtsson, T.T., 76, 88
Beresford, P., 11, 18, 45, 84
Berg, B., 71, 73
Berger, Peter, 29
Bernard, C., 88–9
Bernard, M., 51
Bernstein, Richard, 34
bias
  in group discussions, 153–4
  in surveys, 188–9, 193–4
Bicknell, J., 51
Biggs, S., 196
Bishop, B.J., 52
Blair, T., 19
Blake, M.K., 75
Blee, K.M., 135
'blending in', 136–7
Bloor, M., 159
Blumer, Herbert, 28
Bock, J.G., 47
Boellstorff, Tom, 120–1, 127, 139, 145
Bogardus, Emery, 150
Bond, M., 15, 99
Booth, D., 63
Borland, M., 54
Boser, S., 75–6
Boyd, S., 64
Boyden, J., 16
Bradbury, H., 101
Brady, B., 65
Brady, L.M., 16, 54, 56
brainstorming, 169, 174
Braithwaite, R., 59
Brannick, T., 98–9, 108
Braun, K., 63
British National Survey of Sexual Attitudes
  and Lifestyles (NATSAL), 184
Brodie, E., 17–18
Brossoie, N., 58
Brown, L.D., 104
Browne, K., 58
Brownlie, J., 15–16, 74, 77, 86–7
Brydon-Miller, M., 30, 34–5, 74–5, 79, 85, 88,
  102–3

Bryman, A., 24–6, 70–1, 76, 120, 189–90, 194
Buckles, D.J., 3, 45–9, 52–3, 103–6, 115–16, 189, 213
Buettgen, A., 60
Burgess, R.G., 119, 121, 130
Burke, J., 61
Burke, T., 16
Burns, D., 48, 110

California Health Interview Survey, 201–2
capacity-building for research, 78, 204
capitalist system, 33
care settings, 66
Carey, P., 51
Carney, G.M., 115
Carr, S., 11, 18–19, 45, 82–4, 87
Casey, M.A., 155–6, 165
Castleden, H., 79
censuses, 183
Chambers, R., 45, 168
Chantraprayoon, O.S., 131
Chavkin, W., 116
Cheng, Y., 52
Chevalier, J.M., 3, 45–9, 52–3, 103, 105–6, 115–16, 189, 213
Child and Youth Resilience Measure, 201
children
    born of war (CBOW), 196–7
    contribution to social change, 36
    rights of, 54, 65, 206
    used as co-researchers, 1, 19–20, 65, 77–8, 82, 84, 89, 160, 207–8
    'voice' of, 66
Chopel, A.M., 134
Christopher, S., 197
citizen science, 48–9, 55, 130
citizenship, 16, 18
Clark, Alison, 65, 122–3
climate change, 110, 213
closed questions, 200
Cloutier, G., 110
co-construction of meaning, 153
codes of practice, 71
Coghlan, D., 98–9, 108
Cohen, A., 190
Cold War, 11
Cole, S., 126, 143–4
collaborative research, 2, 13–15, 20, 23, 32, 40, 44, 48–50, 56, 67, 78–86, 91, 104, 125–7, 142, 145–6, 161–3, 190, 194–6, 209, 212–13
    as distinct from participatory research, 18
collegiate mode of participation, 196
Collins, K.J., 48
communicative skills, 134
communicative space, 34

community-based participatory research (CBPR), 43–5, 55–9, 64, 67, 79, 112–13, 175, 196–7, 203
    core principles of, 44
community members and organisations, role of, 100, 111, 128, 131, 134, 142–3, 162, 204
community regeneration, 59
compensation of researchers, 81–2
computer-assisted personal interviewing (CAPI), 206
computer-assisted qualitative data analysis (CAQDAS), 176
computer-assisted telephone interviewing (CATI), 206
computer technology, 4, 159
Concerns Report Method (CRM), 111
Conder, J., 62, 87
confidentiality, 78–9, 84, 92, 156, 171–2
conflicts of interest, 85
'conscientisation' (Freire), 103
consciousness-raising, 152
consent
    of the individual and the group, 77
    to participate in research, 172
    see also informed consent
consent forms, 92
constructivism, 24, 32, 214
consultative mode of participation, 196
contextual factors, 20–1, 29, 80–1
contracts, 82, 117, 163, 172
contractual mode of participation, 196, 203
conventional research methods, 2–3, 10–12, 20, 31, 56, 67, 75–80, 112, 130, 212, 214
conversation analysis, 174–5
Cook, J.A., 32–3
cooling-off periods, 172
'co-operative inquiry' (Heron), 13
Cooperrider, D., 114
co-production of knowledge, 3, 11–14, 28, 40, 48, 212–14
    skills and characteristics required for, 22
Coquillon, E., 104
Corbin, J., 17
co-researchers, 1, 3, 77–80, 85, 90, 102, 105, 128, 131–2, 142–4, 161–6, 175–6, 194, 206–8
    involved in data collection, 203–6
    involved in survey translation, 202–3
    in participatory group discussions, 161–2
    reasons for involvement of, 26
Corman, M.K., 142
Cornish, F., 57, 134
Cornwall, A., 6, 12, 43, 111, 115–16
Cotterell, P., 24
covert research, 73, 133
Crabtree, J.L., 65

Craig, V.J., 110
'credibility gap' in traditional research
    practices, 104
Crishna, B., 53
critical pedagogy, 52–5
critical perspectives, 12
critical reflection, 108
critical research, 103–4
critical theory and critically-informed inquiry,
    34–5
Crotty, M., 24–5, 31–3
crowd sourcing and crowd funding, 49
Cuskelly, M., 62

dance-theatre, participatory, 51
Daniel, B., 51
data analysis, 109, 142, 206–7
data collection, 4, 129–30, 149, 175, 203–6
data protection, 74, 159
Davis, J., 194, 204
Dearry, A., 44
de Bok, C.F., 49
deception as part of research, 71
decision-making processes, 109, 153, 198
'deep understanding', 27–8
Delamont, S., 120, 123, 134, 137
Delport, A., 50
Delve, R., 51, 141
Denzin, Norman K., 25, 71
de Vaus, D.A., 189–90
digital revolution, 4
disabled people, 54, 60–2, 114
disadvantaged groups, 2, 16, 56, 87, 91,
    190, 213
disciplinary boundaries, 12
discourse psychology, 174–5
dissemination of survey results, 207, 209
domestic violence, 32
domineering participants, 170–1
Dorsner, C., 47
drop-outs from research, 164
Due, J.M., 47
Dundon, T., 115
Durand, C., 190
Durham Community Research Trust, 77
Durkheim, Emile, 34, 37–40
Dwyer, P., 63
Dwyer, R., 18

education reform, 103
Edwards, M., 63
'efficiency rationale' for participatory
    research, 74
Elwood Martin, R., 64
emancipatory approaches, 14, 99, 145, 152
Emerson, L., 54, 160, 206–8
emic perspectives, 137

emotional responses to research, 107
empowerment, 15–16, 74, 84, 105, 214
    at community level, 19
English, L.M., 47
Ennew, J., 16
epistemology, 24, 41, 214
Erdtman, E., 60
Eriksson, C.C., 19
ethical issues, 69–70, 76, 146, 171–2, 212
    awareness of, 128
    common standards and review processes,
        70–4
    deontological and *consequentialist*
        stances on, 71
    principles underlying, 71–4, 91
    questions to ask when planning research, 73
    situationist stance on, 70–1, 91
    specific to participatory research, 74–5
    in survey research, 208–9
    universalist stance on, 70–3, 90
ethnic groups, 63
ethnography, 72, 120–30, 133–6, 140–2, 145
    flexibility of, 128–9
    participatory and collaborative forms of,
        124–6
    visual, 140–1
ethnomethodology, 29
'ethno-mimesis' (O'Neill), 141
etic perspectives, 137
European Union, 74
evaluations, participatory, 53–5
Evans, R., 120, 124, 126, 130–1, 145
Evans-Pritchard, Edward, 121
Evered, R., 10, 98
expectations of research participants, 86–7
experiential knowledge, 26
experts, use of, 27–8
external aspects of the research process, 108

face-to-face data collection and surveys,
    204, 208
facilitators, 156–7, 163, 167–9, 173–4
    challenges for, 170–2
Fals-Borda, O., 102
Fascism, 11
feedback, 168, 172
female genital cutting (FGC), 113
feminism and feminist research, 31–3, 39,
        104, 127–8, 142, 145, 152, 161
Fenge, L.-A., 58, 112
Fern, E.F., 156–7, 162
Fetterman, D.M., 53
Feuerbach, L.A., 99
Fieldhouse, J., 113
fieldnotes, 141–2
fieldwork, 163
    ending of, 143

Fine, M., 64, 66
Fiorelli, S., 65, 86, 88, 90
Fiske, M., 154–5
Fiske, S.T., 40
Fitzgerald, L.J., 57, 112
Flick, U., 30, 151
Flicker, S., 77, 88
Flippen, C.A., 197
focus groups, 148–52, 157–72
  applications of, 150
  dialogic nature of, 152
  motivations for use of, 162
  popularity for social research, 149
  proliferation and diversity of, 151
  scheduling and question development for, 165–70
  seen as a low-cost option, 151
  size of, 172
  use of the term, 150
  virtual, 159
Fonow, M.M., 32–3
'foreshadowed problems' (Malinowski), 129
Formea, C.M., 194, 202–3
Foster, V., 50, 194–5, 201
Foucault, Michel, 80
Fournier, Jacques, 121
Fowler, F.J., 193
Fox, M., 66
Fox, R., 20, 78
Francisco, V., 112
Frankfurt School, 34
Franks, M., 56
Franz, N., 47
Fraser, Nancy, 112
free riding, 157
Freire, Paulo, 52–3, 80, 99, 103, 111, 152, 161
Freyer, B., 51, 141
Friedman, V.J., 48
friendship with research participants, 83
Froggett, L., 50
Fry, C., 18
Fulcher, J., 30
functionalism, 38

Gahagen, B., 79, 83
Gaiser, T.J., 159
Gallagher, L.A. and M., 84
Galvao, H.M., 203
Garcia, C.M., 195, 197
Garcia-Iriarte, E., 62, 111
Gardner, K., 51
Garfinkel, H., 27
gatekeepers, 133–4, 164
Geertz, Clifford, 129, 142
generalisability of findings, 187–93
Ghaffar, A., 47
Ghosh, R., 57, 134

Gilchrist, F., 54
'Gillick competency', 89
Gitonga, P.N., 50
Godin, P., 34
Goffman, P., 29
'going native', 90, 134, 144
Gold, R.L., 123
Goodfellow-Baikie, R.L., 47
Gotschi, E., 51, 141
Gough, K.V., 60
Gramsci, Antonio, 34
Graybill, P., 202–3
Greenwood, D., 75, 79, 85, 88
Groeben, N., 30
ground rules, 157, 163, 214
grounded theory, 160
group discussions, 3, 5, 148–70
  analysis of data from, 173–6
  applications of, 149, 158–9
  benefits from, 160–1
  characteristics of, 158–60
  composition of groups for, 155, 164–5
  conditions for success of, 154–7
  diversity and flexibility of, 150, 161
  exploratory, 162
  history as a method of research, 150–1
  potential strengths and weaknesses of, 153–4, 165
  pre-existing groups in, 164
  purposes of, 161–2
  scheduling of, 166–7, 177–82
  suitable venues for, 155
  theoretical perspectives on, 151
  use of the term, 150
  used in combination with other techniques, 159–62
  used for data collection, 149
group dynamics, 153, 159, 170–1, 173
Groves, R.M., 184, 193
Gubrium, A.C., 88
Gundersen, C., 190

Habermas, Jürgen, 34–5
Halkier, B., 174–5
Hall, B.L., 10, 106
Hall, K., 19
Hammersley, M., 121, 124, 128–9, 133–4, 145
Hampshire, K., 19
Hardill, I., 63
Harding, S., 32, 104
Harkness, J.A., 202
Hart, E., 99
Hawthorne experiments, 135
health inequalities, 43–4
Heinonen, P., 122, 125, 132–3
Heron, J., 13
Hesse-Biber, S.N., 31

Higgins, K., 141
Hill, A.L., 88
Hill, R.P., 64–5
Hillier, A., 204
Hilsen, A.I., 80, 83–4
Hine, C., 138
hip hop, 50
Hoff, L.A., 32
Hogg, B., 62
Home, R., 115
Honneth, Axel, 36
Horkheimer, Max, 34
Horsfall, D., 54
Horsfield, E., 206
Howe, G., 190
humanitarianism, 80
humour, use of, 156
Humphreys, L., 70

'ice-breakers', 167–8, 177
'idea circles', 60
'ideal speech situation', 34
immersion in the field, 144
imprisonment, 63–5, 87
incentives for research participants, 17–18, 171
inductive approaches to research, 24
informed consent, 73–4, 77, 79
institutional ethnography (IE), 121
institutional review boards (IRBs), 71–2, 75,
    106, 212
interaction analysis, 174
interactive activities, 168, 170
'interlocutors', use of the term, 127
internal aspects of the research process, 108
internet access, 185
interventionist ethnography, 145
interviewer effects, 159
interviews, one-to-one, 160
involvement in research, 10, 12, 150
    reasons for, 14, 16–18
    levels and types of, 162–3

Jewkes, R., 6, 12, 43, 111
Johnson, K., 15
Johnson-Agbakwu, L.E., 113
Jones, V., 61
Jordan, J., 172
Jupp Kina, V., 16, 80, 86

Kaftarian, S.J., 53
Kaplan, S.A., 204
Kaur, J., 205
Kawulich, B.B., 122, 124, 130, 135–7
Kelly, B., 61
Kelly, George, 30
Kemmis, S., 34–5
Kendal, P.L., 154–5

Kendall, S., 64
Kershaw, G.G., 79
Khan, M.Q., 47
King, J.A., 10, 12, 14, 26, 161–3, 175
'knowing', ways of, 26
knowledge
    construction of, 29, 31, 169
    different kinds of, 29
    see also co-construction of meaning
knowledge mapping, 173–5
Kozol, Jan, 152
Kramer, J.M., 61–2
Kreitzer, L., 113
Krueger, R.A., 10, 12, 14, 26, 155–6, 161–5, 175
Kuo, T., 197
Kwan, A., 116

'ladder' of citizen participation, 13–14
Ladkin, D., 98–101, 107
Lakwo, A., 190
Langevang, T., 60
Laroque, C.P., 79
Larsen, M.D., 190
Lassiter, L.E., 126–7
Lather, P., 32
Lavelle, B., 190
learning disabilities, 60–2
learning from other people, 19
Léime, A.N., 115
Lengwiler, M., 11
Le Roy Ladurie, Emmanuel, 121
Leung, M.W., 43
Lewin, Kurt, 15, 98–102, 109, 115
LGBT communities, 58
Liamputtong, P., 150–6, 161,
    164, 171–2
Likert scales, 200–1
Lim, J., 58
Little, R.M., 50
Littlechild, R., 19
Lloyd, K., 54, 160, 206–8
Lorenzo, T., 114
Lowe, C., 141
Luckman, Thomas, 29
Luhmann, N., 35–7
Lund, F., 60
Lundy, L., 20, 54, 86
Lundy, P., 101
Lune, H., 71, 73
Lykes, M.B., 104

McAlister, S., 58
Macaulay, A., 44–5
Macazaga, A.M., 126
McConnell, T., 61
McCormick, A.K.H.G., 197
McDonnell, O., 24.38

McEvoy, L., 54
MacFarlane, A., 76
McGee, R., 46–7
McGovern, M., 101
McIntyre, A., 106–9, 114
McKay, A., 190
MacKinnon, S., 111
Macnaghten, P., 171
McNeill, F., 65–6
Maconochie, H., 65–6
McPherson, M.C., 58
McQuisten, C., 197
McTaggart, R., 12, 107
Maguire, P., 31
mainstreaming of participatory and
    collaborative approaches, 212
Maiter, S., 83
Malinowski, Bronislaw, 121, 129, 139
Mand, K., 51
Mannan, H., 62
Marcuse, Herbert, 34
marginalised groups, 56, 87, 190
market research, 151, 153
Martin, R.E., 64
Marx, Karl (and Marxist theory), 33–5, 39, 99,
    121, 161
Mason, J., 24–5
Mayall, B., 36
Mead, G., 28, 115
Mead, Margaret, 121
Mears, A., 122
medical research, 43
Menec, V.H., 52
mental health, 64
mental shortcuts, 40
Merton, R.K., 154–5
Mhlongo, P., 60
micro-sociologists, 38
Milner, P., 61–2, 87
Minkler, M., 43, 43
minority groups, 188
Mirfin-Veitch, B., 62, 87
Misgav, C., 47
mixed-methods research, 120, 160
mobile phones, 142
mobile surveys, 204–6
Mochmann, I.C., 196–7
Mohler, P.P., 202
Mølholt, A.K., 76, 88
Moni, K.B., 62
Morawski, J., 31–2
Morgan, D.L., 150, 153–4, 158, 164, 169
Morgan, M.F., 62
Morse, J.M., 17
'Mosaic approach', 65
Mosavel, M., 44
Moschitz, H., 115

Moss, P., 65
motivations for taking part in research,
    17–20
Mulder, H.A., 49
Myers, G., 171

Namatovu, R., 60
narrative research methods, 32
Neill, G., 58
'netnography', 138
New Zealand, 112, 206
Newbigging, K., 63
nonresponse to surveys, 193
Northern Ireland, 1, 101, 141, 165, 206
Novek, S., 52

objectivism, 24, 214–15
objectivity and objective truth, 10, 138,
    144, 187
observation
    descriptive, focused or selective, 136–7
    length of sessions, 137
    skills of, 147
    structured and unstructured, 131–2, 135–7
    use of, 130–1
O'Donnell, K., 65, 86, 88, 90
O'Fallon, L.R., 44
O'Hara, L., 141
Ohm, D., 65
older people
    research focused on, 62–3
    involvement in research, 19
Ollerton, J., 54
O'Neill, M., 112, 140–1
online communities, 138
online surveys, 204–6
ontology, 24, 215
open questions, 206
opting into and opting out of participation in
    research, 73, 79, 85
O'Reilly, K., 130, 144
organisational development (OD), 109–10
Orza, L., 205–6
Osteria, T.S., 111
Ostrow, L., 197
'overrapport', 144
'ownership' of the research process, 194

Panek, J., 141
Parrado, E.A., 197
Parsons, Talcott, 37–40
participant observation, 3, 5, 119–46, 160
    critique of, 144–6
    in cyberspace, 138–40
    as distinct from participant involvement,
        12–13
    levels of, 13–14, 211

as a method of data collection, 122–4, 129–30
participatory action research (PAR), 3, 5, 26, 36, 48, 52–3, 57–66, 75, 97–110, 116–17, 141, 175, 189
aim of, 102, 109–10
characteristics of, 100, 102, 108
diversity of projects and common principles in, 108–10
process and design of, 105–6
theoretical background and conceptualisation of, 103–5
typical questions in, 106–7
unique features of, 108
participatory learning and action (PLA), 45–8
participatory observation, 142
participatory organisational research (POR), 48, 109–10
participatory poverty assessment (PPA), 45–6
participatory research
aims of, 12, 161
application of, 56–9, 67
benefits from, 78
challenges for, 78, 80, 212
characteristics of, 12, 76, 146
critical review of, 18–20
as distinct from collaborative research, 18
inherent contradictions in, 88
key principles of, 15
origin of, 10–11
people and communities involved in, 59–66
potentially damaging consequences of, 90
recognition of, 146
risks run by co-researchers, 144
theoretical background to, 211
use of the term, 2, 10, 190–1
weaknesses of, 209
participatory rural appraisal (PRA), 45–8, 55
'participatory turn' in social research, 2–4, 10–12, 15, 50, 85, 97, 104, 212
partnership approaches, 14
paternalism, 45
patient-centred care and research, 38
patriarchy, 31
personal information, 171
Petrie, S., 65, 86, 88, 90
photography, use of, 141
Photovoice, 50–2, 55, 168
piloting of questionnaires, 199
Pink, S., 138, 140
play, 66
politicisation of science, 11
positioning analysis, 174–5
positivism and positivist research, 10, 32, 75, 98, 104, 121–2, 145–6, 152

Povee, K., 52
poverty, 46, 59–60, 190
power relations, 12, 14, 20, 31–2, 58, 80–5, 104–5, 127, 141, 146, 149–50, 154, 162, 168, 212
practical knowledge, 26
Pratchett, L., 19
prediction of research outcomes, 75–6
'production blocking' (Fern), 157
professional organisations, 71
professional research fields, 43
promotional communication systems, 36–7
Prosser, S., 77, 85–8
psychological frameworks, 30–1
Puente-Rodríguez, D., 48, 110

qualitative interviewing, 17
qualitative research, 6, 25, 33, 74, 83, 189, 192
quality of life, 87
quantitative methods of data collection, 175
Queen's University, Belfast, 207
questions, formulation of, 165, 198–200
quorates, 85

Ramos-Jimenez, P., 111
randomised controlled trials (RCTs), 61
rapport, 128, 134–5, 146, 159, 167
Reason, P., 13, 291 101
reciprocity, 17, 83, 126–7, 135
recording equipment, 170
recruitment of research participants, 164–5 194
Reese, D.J., 113
Reinharz, S., 104
Rekalde, I., 126
relationships between researchers and participants, 30–1, 70–6, 81–3, 135, 143, 146, 188, 191–2
reliability of research findings, 187
Renold, E., 57
representativeness, 188
research ethics committees (RECs), 71–2, 75, 106, 212
research questions, 106–7, 125–6, 130–1
'results-oriented philanthropy', 43
rewards for research participants, 17–18, 171
Rickaby, C.E., 51
Riecken, T., 82
rights-based participatory approaches, 54–6, 67
Rimmer, A., 59
Ringstad, R., 113
risk audits, 90
Roberto, K., 58, 161
Roberts, L.D., 52
Robins, S., 130, 145
Roche, B., 76

roles adopted by researchers, 76, 213
Roll, J., 64
Romero, D., 116
Rose, G., 140
Rosenhan, D.L., 70
Rosenthal, G., 17
Ross, N.J., 141
'rubber-stamping' of decisions, 84

Sabbe, A., 154
Saisana, M., 190
Salmon, D., 51
Sample, P.L., 60–1, 102
sampling and sampling grids, 164–6
Sarri, R. and C., 111
'saturation', 143, 165
scaling-up of projects, 116, 189, 213
Schön, D.A., 48
Schurr, H., 62
Schütz, A., 29, 124
science shops, 49–50, 55
Scott, J., 30, 197–8
Second Life, 139–40
self-disclosures, 156
sense-making processes, 13
sensitive topics, 154, 172, 177, 204
Severtsen, B., 64
sex workers, 57–8, 112, 134, 140–1
sexual health, 56–7
Shamdasani, P.N., 169–70
Shannon, K., 57
Sherwood, J., 64
shy participants, 171
Silver, C., 2, 14–15, 99
Simmel, Georg, 27, 34, 121, 124
Singla, N., 205
Siqueira, C.E., 203
Siri, R., 131
'situated ethics' and 'situation ethics', 76
Skeggs, B., 127
Skivenes, M., 89
Smith, A., 197
Smith, Dorothy, 121, 127–8
Smucker, T.A., 47
social background of research participants,
    156–7
social construction, 24, 29–30. 39
social desirability bias, 153–4, 173
social interaction, 29–30, 152
social movements, 11
social networking, 4, 138
social psychology, 30
social research
    aims of, 15, 27, 98
    influences on, 25–6
    criticisms of, 159
social systems theory, 35

social theory, 40
    research linked to, 26–7
societal impact of research, 211–12
software packages, 109, 184, 205
South Africa, 101
Spinney, A., 58
SPSS, 184
Stacey, J., 146
standardisation in surveys, 190–3
standpoint theories, 127–8
Stanford prison experiments, 70
Stevenson, M., 56
Stewart, D.W., 169–70
sticky notes, 168
Stoecker, R., 12, 14, 76
story-telling, 17, 50, 88
Streng, J., 52
structural functionalism, 37–40
Strydom, H., 63
study circles, 161
study groups, 152
Suarez-Balcazar, Y., 111
subjective theories, 30
subjectivism, 24
survey methods, 3–6, 160, 183–210
    attractions of, 186
    criticisms of, 189–90
    ethical issues for, 208–9
    ideal-typical use of, 186–7
    ingredients of success, 191
    objectives of and benefits from, 191–3
    planning and co-design of, 198
    potential strengths and weaknesses of,
        188–9
    responsibilities and remits in, 195
    rigour in, 187–8
    as a tool in social research and policy-
        making, 185–8
    two kinds of, 195
    use within collaborative and participatory
        research, 190–1
    usefulness of, 209
Susman, G., 10, 98
Sutherland, C., 52
Sutton, L., 66
Sutton, S., 51
Swantz, Marja Liisa, 10, 209
symbolic interactionism, 28–9, 38–9
synectics, 169–70
systems theory, 35–9

tacit knowledge, 128
Tajik, M., 203
Tandon, R., 104
Tanner, D., 19
Tavistock Institute, 98
tax, 82

Taylor, S.E., 40
team ethnography, 130
telephone surveys, 204
Temple, B., 111–12
Temu, A.E., 47
theoretical perspectives on participatory
    research, 23–40
theory development, 115
'thick description', 129, 142
Thomas Theorem, 28–9
Tisdall, E.K.M., 65
tokenism, 86–7, 116, 163, 193, 212
Tolman, D., 30
Tong, R., 31
Torbert, W.R., 13, 101
Torre, M.E., 64
Torronen, M.L., 66
training for researchers, 77–9, 131–2,
    172, 188
translation of surveys, 202–3
Treseder, P., 16
Truman, C., 71–2
trusting relationships, 79, 83–4, 107, 135, 143
truth-telling, 101
Turnbull, H.R. and A.P., 104

Ullah, N., 47
Ungar, Michael, 201
United Nations Convention on the Rights of
    the Child (UNCRC), 54, 65, 89
up-scaling see scaling-up of projects
user-led research, 45, 55, 84, 87

validity of research findings, 145, 187
Vandemause, R.K., 64
Van de Vijver, F.J.R., 202
Vermeulen, H., 120
Verstehen, 27–9, 39
VIPER project, 61
virtual reality and virtual worlds, 138–9
Viswanathan, M., 189, 198

Vizcarra, M., 126
'voice', 2–3, 12, 15, 19, 51, 66, 79, 87, 114,
    127, 146, 149
volunteers, use of, 143
Vormanen, R.H., 66
VOYPIC, 66
vulnerable groups, 15, 73, 79, 87, 93, 110

Wacquant, L., 144
Wall, J.M., 65
Wallerstein, N., 43
Walmsley, J., 15, 62
Wandersman, A., 53
Wang, H. and C., 205–6
Ward, J., 64
Ward, L., 79, 83
Warming, H., 36
Warrington, C., 58
Webb, B., 121
Webber, W., 201
Weber, Max, 27–9, 34
Webster, M., 112
Weeks, L., 161
Weiss, J.A., 57, 204
welfare state provision, 184
Whittington, D., 194, 204
Whyte, W.F., 102–3, 134
Williamson, G.R., 77, 85–8
Winter, K., 56
women
    communication of their experience, 152
    oppression of, 31
    as prisoners, 64
Woods, P.A., 112
Wrentschur, M., 51

Yen, I.H., 43
Young, A., 194–5, 201

Zarb, G., 14
Zeitlyn, B., 51